Justice Older than the Law

Photograph by Margaret Thomas, courtesy *Washington Post*

Justice Older than the Law

The Life of Dovey Johnson Roundtree

KATIE McCABE

AND

DOVEY JOHNSON ROUNDTREE

UNIVERSITY PRESS OF MISSISSIPPI • JACKSON

MARGARET WALKER ALEXANDER SERIES IN AFRICAN AMERICAN STUDIES

www.upress.state.ms.us

The University Press of Mississippi is a member of the Association of
American University Presses.

Photos courtesy of Dovey Johnson Roundtree, unless otherwise credited.

Paperback ISBN 978-1-61703-121-2
Ebook ISBN 978-1-60473-774-5
∞
The Library of Congress has cataloged the hard cover edition as follows:

McCabe, Katie.
Justice older than the law : the life of Dovey Johnson Roundtree / Katie McCabe
and Dovey Johnson Roundtree.
p. cm. — (Margaret Walker Alexander series in African American studies)
Includes bibliographical references and index.
ISBN 978-1-60473-132-3 (cloth : alk. paper) 1. Roundtree, Dovey Johnson,
1914– 2. Lawyers—United States—Biography. 3. African American lawyers—United
States—Biography. 4. Women lawyers—United States—Biography. 5. Segregation in
transportation—Law and legislation—United States—History. 6. Segregation—Law and
legislation—United States—History. 7. United States—Race relations—History. 8. Civil
rights—United States—History. I. Roundtree, Dovey Johnson, 1914– II. Title.
KF373.R686M34 2009
340.092—dc22
[B]   2008045574

British Library Cataloging-in-Publication Data available

To the memory of my grandmother, Rachel Bryant Graham,
the greatest warrior I ever knew
—D. J. R.

and

To the memory of my parents: John T. Burns, who loved the law,
and Kathleen Hynes Burns, who loved the dawn; and to both of
them, who loved words and taught me to love them too
—K. J. M.

CONTENTS

ACKNOWLEDGMENTS

When two lives intersect as fruitfully as have Dovey Roundtree's and mine over the past thirteen years, there is much to be grateful for—more than can be articulated in any conventional reckoning. For Dovey, *Justice Older than the Law* is one long, sustained, profound "thank you" to each of the great figures in her life, from the grandmother to whom she has dedicated this book to the staggering procession of legal, intellectual, and spiritual mentors who shaped her.

"I have found that there is always somebody who would be the miracle maker in your life, if you but believe," she told the *Washington Post* in February 1995, and it was that utterly unlawerly statement, printed under the photograph that appears on the cover of this book, that compelled me to seek her out and attempt to capture her life in words. In that journey, I encountered many a miracle maker of my own.

Without my colleague and friend Adina Rishe Gewirtz, this book simply would not exist. It was her belief in the importance of Dovey's story and in my ability to tell it that sustained me in this endeavor, beginning with my first foray into writing about Dovey's career in a 2002 *Washingtonian* magazine article and continuing through every stage of the book's preparation. To capture the voice of a human being as complicated and multifaceted as Dovey Roundtree and discern the narrative shape of her life proved so difficult that had it not been for Adina's story genius and unwavering faith, I do not believe that I could have completed the task. To her and her husband, Danny, who patiently tolerated our endless consultations and made deeply insightful contributions of his own as the manuscript took shape, I say, inadequately but sincerely, "Thank you."

I thank, too, writing colleagues Judith Hillman Paterson and Nancy Ruth Patterson, whose unflagging enthusiasm kept me going. Judith's unerring sense of voice, pacing, and style were critical in the early chapters especially, and I am deeply grateful. To Nancy I owe a special debt for accompanying me on the road trips to Charlotte that enabled me to complete the all-important task of reviewing the manuscript with Dovey. Those were truly the project's golden hours, when Dovey and I were given the great gift of seeing the work coalesce, when Dovey, despite the onset of the blindness that prevented her from reading the manuscript herself, was able to walk every last mile with me.

Dovey's extended family and lifelong colleagues also became inextricably entwined in our endeavor, and I would like to pay particular tribute to her goddaughter, Charlene Pritchett Stevenson, a woman with as large a soul as Dovey's own, and to the incomparable Dr. Walter J. Leonard, who supported us in ways both large and small as we struggled to complete the book. At every stage, they stood on the sidelines, and sometimes even in the middle, cheering us on. Dovey's friend Ella Scarborough was another mainstay, endlessly facilitating the long-distance phone conversations that made it possible for me to continue the interviewing process with Dovey even after her failing health necessitated a move to a nursing home in Charlotte.

In striving to build a deep understanding of Dovey from as many perspectives as possible, I turned to dozens of people who knew her in one or another of the various aspects of her life. I am especially grateful to Dovey's "first child," Peggy Pledger, who shared with such honesty the story of the painful journey that placed her under Dovey's wing; to the family of Dovey's Spelman professor Mary Mae Neptune; and to Dovey's many colleagues at bench and bar who took the time to speak with me about their memories of Dovey and their insights into her approach to the law.

Thanks also to the staff at the National Archives and Records Administration, who assisted me in locating what remained of the ICC case file in *Sarah Keys v. Carolina Coach Company* in the records of the Department of Justice; to Steve Plotkin at the John F. Kennedy Presidential Library and Museum in Boston, who unearthed, in the papers of Attorney General Robert F. Kennedy, the ICC petition that figured so critically in the *Keys* case; to Kenneth Chandler at the Mary McLeod Bethune Museum and Archives for his invaluable help with materials in the collection pertinent to the Women's Army Corps during World War II; to Joellen El Bashir at Howard University's Moorland-Spingarn Research Center for making available to us the papers of James Madison Nabrit, Jr.; and to writer Peter Janney, for sharing with Dovey and me materials related to his ongoing investigation of the Mary Pinchot Meyer murder.

Every writer should have editors like the two who first published Dovey's story as a magazine article—Jack Limpert and Ken DeCell at the *Washingtonian*. It was their publication of my profile of Dovey in March 2002 that launched the book process, and I thank them for believing in the story and giving it the space to flex its muscles. To Ken and to writer Nick Kotz, who took the time to guide me in pitching the book and who directed me to his magnificent agent Tim Seldes and Tim's formidable young associate Jesseca Salky, I owe a monumental debt. No agent could have embraced a manuscript more passionately than Jesseca, nor championed it more expertly than she did as we undertook the process of finding the right home for it. What a stroke of brilliance it was to put the manuscript in the hands of University Press of Mississippi director emerita Seetha Srinivasan, who before her retirement in June 2008 acquired the book, saw to its launching, and passed it along to her superb associate Walter Biggins and the production staff, who shepherded it to completion.

And finally, I must thank my family. Dovey had a whole book to pay tribute to hers; I have but a paragraph. Let the record show that I owe this book and any success I've had as a writer to my parents, John and Kathleen Burns, who prized the precision and beauty of language and passed that along to me, and who believed I could do anything. It was their courage, their nobility, their vision of hope and goodness, that defined the world for me and shaped the way I chose to tell Dovey's story. Although neither of them lived to see this book finished, their influence upon me was profound and it continues to this moment. Soldiers that they were, they urged me onward to completion, along with those two most important of all people, my son Luke, who has spent half of his twenty-seven years on earth watching me write about Dovey and patiently bailing me out of innumerable computer disasters, and my beloved husband, Jack. It is Jack who gave me the greatest of all gifts: the gift of time. Although he frequently compared the duration of this project to the painting of the Sistine Chapel, and wondered, as Pope Julius II did as he regarded Michelangelo's seemingly interminable labors over a period of two decades, when I was going to "make an end," he never gave up. Thanks mostly to his faith, I didn't give up. And at long last, I did make an end.

PREFACE

Justice Older than the Law was born, in the form presented in these pages, at the funeral of a child. His name was Damion Dwayne Blocker, and on the nineteenth day of January in 1996, in his fourteenth year, he was gunned down in the stairwell of the Washington, DC, elementary school where he'd gone to pick up his five-year-old cousin. The two masked gunmen who shot Damion had, the newspaper said, been aiming for someone else. It seemed a death without meaning, the kind that breeds searing rage. The moment I entered the church, I felt it. Like a living thing the anger moved through the great chapel they call "the cathedral of Southeast," charging the air in a way that frightened me.

Had it not been for Dovey Roundtree, the lawyer whose biography I'd begun writing a few months earlier, I would never have been in this place. But she had pressed me, hard, to accompany her on this painful errand—one from which she simply could not turn away. For thirty-five years, since her earliest days in Washington, she'd been a minister here, and I saw that nothing, neither the urgency of courtroom matters nor the office full of clients hungry for her counsel, would deter her. Damion Blocker was, after all, part of her congregation, the one she'd helped build and nurture before that thing she called "the demon of violence" had turned the streets of her beloved Anacostia into killing fields.

I fully understood Dovey's overwhelming sense of obligation, but I did not share it. What place, I remember thinking, did I have inside this circle of pain? As she and I walked together past the casket of Damion, this boy so lately out of childhood, a boy almost exactly the same age as my own son, I felt that perhaps I should have taken my leave of Dovey after our interview at her law offices on the other side of town. There, at least, order prevailed. Hers was the sort of story toward which I'd gravitated ever since I'd begun writing ten years earlier. Over and over, it seemed, I sought out stories of improbable heroes—most of them black. And though I was often asked what drew me, a white woman, to choose African Americans almost exclusively as my subjects, I found it not in the least strange. In the tales of courage, of dignity, of brilliance that transcended the constraints of time and place, I found an affirmation of my own deepest values.

There was something steadying, for me, in what Dovey had managed to accomplish against overwhelming odds: her challenge to Jim Crow in a World War II military; her triumph over segregation in interstate bus travel; her fearless defense of black clients in Washington's all-white judicial system. I am a lawyer's daughter, and I relished the endless sifting and sorting through facts—the facts that defined the life of this legal giant who'd rewritten history again and again over five decades at the bar. But Dovey, with her request that I come with her to the funeral of Damion Blocker, had taken me, abruptly and without warning, into a world both unfamiliar and unsettling.

There was, to begin with, nothing of the civil rights warrior in her that morning. Robed in clerical garb, she moved with slow deliberation past the rows of mourners to join the dignitaries who'd come to offer solace to the family and the community. No one, Dovey had told me in the car a few moments earlier, could make sense of the murder of a child by other children. In fact, she confided, she had no idea, none at all, what she would say when her turn came to address the congregation.

"Always, there must be something to fasten onto as we march out of death," she'd told me, "but this time, I cannot find the rung of hope." In our entire acquaintance up to that point, even when Dovey had spoken of the wrenching loss of her father in childhood, the pain of her life under Jim Crow, her impatience with the law's slowness, and the elusiveness of freedom, I had not once heard that note of despair.

What I had heard her recite, many times over, was the litany of pleas being made by her colleagues seated in front of the altar, as one by one—mayor and judge, pastor and lawmaker—they stood at the pulpit and began sounding the call for stricter gun laws, better police work, heightened security, and punishment, swift and severe, for the crime of murder. As I watched Dovey sitting above me in a great carved cathedral chair, her brow furrowing at the cries for justice that rose softly but clearly from the rows of teenagers in the front of the church, what struck me was how heavily her eighty-one years seemed to weigh upon her. She looked inexpressibly sad, and small, and old.

Until she rose to speak. She changed, then. Her age dropped away, somehow, as though she'd shaken it off like an inconvenient outer garment, and as she stood there, silent, for a very long moment, the fifteen hundred mourners grew silent, too. Dovey looked down at Damion, laid out in white T-shirt and blue jeans at the foot of the altar, and she reached downward with both her hands.

"The caskets," she said, "grow shorter and shorter."

That statement hung in the air in all its breathtaking honesty, waiting to be faced and owned up to even as Dovey consoled the family. What she had dared to put before grieving people was a truth more frightening even than the death of their own—the certain knowledge that what had killed Damion Blocker was not the bullets he took to his face and right shoulder, but a whole world gone mad.

"Somewhere, another boy is crouching," she said, rolling over the gasps of the mourners as they realized she was talking about the perpetrator. "He, too, needs our love." To heal their community, she told them, perpetrator and victim alike needed their care. Justice would come; indeed, it must come. The murderer, or murderers, must walk out of the shadows, own up to their deed, and pay for it. But in the end, it would be necessary to move past the kind of justice provided by the law, past the need to hurt and avenge, to forgiveness, if their broken world was ever to be made whole.

At that moment, I began to understand that no ordinary biography could possibly capture the essence of a woman who took fifteen hundred mourners and made them look their own responsibility in the face. No mere chronicle of accomplishments, however stunning, could convey the worldview of a woman who, having spent her life in the pursuit of simple justice under law, who had indeed loved the law in all its possibility, now so powerfully articulated the need to go beyond it.

I knew, too, that Dovey's story must be told in her own voice. It was her voice, in all its richness, in its biblical rhythms and the easy grace of its southern cadences, that had lifted up row upon row of people in chaos and moved them almost invisibly from the brink of destruction to the beginning of healing. In Dovey's voice was her soul, the expression of her spirituality, her passion for goodness, her fire, her softness, her wisdom, and her pain. My job as a writer was, from that day onward, clear.

I set about to capture her voice and draw out the themes of her life, and in so doing I learned how to tell a new kind of story, about challenges to the spirit as well as to the mind, about the places a human being discovers when there is nowhere left to go. I began to understand how one might, in the words of the hymn Dovey's grandmother so loved, "make a way out of no way." In the midst of all that, Dovey and I created this book together, she telling me stories in the magnificent oral tradition of her grandmother, I trying to capture that as a writer. The voice is Dovey's; the words are mine; the vision is one we share. The fact that the two of us are separated by forty years in time and the divide of race that even now splits America seems to me insignificant in comparison to what we wish to pass on together. *Justice Older than the Law* is more than an account of a remarkable life. It is a collaboration between two women with a common vision of the family, of children, of the future and the shape it must take if we are to survive.

This is the story of that vision.

KATIE McCABE

Justice Older than the Law

1. WALKING UNAFRAID

Every evening, in the tiny kitchen of the old frame shotgun house where I grew up in Charlotte, North Carolina, my grandma Rachel marked the day's end by a ritual etched in my memory with a clarity that belies the eighty years since then.

She ceased to rush, as she did endlessly in the hours between dawn and darkness, and she commenced to draw water and lay out clean towels and mix an ointment she made of turpentine and mutton tallow. I would stand, quiet, watching her heat the water on the wood stove, pour it into a metal pan, then remove her stockings and hoist her skirts as she lifted her feet into the steaming bath.

Her feet were broken. They were gnarled and twisted and horribly misshapen, with the bones sticking out in strange ways. As she lifted them into the steaming water, she winced. And I would know, though she had spoken no word and given no sign, that all day long her feet had been paining her.

How frightened I was the first time I saw those poor broken feet. I was five years old, and my mother and my three sisters and I had just moved to my grandparents' home after the death of my father, James Eliot Johnson, in the influenza epidemic of 1919. My grandmother had scooped us up and taken us under her wing, whisking us from my parents' house to the little parsonage where she lived with my grandpa. All day long, she hovered over us, even as she flew about the house and garden, baking communion bread and hauling water and starching altar linens. Like a tiny whirling dervish she moved, and so, when I first saw her grow quiet, I was startled.

Then I saw her feet, so large and misshapen they seemed to belong to another woman entirely, and I drew back, frightened. Every night after that, I'd look at her scarred, twisted feet, at the skin stretched taut over the jutting bones, and I'd want to ask her what had made them that way. But something in her silence warned me not to.

Over time I grew to cherish this part of the evening, for it was one of the rare moments when I could actually be of help to my grandmother, who appeared in daytime hours, so far as I could tell, to hold the whole earth and sky under her command. I learned to wait by her side as she began the bathing process and watch for the moment when her face began to relax, the sign that the steaming water had done its work. I'd stir the ointment, and gently as I could, I'd rub her feet, taking care not to hurt the sores and bruises and bleeding places. The salve, like most of my grandmother's homemade medicines, smelled worse than sin itself, but it had mighty healing powers. For in the morning, she was moving once again about the house and garden, swaying and swinging on the outsides of her feet, awkwardly, but swiftly.

The day came, finally, as I was just beginning to mature into womanhood, when Grandma took me to her in private and spoke to me of what had happened to her feet.

A white man had broken them.

It had happened a very long time ago, Grandma said, when she was a young girl, just coming into womanhood herself. She was only thirteen years old, but she had developed early, and she had seen the man watching her with a look that told her he meant to do her harm.

"The slave master," she called him, though in point of fact the days of slavery ended ten years before my grandmother was born. He was the overseer on the farm near Henrietta, North Carolina, where her father worked, and when she spoke of what he had tried to do to her, a look of anguish crossed her face unlike any I had seen before or would see after.

"He was meanin' to bother me, Dovey Mae," she told me, in the delicate way she had of speaking about things sexual. "I ran and fought every way I knew how. And I hurt him. Then he grabbed hold o' me and he stomped, hard as he could, on my feet—to keep me from runnin' for good, he told me. But I kept on runnin'."

"Wasn't nothing to do but fight him, hard as I could," she said. "He wasn't goin' to have his way with me."

Grandma's mother had wrapped her smashed, bleeding feet in cloth and rubbed them with the mutton tallow and turpentine ointment Grandma would use for the rest of her days. But the bones had been so crushed that her feet were forever misshapen, and so twisted that for a while she could not walk at all. When she did, it was with a swaying awkwardness that late at night became a limp.

And yet, for all of that, she had won. He had not, as she said, had "his way" with her.

I saw my grandma Rachel fight everything with that same fierceness—poverty, sickness, injustice, and even despair. Like a mighty stream, her courage flowed through my childhood, shaping me as rushing water shapes the pebbles in its path.

She was not, of course, the only influence upon me in my early years; my mother, with her keen intelligence and her quiet ambition, and my grandpa, with his passion for books and education, set me on my way toward learning and goodness. But my grandmother was the warrior in the family. It was she who armed me for battle, with weapons both soft and fierce, imprinting me with a mark so deep it seemed to go down into my very soul.

There was, to be sure, nothing of the warrior in her tiny person, for she was small of stature and ever so feminine. Many a time as a girl I would study the faded old photograph of Grandma on the parlor wall and wonder how the delicate black-eyed young woman who looked part African queen and part Indian princess had fought that white man with such ferocity, whence came the iron that carried her through the sorrows that befell her in the years after that portrait was made. She had married, given birth to my mother and her two brothers, and then in the way of so many black women of her time, she'd had to stand by helplessly as the wrath of the Klan fell upon the head of her young husband. No one knew what had incited their rage, nor did Grandma ever learn the particulars of his fate after she bade him farewell in the woods outside Henrietta. She'd sent him on his way with all the money she had in the world—a quarter she'd kept in her apron pocket—and had never seen him again. Somewhere in his flight northward, he'd met his death at the Klan's hands.

She had to push onward after that, to do what generations of black folk had done before her—to "make a way out of no way." I am persuaded, thinking on it now, that my grandmother spent all her days making a way out of no way. And she'd done it with no more than a third-grade education. She'd picked herself up after the loss of her young husband and rebuilt her life with the great man who became my grandfather, the Reverend Clyde Graham, but that, too, had its hardships. Again and again she had to uproot her family, for the life of an itinerant preacher in the South meant endless movement from one country church to another. At last, Grandpa's reputation as a preacher won him an appointment as pastor of East Stonewall AME Zion, one of Charlotte's largest black churches. Grandma settled with Grandpa into the parsonage, watched her daughter, Lela, marry, give birth to me and my sisters, make a home of her own.

And then my father was stricken.

I was too young to grasp the terrible sweep of the influenza epidemic that the returning soldiers brought home after World War I. I understood only that my tall handsome papa, who one moment had been riding me on the handlebars of his bicycle in the autumn sunshine, was gone, and my mother was crying. The next thing I knew, we were in my grandmother's home, to stay. So ferociously did she take on our sadness that if grief had been a wild animal at large in the house, she could not have attacked it with greater vengeance.

I have thought many times since then how defeating it must have been for Grandma—a woman who knew what it was to lose a husband and be left with young children—to watch my mother disappear into a netherworld right in front of our eyes. My beautiful mother, so young she seemed more like a big sister, the playmate who loved to beat us at jacks and hike up her skirts and jump hopscotch with us, grew silent and thin. She took no care of her person, wore her long wavy hair in a tangle down her back, and refused to eat. It was terrifying to me and my sisters, and surely my grandmother must have been horrified.

Yet she took us in hand so fiercely and so firmly that for the rest of my life I have remembered that time as one when I was swallowed up in love. Against the tidal wave of sadness, Grandma pushed back with a tidal wave of her own, launching what amounted to a one-woman assault on despair. In such things as the baking of cinnamon pastries and the pounding of herbs and the serving of sweet potatoes and the setting of bread to rise she undertook to push the darkness out.

Soft weapons, those, and yet in my grandmother's hands they were as formidable as any I have seen in my time. Only someone who has lain in the early morning darkness breathing in the smell of bread baking and beans and ham hocks bubbling, as I did every day of that long winter of 1919, can know the potency of such small things to heal. It was not simply the food, of course. It was my grandmother herself, all five feet of her, that filled the house from morning to night, her fiery spirit that displaced the darkness.

The stiller my mother became, the more quickly my grandmother moved, rushing back and forth between the kitchen and the bedroom, serving up tea, endlessly tempting Mama with treats for weeks on end, until finally, one day, Mama laughed.

It was not a little chuckle, but a great loud laugh. When the rest of us heard the sound of my mother's laughter coming from the back porch where she and Grandma were stringing beans, we all burst out laughing—Grandpa, who'd been studying over his Bible as he prepared his Sunday sermon, my older sister Beatrice and my younger sister Eunice and even baby Rachel in her high chair. I had no earthly idea what the joke was, nor did I care. I joined right in with the laughter, too, and in that moment, the world righted itself.

The sadness never completely vanished, of course. It never does, after death. My father's passing left a hole in my heart that was to stay with me for the rest of my life. Even to this very moment, the emptiness remains with me. But after my mother laughed at whatever little joke Grandma made that day, our family was able to move forward, to get on with the business of living, in all its goodness. And my childhood, which had begun with the terrible darkness of my father's death, opened up at the hands of my grandmother into a time shot through with light.

Everything Grandma did seemed woven with magic. Even before dawn, summer mornings came alive for me, as I trailed behind her into the woods in search of blackberries. They grew along the creek, amid stickers and bushes, and Grandma knew how to find the ripest, the best. She knew how to follow the birds to the places where they grew thickest. And in some otherworldly way I could not fathom, she could read the darkness simply by listening to the sounds that came out of it.

With autumn came the time for the making of lye soap, a rite that drew the neighbors from blocks around to our backyard as Grandma turned fat drippings into soap that bleached clothing so white the ladies had a name for it: "Miss Rachel's clean." It was made, my grandmother said, by the "right sign of the moon," and she alone among all the women knew when that sign came. I'd dart in and out among the fig trees that grew tall around our property and breathe in the cool air as Grandma lit the fire beneath the great cauldron. Moving in as close as I dared, I watched as she poured boxes of Red Devil lye into the mixture of cooking grease she'd collected all year from the neighbors. The liquid in the cauldron boiled, the ladies sang and gossiped and laughed,

Grandma ladled foam from the top, and then all at once, the bubbling mass cleared. Closely as I watched I never could tell the precise moment at which that filthy mess turned beautiful. But the white cakes of soap, gelled and molded and placed on butcher paper for the neighbors to take home, were as perfect and pure as the liquid in the cauldron was greasy and dark and foul smelling.

Enfolding it all, week in, week out, was the Sunday ritual that pulled us up tall with pride, my sisters and me, as we rushed to take our places with Mama in the grand procession Grandma and Grandpa led from the parsonage to East Stonewall AME Zion, where Grandpa pastored. Behind us marched the whole world—the dozens of families who made up Grandpa's flock, wending their way through the clay streets and alleyways of the neighborhood known as Brooklyn. At the head of the parade walked Grandma, starched altar linens draped over one arm, the other linked with Grandpa's, as she led the crowd in the chorus of the hymn she loved best, the one she hummed from morning to night.

Blessed Assurance, Jesus is mine.
O what foretaste of Glory Divine.
This is my story, this my song,
Praising my Savior all the day long.

People came to Grandma—people whose faces were heavy with sadness, mothers worried about their children, girls in trouble of one kind or another, men who'd gotten mixed up with the bootleggers or card sharks who preyed on the desperate. For all of them Grandma had something—a sermon with plenty of scorch, or as the occasion required, what she called "some straightnin' out." For sick folk she bottled up doses of the cold medicines she pounded from gypsum weed and herbs she found in the forest, the paste that stung and smelled but that somehow sucked the pain from your chest.

So powerful a force was my grandmother in our home and in the neighborhood at large that it never occurred to me as a little child that there was anything she could not shape, or mold, or fix, any darkness she could not chase away. But the day came, as it had to, when I grew old enough to venture forth from the cocoon I inhabited. And I saw for the first time an ugliness Grandma could not banish. On that day, I looked Jim Crow full in the face.

Nothing about that morning, in the spring of my sixth, or perhaps my seventh year, betokened ill. The sunshine warmed the earth beneath my feet the moment I stepped outside; the birds called, and the forbidden creek beckoned. Before I'd even had a chance to weigh the prospect of chasing butterflies against the possibility of a whipping, though, Grandma surprised me.

"Dovey Mae," she said, using the name she herself had given me at birth, "you may come with me to town this morning."

I nearly jumped out of my skin. The prospect of accompanying my grandmother on such an adult errand as business in town sent me ripping into the bedroom to change into a dress and a sunhat as fast as I could go.

As Grandma and I came up the block, I could hear the Biddleville trolley clanging and squeaking its way down McDowell Street, the thoroughfare that connected the city's Second Ward, where we lived, with the neighborhood known as Biddleville. Wild as a buck to begin with, I was so excited on this occasion that Grandma had all she could do to keep me by her side, no matter how much she threatened to wear me out if I didn't hold tight to her hand. The minute the trolley doors swung open and I spotted an empty seat behind the driver, I shot up the steps and settled right into it. There I was, with a perfect view of just about everything worth looking at on that trolley car, so far as I was concerned. I sat up straight in the cane-bottomed seat and grinned at Grandma.

But she wasn't smiling, and neither was the driver, who had turned around to look at me. The color rose in his face, and when he spoke, he spat.

"Get that pickaninny out of here!" he shouted at my grandmother, with such venom that my cheeks burned. "You know she can't sit there."

I had never heard the word "pickaninny" before, but I could tell immediately from my grandmother's face that she had. It was a moment that was replayed hundreds, perhaps thousands of times across the country in the years when segregation held the South by the throat. More than three decades would pass before Rosa Parks refused to move to the rear of a Montgomery, Alabama, bus and launched a movement.

In the twenties, such behavior was unthinkable. My grandmother, a middle-aged black woman abroad in a North Carolina town with a small child in tow, did the only thing she could do and still hold on to both her dignity and her life. She got off the trolley.

In one motion she grabbed me by the hand, whirled around and yanked the cord so hard I thought it would snap. The moment the trolley stopped, she pulled me down the car's back steps and turned, face set, toward town.

Then she began to march.

Block after block we walked, round the corner of Brevard, past Meyers Street Elementary School, across Alexander Street, half a mile to town. There was no sound but the rustle of Grandma's stiffly starched apron, and there was no stopping. She had me tight by the hand, all the way up the steps of the brick insurance building where she did her business, and back again. We crossed the square and made our way down East Trade Street, heading for home.

That was the longest mile I ever walked. I had to run to keep up with my grandmother, who quickened her pace with each block. And the faster she walked, the more awkwardly she swung her legs, rocking and swaying from side to side the way she did at night when she was very tired. Though trolley after trolley passed us, my grandmother never slowed or even turned her head. What frightened me more than anything was her silence.

It wasn't until after dinner that she finally spoke about the trolley car. Just as she did every night, she lit the kerosene lamp in the sitting room and cleared a space for my grandfather to open the old family Bible. Then she disappeared into the kitchen to take her cinnamon and butter pastries—"stickies," she called them—from the oven. It seemed to me that she was gone an unusually long time.

When she came back, she set down the tray and wiped her hands on her apron.

"Something bad happened to Dovey Mae today," she said.

I felt my cheeks grow hot, and I looked down.

"The mean old conductor man on the trolley car called her a bad name." No one spoke. In the lamplight, I looked up into Grandma's face, and I knew she was almost as angry as she'd been that morning.

"I want to tell you all something," she said. She looked around the table at each of us. Her gaze rested last on me.

"Now hear me, and hear me good," she said. "My chillun is as good as anybody."

Only from a distance of years is it possible for me to fathom the courage required for my grandmother to pick herself up from such humiliation and speak those words. I believe, now, that in the long moment when she vanished into the kitchen, Grandma was crying. Certainly she was reaching down into her heart's core, for she was wrestling with the greatest curse of segregation: the horror of having to watch one's own children and grandchildren face its degradation.

In the course of my life, I have heard black people say they got used to the pain of segregation, eventually. I weep for the numbness of mind and the brokenness of spirit that motivates statements like that. Let me say here for all time that never for one moment of my life under Jim Crow did I grow accustomed to being excluded, banned, pushed aside, reduced. I was never to take a back seat on a trolley or bus, drink the rusty water that trickled from the "Colored" fountains, smell the garbage in the back-alley entrance to segregated movie theaters, or scratch myself on the rough toilet paper in the black restrooms but that I felt personally violated. And I know, having seen the look on Grandma's face that night, that she felt the same way. Powerful as she was, she could not protect me from the thing she most hated.

But she could arm me. And arm me she did, with words that lifted me up and made me forever proud: "My chillun is as good as anybody."

2. Making Somethin' of Yourself

In the 1920s, the most famous black woman in America, if not the world, was Mary McLeod Bethune—educator, activist, and consultant to President Coolidge. That such a woman should have called upon my grandmother, should have huddled with her in close conference upon the broken-down sofa at our house at 905 East Boundary Street, should have consulted with her on the future of Negro children, defies the laws of chance and, indeed, every reality of the social hierarchy, at least as we know it today.

Yet consult with Grandma she did. The first time I laid eyes on the great woman, I was perhaps ten years old. She was nodding gravely as my grandmother spoke and sipping a tall glass of Grandma's homemade locust beer. Though Grandma's schooling had ended at the third grade, and Dr. Bethune presided over the education of college students at the Florida institute she herself had founded, they addressed each other in the manner of old acquaintances and trusted allies. She called Grandma "Rachel," and Grandma in her turn called her renowned visitor "Mary."

I never did come to know precisely how the two of them met, but this was the era of the black women's club movement, which cut across class lines in a way that has no modern counterpart. Any one of my grandmother's connections—her close friendship with Charlotte's NAACP president, her relationships with wealthy black ministers' wives, her office in the prestigious Order of the Eastern Star—might have placed her in Dr. Bethune's path as she barnstormed through the South in the twenties, recruiting women for the National Association of Colored Women's Clubs. Whatever their initial connection, I am entirely persuaded that having met once, my grandmother and Dr. Bethune were drawn together in the way kindred spirits are in great struggles.

No two women I have ever known—and in adulthood I would come to know Dr. Bethune very well indeed—fought for justice quite so fiercely as those two.

Even as a child of ten or twelve, I sensed in Dr. Bethune something powerful, almost regal. Ebony-skinned and crowned with an enormous feathered hat that matched her silk suit, she spoke in a voice so rich, so cultivated, so filled with authority that it held me fast. By the time my grandmother knew her, she was already a figure of legend, a woman who had done the unthinkable: she had defied the Klan, alone. I knew what that meant, for I carried with me from one terrible night in my earliest childhood the shadowy memory of men howling and whips lashing and horses' hooves pounding outside our house, of hot darkness pressing on my neck, of the muffled sound of my sisters' sobbing, of Grandma's feet dragging on the floorboards as she paced, and the clear awareness that not even my grandmother for all her boldness could have protected us if the men in the white hoods had determined to do us harm.

That Dr. Bethune had taken on that nameless horror stunned me. But she had, rather than abandon her campaign for black voting rights. She'd faced down the Klansmen who'd threatened to burn her college to the ground, so the story went, turning the campus floodlights upon the horde of hooded men with their torches and leading her girls in the singing of spirituals, one after another, until at last the men turned their horses around, and rode off into the night.

And there were so many other stories, told and retold among church folk and the ladies' societies Grandma entertained. They spoke of the world-renowned woman who'd begun life as Mary Jane McLeod, daughter of freed slaves. Alongside her sixteen brothers and sisters she'd picked cotton in the fields of Mayesville, South Carolina, until with her brilliance she captured the attention of a black missionary who'd seen to her schooling. Barred because of her race from the missions of Africa to which she felt called, she'd taken on the fight for Negro advancement as her life's work. In a tiny cabin with five pupils, she founded the Florida normal school that would eventually become Bethune-Cookman College, and as a child I loved to hear the tales of how she'd used packing crates for desks and elderberry juice for ink and raised funds by selling sweet potato pies. Later, when poll taxes shut blacks out of the voting booth, it was said she took to bicycling around the countryside collecting money to pay them.

No church paper in those days failed to mention her, and when the weekly newsletters arrived from the AME office, Grandma would scan the headlines in search of Dr. Bethune's name, then command Eunice or Bea or me to read the article aloud, often more than once. If Dr. Mary McLeod Bethune, child of slaves, could rise from poverty to command the attention of presidents, Rachel Graham's granddaughters could do the same. In fact, Grandma insisted, we *would* do the same—or she'd know the reason why not.

"Girl, you are goin' to make somethin' of yourself, if I have to beat it into you," Grandma would tell me when I'd come home dripping wet from my forays into the forbidden creek. In her eyes, the world was locked in a mighty battle between good and evil, and the line between the two was as sharp and clear as the fence that separated our nest of shotgun houses and good church folk from that place of sin and damnation on the other side, the black ghetto known as Blue Heaven. So vile were the goings-on in its speakeasies and brothels that Grandma judged the mere *sound* of it dangerous, and she'd whisk us girls off the porch on summer evenings, lest we drink too deeply of the raucous jazz music and wild laughter floating on the breeze. Satan himself, Grandma insisted, walked buck naked down the streets of Blue Heaven on Saturday nights, and her folk would have no truck with it—not even at a distance.

It was a way of looking at the world that entirely suffused my sisters and me, for my grandfather and my mother lived by the same iron law of decency and hard work and goodness. And they held us unflinchingly to the goal of a college education, which was, after all, the "way out" for black people.

We heard that like a mantra all day long during the week, and on Sundays my grandfather sounded the theme from the pulpit at East Stonewall, weaving it together with the dozens of other threads of his elaborate sermons. From the books he spread out on the kitchen table in the evenings came ideas about freedom and democracy and education and hope for a better future, all tied into his biblical text for the week. A man with only a high school education, my grandfather was nevertheless a person of true greatness of mind, and what he was preaching, in his own way, was a brand of religious activism that would come to be known during the civil rights period as the "social gospel." Nobody called it that back in the twenties, of course, but that is precisely what it was—a rich tapestry of Holy Scripture and political protest, all strung together in a way that shot through you like something electric.

There was nothing abstract about any of it, in Grandpa's mind—particularly not about the need for what he called "an educated black youth." His four granddaughters were the youth he was bent on educating, no matter what else he had to give up. We pieced out our existence in pennies, it seemed to me, and had it not been for the donations of food we received as a minister's family, we might not have made it at all. Still, by the time I was in the fourth grade, Grandpa had managed to buy us the entire set of *The Book of Knowledge*, one volume at a time, on the change he eked out from the proceeds of the little store he ran in town. How I loved those red leather–bound books with their maps of faraway places and their color illustrations of all the insects and birds and creatures I was forever bringing home for study and nurturing. On the appointed day each month, I waited for the newest volume to arrive in the mail, ripping open the brown paper wrapping and diving into a corner to devour the contents. The books held the answers to questions I hadn't even thought of asking. All this, from a man who was no kin to me.

That was the way of things in our house—and it had been long before I was born, from the time Grandma married Grandpa and he took my mother and her brothers to raise as his own children. When Mama married my father as a widower, she had in turn taken his daughter, Beatrice, to raise. No daughter—or sister—could have been more beloved than Beatrice, for blood ties counted but little with my folk where love was concerned. Bea was a born teacher, our reading coach and tutor from the time Eunice and Rachel and I could hold a book, and when she set her sights on Winston-Salem Teachers College, Mama and my grandparents found a way to send her there, using the small inheritance Grandma had received upon the death of her brother. College was as essential to life as breathing in our family. And Bea was family.

In all the ways, great and small, in which a group of people living under one roof bond tighter than glue, the seven of us were bonded. Nothing that happened beyond the reach of that table ever broke the bond among us, though the terrible times that came with the Great Depression pushed our family almost to the breaking point. Chaos descended on Charlotte following the stock market crash in the fall of my sophomore year, and our little world disintegrated as well. The bankers who'd brought their shirts to Grandma no longer sought out her laundering services, and the food donations dwindled to almost nothing. My grandfather's little store went under. Crushed by the hopelessness of our situation, he began to drink; his parishioners began to whisper; the bishop called for his removal from East Stonewall. Finally, the day came when we were forced to vacate the parsonage.

That was when I learned how great a thing love is, that it is greater even than shame. And there was shame in those years. I saw it in my grandmother's face when we were turned out of our home, when Grandpa was shunted from one church to another, first in the city and then out in the country, until finally he lost his stature as a minister altogether. As we moved from the parsonage and struggled to pay rent with the money Mama earned cleaning houses, Grandma aged before my eyes.

Still, she never gave up, and neither did Grandpa. The year we moved from the parsonage, they took in two foster children, in the hope that the stipend from the county would help us to pay the rent in our new home. It was, Grandma said, a way to survive, and yet, even in that, she and Grandpa and Mama transformed it into something more. No other family in Mecklenburg County wanted Tom and Pete, the eight-year-old twin boys my grandparents took to raise, for they were the product of that most despised of all unions—the one between a white woman and a black man. Boldly, my grandparents and my mother embraced those two sad, bewildered little boys. On the one occasion when I heard a neighbor whispering about Tom and Pete's parentage, Grandma turned on the woman, her black eyes snapping fire.

"I'll tell you exactly whose children they are," she said. "They're *mine!*"

When all was said and done, I am not sure the allowance my grandparents received from the county ever did much more than cover Tom and Pete's expenses. As the Depression deepened, my grandfather opened yet another store. So often, as I saw him struggle to provide for all of us, I thought of what he'd said to my sisters and me the night he'd brought our family to live in his home. He had drawn us close, lifted Rachel into his lap, and promised that so long as he was alive, we would never go hungry. In spite of everything, he kept that promise.

During those years when Grandma fought with fire and Grandpa with tenderness, I watched my mother emerge from the shadows in the wake of my father's death as a woman of steel in her own right.

I'd known even as a little girl that it was quite a thing, in Charlotte, to be the daughter of Lela Bryant Johnson, to sit in the front row at East Stonewall as she led the choir with her rich alto, to walk down the street and watch heads turn at her delicate beauty. Her fingers teased the most beautiful music from the creaky old upright piano we inherited with the parsonage, and her voice danced over the hymns Grandma hummed from morning to night, filling in the tunes with the words that became such a part of me they would forever shape the way I conceived of things spiritual.

But there was far more to my mother even than that. As my sisters and I advanced in school, I discerned in her a deep ambition. She was the one who brought in the bulk of our income during the Depression, working long hours as a domestic for one of the wealthiest white families in Charlotte. I, too, began working for them on weekends as a nanny to their little boy, but it was Mama who carried the load. Every night after dinner, she marched off to night school to study dressmaking and tailoring, turning those skills to such account that we were able to hold our home when others were losing theirs. Had the times been different, she would unquestionably have pursued higher education. The times being what they were, she held to that vision for us.

Mama was a woman who could see things where others could not, who could conjure up in her mind's eye the entire picture of a tailored, lined, and finished coat or suit from a length of fabric lying folded on a table. How she turned a bolt of crepe or wool into something that fit the curves of a person and swished and swung when that person walked, I never knew. It was a process as fascinating to me as the making of lye soap, and every bit as impenetrable. Grandma, I reckoned, had secrets; Mama just *saw*.

In her eyes, we girls were women of destiny, with futures as golden as if we'd been daughters of privilege. How proud Mama was when Beatrice set out for Winston-Salem Teachers College, at that time the only black institution in the country which granted not merely a teaching certificate but a baccalaureate degree in education. Her oldest daughter was a young woman of exceptional talent, Mama said; she deserved no less.

I was the child who put Mama most in mind of Papa. I spoke like him, she told me often, used my hands in the way he did, had his ability to command the attention of a roomful of people. Someday, my mother told me, I would live out his legacy, walk where he could not, do the things of which he'd only dreamed.

From out of her dresser drawer one day came a tiny black book of devotions, in which my father had written one simple sentence. Mama called me to her, giving me the book to keep—as a reminder, she said, of Papa's deepest passion.

"By all let it be known," my father had penned on the fly leaf, "that I, James Eliot Johnson, have loved the teaching of Sunday school." I read the proclamation aloud, puzzled at the import my mother assigned to it. In those words, as in all things, Mama saw something beyond what lay before her. My father, she told me, was brilliant. Had he lived, she believed he would have become far more than a Sunday school teacher. His gifts would have made him one of the great ministers of the black community, a man who would have changed the lives of people far and wide. She insisted that I would do the same—whether as the doctor I aspired to be, or in some other profession. I was destined, she said, for my own brand of greatness.

The college upon which my mother set her sights for me was truly an impossible dream, and would have been even if the Depression had not wiped out our savings: Spelman College, the elite undergraduate institution for girls of wealth and privilege, in Atlanta, Georgia. Had the person who brought it to our attention been anyone other than my beloved eighth-grade teacher Edythe Wimbish, the notion would have been discounted immediately. But Edythe Wimbish was no ordinary woman. She hailed from one of the most influential black families in Atlanta, a family that traced its lineage to Reconstruction days, when her father had wielded political power as a Republican Party "wheel" and federal customs inspector. That someone of Edythe's breeding and education had come to Charlotte to teach at Meyers Street Elementary, the broken-down old frame building where I attended grade school, was a stroke of remarkable good fortune. That she then took me under her wing and came out to our home to speak to Mama and my grandparents about my future seemed downright miraculous.

What Miss Wimbish said about Spelman and its opportunities took such hold of my mother's imagination that she did something no one in the family had ever dared to do: she took a position against my grandmother. In our household, Grandma's word was law; in all things great and small, Grandpa and Mama deferred to her. But in this matter, my mother pressed and pushed as I had never seen her do before.

"It's such a wonderful chance for Dovey Mae, Mama," she'd say to Grandma, who would nod, and grow quiet, and turn and stir her pots when Mama talked of the ties Spelman had to the other black universities in Atlanta, the doors it would open for me, the preparation I'd get for medical school at such a college. It was not that Grandma wanted anything less than the very best for my sisters and me; she'd held us to the example of Mary McLeod Bethune from the time we could think. And no one was prouder than Grandma that a woman like Edythe Wimbish had taken such an interest in me. When she appeared at our door, Grandma received her with almost as much awe as she did the great Dr. Bethune. When Miss Wimbish praised my academic achievements, Grandma's face shone.

But Spelman troubled Grandma, for two reasons. First, the cost of attending such an elite four-year institution staggered her: the yearly tuition was $75, room and board $225. That came to $1,200 for four years—more than eight times what it had cost to send Beatrice to Winston-Salem Teachers College, where the state paid the tuition and students had only to cover their living expenses. Then, too, for all its prestige and opportunity, Spelman was in Atlanta, the heart of Klan country, a place torn by race riots so terrible in 1906 that twenty-five years later, black folk of Grandma's generation spoke of them as though they'd just happened. To send her "chillun" 250 miles into the Deep South, to a city where blacks feared to walk the streets, even in the daytime, was more than my grandmother could contemplate. Silent as Grandma was on the subject, I well understood what terrified her.

And yet, I yearned with all my being to go to Spelman. Even the prospect of grave danger did not wipe out the feeling that came over me when I sat studying, late in the evenings, pondering the things Miss Wimbish had said about the school before she'd left Charlotte for her native Atlanta at the end of my eighth-grade year. She herself had graduated from Atlanta University, but she viewed Spelman as the ultimate academic institution for women. At Spelman, she told me, I would learn at the feet of extraordinary professors both black and white, study not only premed subjects but the classics and music, perhaps pursue the study of the French horn I'd begun in high school. As a Spelman student, I'd have access to the facilities of Atlanta's other fine black institutions, even of its graduate schools. Danger paled, in my eyes, alongside that prospect.

A strange turn of circumstance opened the door to Spelman shortly before my graduation from high school. The family for whom Mama and I worked, the Hurleys, were moving to Atlanta, Mama announced one night. Mr. Hurley had been offered a new job, and Mrs. Hurley had asked Mama and me to accompany them. We would have a place to live, with good, decent white people, Mama told Grandma and Grandpa. Sheltered from the horrors of the Depression in the safety of their home, we could survive even in Atlanta. And in two years' time, if all went well, Mama believed we could save enough for my first year's tuition. Then she would return home.

At that, Grandma shut her eyes and shook her head. We all grew quiet, for every one of us, even little Tom and Pete, knew what she meant. Our family would be split apart. Mama would have to leave behind Eunice, a year younger than I, and Rachel, just finishing elementary school, and Tom and Pete, coming up right behind her.

The thing that Grandma had always feared was about to happen. Through all the years when she and Grandpa had moved from place to place as a young couple, when my papa had died and we'd left our home, even when the church conference had turned us out of the parsonage, Grandma had managed to keep us all together. Nothing was more hateful to her, the child of slaves, than the prospect of breaking up her family.

My mother, too, looked sad. But she did not back down. It would be for only a little while, she argued in her quiet way, just long enough to save up tuition money for my first year at Spelman. There was no work in Charlotte, no chance for us at all. Grandma knew that as well as Mama did.

For several weeks, I said my own silent prayers as I watched Grandma struggle and heard my mother's quiet, persistent arguments: that Edythe would be there, that the Hurleys were good people, that we would not be alone.

At last Grandma relented.

"Well, Lela," she said one evening. "I reckon you and Dovey Mae won't be alone down there in Atlanta. I'll be at the Throne of Grace, prayin' all the time."

3. "PASS IT ON":
Spelman and the Legacy of Mae Neptune

I thought I had arrived at the Throne of Grace the first time I saw Spelman.

When Mama and I visited the campus not long after our arrival in Atlanta in the fall of 1932, we stood staring—staring, without saying a word—at the stately white-columned buildings, the magnificent Sisters Chapel, the lush green lawns ringed by dogwood and magnolias, all so flawless they looked like they'd been painted. That such a place lay within my grasp—I, who'd begun my education in a rotting frame building with rickety outdoor stairways and privies and a play yard of bare clay—seemed barely comprehensible. Right then and there, I decided Spelman was God's answer to the prayers of the world.

Yet twenty feet from the place where the trolley stopped, that vast expanse of sheer perfection changed into a filthy, poverty-stricken, hate-filled city. Atlanta had always been a racial hell, just as Grandma had told us, but the grinding poverty of the Great Depression made it worse. Whole families—black as well as white—lived on the streets and in the alleyways; men walked aimlessly about looking for jobs that didn't exist; women foraged for food in garbage cans. What few pockets of goodwill might have existed between blacks and whites before the Depression, the fear of starvation and homelessness killed. Each time Mama and I boarded the trolley, we took seats all the way in the back and held our breath at every transfer point on the fifteen-mile route from the city to the Hurleys' home in the town of Decatur. I watched the black and white passengers crowd onto the cars, jostling and elbowing their way down the aisles, my whole body stiff with dread until we reached the Hurleys' home, a safe haven in the midst of that awful city.

At least, that was the way Mama and I perceived it in the two years it took for the two of us to save the seventy-five dollars for my freshman tuition and see to my admission to Spelman. Had my mother sensed anything amiss in the home where I was to live, she would never have departed for Charlotte in the spring of 1934. It was in fact only after Mama left that Mrs. Hurley began to change toward me, to grow ever so slightly cooler and more distant. At first, I told myself I was misreading her. She had, after all, taken Mama and me under her wing, done us a hundred kindnesses over the years. I knew, too, that she held me dear for the care I showered on her little boy, Bailey Hurley, Jr. But on the afternoon when my official letter of admission arrived from Spelman and I held it out for her to see, excited and proud, I sensed that all was not well.

"Well, my goodness gracious," she said, raising her eyebrows and looking straight at me and not at the letter, "why on *earth* do you want to go to Spelman?"

There was a coldness in her genteel voice I'd never heard before. I stared at her, wondering if I'd understood her question correctly.

"Mama wants me to go," I finally answered. I had never imagined that anyone as lovely as Mrs. Hurley could sneer, but she did. Her pretty mouth twisted, and without another word she turned and left the room.

Though she made no move to stop me from beginning classes, I walked on tenterhooks in her presence from that day forward. I felt her eyes upon me as I did my chores, watching me, as though trying to puzzle out something she truly could not comprehend.

"Just look at Mrs. So-and-So's girl," she'd say out of nowhere, naming some young woman who worked in service for one or the other of her lady friends. "She's just doing fine now, isn't she? Without any old college."

Always, she spoke softly and gently. But there was nothing soft about the snatches of conversation I overheard when her friends came to call, as I bustled about, serving tea or entertaining Bailey.

"I certainly wouldn't keep her around," I heard one woman say. Another, eyeing my stack of textbooks on the dining room table, shook her head as I passed through.

"The impudent little thing," she said, so loudly I heard her from the kitchen. "I'll tell you, I wouldn't have it. No indeed. Not in my home."

Something inside me began to harden. I watched Mrs. Hurley as carefully as she watched me, saw her nodding at the pronouncements of her friends. And I understood that in all the years when she'd talked so proudly of how she would "make something" of me, she had not imagined I would actually try to make something of *myself*. In her mind, I had broken a sacred trust.

Never in my life had I hidden my thoughts and feelings, but now, alone in a house where I was despised, I drew up a mask and I took care never to let it slip while in Mrs. Hurley's presence. Only late at night, alone with my books, and in the hours I spent with six-year-old Bailey, did I feel the heaviness lift. I'd taken delight in children from the time Tom and Pete had become my little brothers, and bright and curious as Bailey was, I found no end of joy in reading to him, working with him on his letters and numbers, entertaining him by playing my French horn, and teaching him a bit of music in the process. I sang almost as badly as I played, but Bailey took no notice. We loved each other, that little boy and I. But in Mrs. Hurley's presence I ached with a tension so overpowering that had it not been for my visits to the Wimbishes on Sunday afternoons, I doubt I could have survived.

Sundays were a feast—and not only on the food Edythe's mother served up in heaping portions in her elegant dining room. In the home of Mrs. Maggie Wimbish gathered Atlanta's most distinguished black citizens—lawyers, doctors, professors, educators, and clergymen like the great James Madison Nabrit, pastor of Mount Olive Baptist Church and one of the South's most prominent black preachers. Wide as my grandmother's reach had been in Charlotte's black community, I'd never been exposed to a world remotely like the one in which the Wimbish family moved—one marked not only by wealth but by a deep drive for education. Edythe's brother, C. C. Wimbish, Jr., renowned by the late 1920s as an assistant state's attorney in Cook County, Illinois, had earned a law degree from Northwestern University at a time when few black men reached beyond Howard University for their legal education. When Edythe and her sisters had trained as teachers at Atlanta University, they'd followed in the footsteps of their mother, one of the city's most esteemed high school principals.

Mrs. Wimbish took me to her bosom like a daughter, and her circle of friends did as well, all of them urging upon me the care and caution required to stay alive in Atlanta. No black person—not even folk as privileged as the Wimbishes' inner circle—could walk the streets in safety. Some years before my arrival in Atlanta, the family said, Edythe's brother had been beaten unconscious by a group of white men and left for dead—not in a rough section of the city, but right at the edge of the elegant black neighborhood where the Wimbishes lived. But though they warned me constantly to take care, to assume that danger lurked everywhere, to watch my back at every turn, Edythe and her friends made it clear that I must allow nothing to get in the way of my studies at Spelman. Spelman was a college that reached back to Reconstruction days, I learned from Rev. Nabrit, whose mother, Margaret Petty Nabrit, had been in the school's first group of students in 1881. A freed slave, she'd entered as a newly married woman, along with ten others who attended class at what was then known as Atlanta Baptist Female Seminary, in the basement of Friendship Baptist Church. The pride that filled Rev. Nabrit's voice when he told me of his mother, determined to learn to read the Bible and to write at a time when such abilities posed actual danger to her person, spoke volumes to me about the tradition of which I was a part. My anger, my bitterness toward Mrs. Hurley, my fear of the streets of Atlanta—none of that mattered, really, in comparison with what it meant to attend a place like Spelman. I made up my mind I'd finish if I died in the process.

And so I kept quiet and tread carefully in Mrs. Hurley's home. Each afternoon, I returned to the Hurleys' at exactly the appointed hour, saw to the serving of supper and to Bailey's bedtime, then retreated to my room and buried myself in my textbooks for the night. I nearly ran from the house each morning, I was so eager to board the trolley that would take me to Spelman. There, inside those great iron gates that shut out a white world that loathed me for having ideas of my own, I discovered another sort of white person entirely—a person who held thinking so sacred a right that she put her very life on the line for it.

Nothing Edythe had told me about the white professors at Spelman prepared me for Mary Mae Neptune, professor of English literature, as much a warrior with her Shakespeare text and her red pen as my grandmother was with her broom. She was six feet tall, or close to it, and every bit of sixty years old, with her white hair done up in a bun, but for all her old-fashionedness, Mae Neptune was without question a revolutionary, decades ahead of her time.

What she pulled from Shakespeare's *Othello* and *Merchant of Venice* made me squirm, at first. "The stuff of life," she called it, but no one I knew had ever spoken so forthrightly of race hatred or interracial love. That was the stuff of pain and sadness. Only in private did people of either race refer to the shame of sexual unions between blacks and whites, even as Grandma had spoken behind closed doors to the poor outcast soul who'd earned the contempt of both races by giving birth to my foster brothers, Tom and Pete. To hear a white woman not only speak of such things as miscegenation and racism, but to push and prod us into doing so, and in the bold light of day, stunned me. It seemed nothing was out of bounds: the pain of Shylock, the lone Jew in a Christian world; the isolation of Desdemona, despised for loving a black man.

Just what had brought a northerner like Mae Neptune to the South in the thirties I could not imagine, and it was quite some time before I learned that her journey from her native Ohio had begun forty years earlier when she lost the young man to whom she was engaged. His death nearly broke her, she later told me, but it also set her on some kind of quest—a quest that first led her westward, to Iowa, where she was dean of women at an Iowa university, and then to Columbia University in New York, at the height of the Harlem Renaissance.

She was a distant relative of John Brown and perhaps that, mingled with her Quaker roots, drew her to the black intellectuals of Harlem, particularly to the Atlanta University scholars who spoke of the revolution afoot in the black colleges of the South. How mightily they must have moved her, for she was a middle-aged woman when she pulled up stakes and took a position at Spelman. "The black Vassar," they called the college John D. Rockefeller had deemed worthy of funding in 1884, when he'd moved it from its basement quarters and renamed it for his abolitionist in-laws, the Spelmans. But for all the elegance of its magnolia-shaded campus, Spelman was a bed of insurrection and had been since its founding. To train young black women to think, to hold jobs, to become leaders: that was Spelman's mission. And of all the professors I knew in my years there—black or white—Mae Neptune was its most fiery exponent.

Had life treated her differently, she might have been simply a well-educated farm wife with a fierce heart, or, if a professor, one who ministered to her own people in the colleges of the Midwest. But events had conspired to make of Mae Neptune something of an outsider. She was a woman uprooted by her own choice, a person who seemed to draw her strength not from the beloved family she'd left behind in Ohio nor from her colleagues on the Spelman faculty, but from bonds of the spirit.

Such a bond she forged with me. Whether she sensed from the beginning that I was in my own way an outsider—a poor working student in a sea of black privilege—I do not know. I felt, somehow, that she reached out directly to me, with her penetrating gaze and her relentless questioning. The first time she asked me to commit to a position in writing, in an essay on democracy, I felt that gaze upon me even in the privacy of my room, pushing me to say what I really thought.

Spilling out onto the paper came things I'd heard black people talk about in the quiet times, in the quiet places, when there were no white people around to hear them. And there were no white people to hear me now, for when I locked myself each night in my bedroom at the Hurleys', I breathed as freely as if I'd actually been sitting in Miss Neptune's classroom. Alone with my thoughts and the paper before me, I could shed the hated mask of servility I wore in Mrs. Hurley's presence, forget the fear that suffocated me when I entered her home, forget that at any moment she might decide to throw me out and put an end to the dream of Spelman. I forgot everything but the task before me. And I saw, as I scribbled furiously far into the night, that ever since I'd been old enough to eavesdrop on Grandma's church ladies whispering about lynchings and Klan burnings and black men disappearing for who knew what reason, I'd been soaking up one long lesson in democracy gone wrong. I wrote as though someone had opened the floodgates, about the uneven hand of justice in the "land of the free" and the grotesque thing called "separate but equal," putting into words thoughts I hadn't known were mine.

Miss Neptune answered me in three lines of red ink. Even now, I can see her beaming down at me as she handed the paper back, a few days later. "Would you like to write for the campus newspaper?" she'd penned at the bottom of the paper, in handwriting that looked like copper plate. "You think well enough to. See me."

She had framed it as a question, but I could see in her face that she expected only one answer. When I walked into the *Campus Mirror* office that afternoon, she turned me over to the editor-in-chief, who had an assignment slip waiting for me, with a two-day deadline. At that moment, I ceased to follow the university president's dictates about the measured, graceful way a "Spelman woman" was supposed to walk, running and ripping across the campus at such a pace that Miss Neptune—a lover of Homer and mythology—took to calling me "far-darting Apollo."

Lord knows I was no Apollo. I was more like a half-crazy rabbit turned loose in a briar patch, so wild with excitement at the things that were mine for the taking I barely knew what to grab first. I've had glorious times in my life as a lawyer and minister amidst the headiness of legal theory, of theology and biblical studies, but Spelman was my baptism into the life of the mind, and at twenty years old, I was fairly drunk with it. Most of the time, I was ten feet off the ground, gulping in everything afforded me as a double major in literature and biology in great heady doses, always racing to whatever awaited me at the next corner.

Even the trolley rides I had hated and feared for more than two years turned, abruptly, into something downright wonderful, when one morning in November a young man named William Roundtree took a seat next to me.

He was so tall and so handsome that I'd taken note of him the first time I saw him in the early fall, boarding at the stop near Emory University. Each day after that, I'd find myself looking up from whatever textbook I'd been buried in as the trolley neared the Emory stop, scanning the crowd of passengers climbing aboard. With his satchel of books and his serious demeanor, he seemed to me to have all the marks of a student at Morehouse College, Spelman's brother school.

One morning right before Thanksgiving, as I sat studying biology, I saw him heading towards the back of the car, passing a number of empty seats and taking a seat next to me. He mumbled something about the hateful sign that separated the colored from the white section. Then he cleared his throat.

"I'm William Roundtree," he said. "I see you go to Spelman."

Without looking up from my biology book, I answered, "I'm Dovey Johnson. I see you go to Morehouse."

We both laughed. I looked up at him, grinning down at me, and I promptly decided he was even handsomer up close than he was at a distance. Bill, or "Buster," as he said folks called him, spoke in such a friendly way as he asked me about my studies at Spelman that I blurted out, in a rush, not just the answer to his question about my major, but my plans for medical school. I'd wanted to be a doctor from the time I was a young girl, I told him, and I was going to get myself to medical school no matter what it took.

Bill shook his head, amazed.

"Well," he said after a moment, "I'll tell you the truth. I have absolutely *no idea*, right now, what I want to do."

All my life I've been drawn to people who tell it just the way it is, without pomp or pretense. Bill was a straight shooter; that I knew immediately. And he understood what it meant to come from plain working folks, though his manners were so refined that at first I thought he hailed from a wealthy background like the typical Morehouse man—or Spelman woman, for that matter. Most of the stylishly dressed, beautifully spoken girls in my classes had been born into the "blue-veined" black world of cotillions and coming-out parties and summers on Martha's Vineyard, a world so different from mine I could scarcely comprehend it. With Bill I didn't have to. His mother worked in service for a white family, just as mine had, and he lived with her in their home.

With his easy laugh and his gentle ways, Bill filled the emptiness I'd felt after Mama returned to Charlotte. We began timing our afternoon trolley rides to coincide, and soon we were seeing each other on weekends, squeezing in a movie, or, every once in a while, a Sunday picnic. Whenever we could, we arranged study dates together at the Atlanta University library, located across the street from Spelman. I loved Bill's company, loved the way he looked at me so intently when I ran on about my courses and Miss Neptune and the newspaper office, the way he laughed when I told him stories of home, but the truth was that when I was surrounded by my books, everything fell away. Looking back on those heady times from a distance of years, I see so clearly that my real love affair at Spelman was with ideas. And what a wild, desperate love affair it was.

There are those, I know, for whom ideas are cold and lifeless. Never have I found them to be so. Writing that first essay on democracy had pierced me, forced me to unleash ideas I'd never before acknowledged, and each day, when I arrived, breathless, at the door of the *Campus Mirror* office, I found more of the same awaiting me. The juniors and seniors who ran the paper were brilliant, serious types, and the place was alive with discussion not just of campus issues, but of the turmoil of the Depression and the tension in Europe in those prewar years, all viewed in minute detail through the telescope of the dozen or more newspapers to which Miss Neptune subscribed. The *New York Times* was our Bible, and she expected everyone who crossed the threshold of that room to read it—not quickly, not at a glance as we typed up our stories, not on the run, but closely and carefully and analytically.

I needed no pushing. I was hungry. I followed the track of Miss Neptune's red pen through the columns of the *Times*, and slowly, I began to grasp the sheer enormity of the Great Depression. I had known it in pieces—in the closing of Charlotte's banks; in the failure of my grandpa's little store; in the faces of the men who wandered the streets of Atlanta and the deafening sound of dynamite blasting the city's black ghettoes to rubble to make way for the New Deal's first housing projects. The newspapers stacked on Miss Neptune's desk turned my eyes outward on a whole country that seemed to me to be despairing. Two years into President Roosevelt's first administration, the Supreme Court had declared his National Industrial Recovery Act unconstitutional. People fought bitterly in the newspapers about the wisdom of the New Deal's programs, and the front pages were filled with pictures of the dust storms and floods that were destroying the West.

How distant and remote and irrelevant the rumblings in Germany would have seemed to me in comparison with what lay right at my feet, had it not been for Miss Neptune. With a prescience I now find stunning, she pushed us to read and reread the stories of Hitler, newly risen to chancellor of Germany, proclaiming to the Nazi Congress in Nuremberg the start of a Thousand Year Reich and an undying hatred for "Jewish intellectualism" and anything—or anyone—that was not pure Aryan. Even then, of course, five years before his invasion of Poland, Hitler's overpowering race hatred was moving the world toward war— a war that was to change the course of my life more profoundly than any other single event. In the fall of 1934, Hitler spoke incessantly of peace even as he targeted a tiny tract of land known as the Saar Basin, carved out of France and Germany by the Treaty of Versailles with a promise that it would decide its allegiance in 1935. The fate of Europe, wrote the bold and brilliant journalist Dorothy Thompson, hung on whether the Saar voted to join France or return to a Fatherland now entirely controlled by the Nazis.

Fascinated, I sought out every word written by Thompson, whose articles, though buried deep within the *Times*, were unfailingly marked for our attention by Miss Neptune's pen. While European leaders lauded Hitler's peaceful intentions, Thompson dared to write of the Nazi terror tactics being brought to bear on the Saarlanders on the eve of the vote that would determine their national destiny. So devastating were her dispatches that Hitler expelled her from Germany, but before she left, she exposed to the world the Nazis' round-the-clock radio onslaught, their transformation of the Saar's newspapers to German propaganda organs, the economic pressures on enemies of the Reich, the flight of the Jews from the Saarland, the SS presence that paralyzed the capital city—all in anticipation of the "free election" Hitler said would prove just how widely his doctrine was accepted.

All this I read, and then, pressed by Miss Neptune, who contended that only through writing could one grasp the essence of a thing, I undertook to dissect the Saar crisis in a research paper that tracked events as they unfolded in the fall of 1934. By the time the Saarlanders voted overwhelmingly in January to return to a Nazi-ruled Germany, I had learned a truth I would carry with me in the years to come: what had cowed those half million folk upon whom Hitler had set his sights was the same kind of intimidation I had known every day of my life. I saw, too, as I spoke of these things with Miss Neptune in the empty newspaper office in the early mornings, or on our walks to class together, that she understood in some deep way how pained I was about matters of race, whether a continent away or right at my feet, in Atlanta.

I was nearly paralyzed by my pain in those years. Decades would pass before I finally let go of the seething rage I harbored toward every white person who had ever wronged me, toward the whole faceless mass of white humanity who might someday wrong me for the mere fact of my blackness. I am persuaded that the walk out of such consuming rage is the journey of a lifetime. It would take the words of the Reverend Martin Luther King, Jr., speaking about peace and nonviolence thirty years later, to finally stanch the avalanche of rage I carried within my breast. But the journey began at Spelman, in the presence of Miss Neptune, whom I came to trust not just as a great professor but as my truest friend. To her I could speak of things I shared with no one else, not even Bill, who looked at me with real fear in his eyes when I railed about the injustice of segregation.

"You keep talking like that, girl, and you'll get yourself killed," he'd tell me. Gently, he'd put a hand on my arm in the protective way he had, and I'd find myself quieting down and moving on to things that did not pain him—or me—quite so much.

With Miss Neptune, nothing, no matter how ugly or painful, was ever pushed aside. It was not that she was oblivious to my hurt; indeed, she winced when I spoke of Mrs. Hurley's betrayal, and on the day I told her of my grandma and the white overseer who broke her feet, I saw something close to shock in her face. But fearless soul that she was, she never retreated. To wallow in what she called "rabid hatred," she told me, was far too easy. What I must do was to take control of what tore at my heart by marshaling the power of my mind.

"It's up to *you*!" she insisted.

Even when I fought her, a part of me listened. This was a woman brazen enough to walk past every white person on the trolley car to sit with me in the rear when we traveled into the city together. The whites who glared at her in disgust, she told me, had been spoon-fed hatred from the day they were born. But she believed that a new day would come, and that I would be one of those who brought it about—if I could set aside the anger that crippled me.

In the quiet of early morning in the newspaper office, or in the apartment at the edge of campus where Miss Neptune made her home, she and I would wrestle with the ideas that ripped me apart. That plain, old-fashioned apartment, lined with great books and photographs of Miss Neptune's European travels, became for me an oasis of peace and wisdom in the midst of my anger. Patiently rocking as I ranted and paced and pounded the table, she counseled patience and the long view in matters of race. One day, she simply stopped arguing and brought me to the place where the greatest black intellectuals of this century were holding forth on the very things that tore at my heart.

I no longer remember whether it was W. E. B. Du Bois to whom she and I listened in a packed auditorium at Atlanta University, or one of the other scholars who'd arrived from Harvard and Columbia that year and were laying out their revolutionary vision right in the heart of the old Confederacy. I know that after that first lecture, I couldn't stay away. I began going on my own to hear Du Bois and his young disciples—the soft-spoken but impassioned sociologist Ira De Augustine Reid, who held up the black experience as a thing of majesty, to be studied and catalogued and dissected; historian Rayford Logan, bent on transforming a country that had shut him out of full citizenship upon his return from combat in the trenches of World War I. These great men hurt, just as I did. But the brand of anger that came pouring out of them seemed not to pull them down; instead, it swept them forward on a mighty tide.

There were, to be sure, ideas I found unsettling in their vision of the future, and how we were to reach it. When Du Bois spoke of the elite percentage of black folk he believed would lead the whole race to true equality—the "talented tenth"—my mind turned to Grandma, pounding herbs before daybreak, bending over her cauldron of lye soap. What place was there, I wondered, for that earthy brand of greatness in his America? Listening to Du Bois, I saw how deeply divided I really was—not only as a black woman in a white world, but as a child of the working class who was being groomed to leave it behind.

The passion that flowed from him about his blackness, though, I embraced without reservation. In the pages of Du Bois's *Souls of Black Folk* and in his wide-ranging orations, I divined a portrait of my race that made me proud beyond the telling. I came to see that the struggle for dignity and respect and equal treatment wasn't only about me. And it wasn't about today. There was an "us" that spanned centuries and continents, that was far bigger than one hundred years of slavery and the degradation of Jim Crow.

No young black person who listened to Du Bois say that we were "equal to every living soul on the face of the earth" could remain unchanged. To stand tall, tall in your blackness: that was the call he sounded. His ideas held a healing power, and so did my long discussions of them with Miss Neptune. More than at any other time in my life, with the possible exception of my early days in law school, I could actually feel myself changing as I soaked up the notions of Du Bois and Logan and Reid and processed them with Miss Neptune, pushing and pressing them as through a great sieve. The fear I'd carried with me from childhood ebbed from me. That more than anything, I now believe, was what lay at the heart of my anger—the kind of fear that comes from powerlessness.

Who can say with any certainty what others saw in me in those glorious weeks? Never consciously did I drop the mask I wore in Mrs. Hurley's presence. And yet, as I now believe, my employer divined some change in me, some subtle difference in my look, my walk, the manner of my speech. In no other way can I explain what happened on the horrible May afternoon when I entered the house to find her gone all to pieces, waving her arms at me and screaming.

That day exists for me only in tiny slivers of memory, like shards of glass that cut me even now. I remember the terrified face of little Bailey, crouching in the corner, the sound of Mrs. Hurley's shrieking, the feeling of my mouth going dry as I slowly made out what she was saying.

I had stolen something. That was it. I had robbed her and I would be punished. I would be arrested. I was a thief, a dirty little thief, and I would be made to pay. I must have asked her what I was supposed to have stolen, and she must have answered me. But I could make nothing of it. I discerned only that single word, flung at me again and again with a venom I cannot describe.

"Thief!" she shouted, flailing her arms. "Thief! You're a thief!"

I can see myself marching, head up, eyes forward, into the old jailhouse in Decatur, determined not to cry, though I was nearly numb with terror. Being swallowed up by the white legal system, without money or legal connections, was a fate dreaded by every black person in the South. Without even realizing I'd made a misstep, I'd walked into the no-man's-land about which I'd heard all my life—the place where black people simply disappeared, in the way my mother's father had disappeared when he'd run afoul of the Klan so long ago.

Yet even in the midst of the horror, there was kindness. The white guard asked me gently for the name of someone—anyone—whom she might call in my behalf. Not a single black person of my acquaintance stood a chance in this situation—not Bill, not Edythe, nor any of her wealthy friends. Even the white authorities at Spelman would steer clear of a mess like this, I thought, remembering the warning of the college president, Florence Read, that we must "take care" when we went into the city.

"Should you get into trouble," she'd told us repeatedly, "it is not clear how far the school could go in helping you."

Of course, it was all too clear. Once we left the campus, we were on our own.

I knew only one white person bold enough to involve herself, and that was Miss Neptune. I gave the guard her telephone number. And then I began praying.

Afternoon was turning to evening when a tall, elegantly dressed white gentleman arrived at the jailhouse, introducing himself as Mr. Slye Howard. He was an attorney sent by Miss Mae Neptune and Spelman treasurer Phern Rockefeller, he said, reaching out to shake my hand.

Up until the moment when Mr. Howard began questioning me, I'd been too frightened to think. But when he asked me, point blank, whether I had stolen, whether I had ever done anything, ever, some little thing, that Mrs. Hurley might have misinterpreted, a flicker of anger broke through the fear that had swallowed me up. I looked Mr. Howard straight in the eye and told him that I had never stolen, would never steal. He looked straight back at me, studying me intently, nodding gravely.

In a matter of hours, the nightmare had ended. Early the next morning, Mr. Howard returned to the jailhouse, had me released, and personally drove me to Miss Rockefeller's office, where she and Miss Neptune were waiting for me. Already, they'd made arrangements for me to move to temporary housing on campus until permanent lodging could be found. In the strongest terms, they urged me to put this matter behind me, immediately, and move on, assuring me that in the hands of an attorney as illustrious as Mr. Howard, my legal troubles were over.

They spoke truly. I never heard another word about the charges. But though Mrs. Hurley vanished forever from my life, that night in the Decatur jailhouse marked the beginning of a long slide toward disaster. I had lost my livelihood, at a time when people far better trained and educated than I were out of work.

No campus job, I knew, would come close to matching the wages I'd made at the Hurleys'. If I'd really understood my financial situation, I daresay I would have packed my bags and headed back home to Charlotte. But I was so young and so hardheaded and so downright ignorant of money matters that I set out to beat the demon of poverty with hard work, the way I'd seen my grandma do it.

For two years and two summers, I ran—actually, physically ran—not in the joyous way I had in my freshman year, but desperately, forever trying to stay ahead of the clock that chimed in the campus bell tower. I ran at such a breakneck pace that I caught the eye of President Read, who called me into her office one day in the spring of my junior year to counsel me on proper carriage and ladylike deportment. Entirely taken aback by her suggestion that I avail myself of the college's "whole personal development program," I explained that I had to work, that I had so much to do that I had no choice but to run.

If only I could move faster, I reckoned, I could clear a little more money and pay off my student account, which had in fact been in arrears even before I left Mrs. Hurley's employ. Neither Bill nor Edythe nor my family understood how dire my circumstances were, primarily because I shielded them, blaming my move on the need to be nearer to campus. I could see Grandma down on her knees, back at home, "pesterin' the Lord," as she liked to say, just about driving Him crazy on the subject of my safety in Atlanta. She and Mama had split our family apart for two years so I could go to Spelman.

If two jobs weren't enough, I told Miss Neptune and Miss Rockefeller, I'd take three. And I did. I lived in a tiny house just off campus that Miss Rockefeller located, and I earned my room and board by cleaning dormitories and picked up a few dollars here and there doing research for Miss Neptune. In the spring, the biology department chairwoman took me on as a paid lab assistant under the work program of the National Youth Administration, through which the great Mary McLeod Bethune had begun channeling funds for thousands of young black folk like me.

For all of that, I never had a chance. Spelman tuition was such that as the Depression deepened, even some of the wealthy girls began leaving. Finally, in the last weeks of my junior year, my moment of reckoning came.

President Read was kind when she summoned me to her office to confront me with my overdue student account, but she left no doubt about the university's position. In these hard times Spelman couldn't afford to carry anyone. She recommended that I take a teaching job in a little town in Georgia, a job for which she was certain I could qualify. In that way, I could pay off my debt and in a few years return to Spelman. The only other option was to come up with the money— immediately. If I could not do that, I must leave as soon as the semester ended.

Miss Read's voice went on for a while in the quiet, but I stopped listening. When at last she rose from her chair, I did too. I thanked her, found my way to the door, and stumbled out of her office into the blinding sunshine.

It was May. On any other morning, in any other spring, I would have drawn a deep breath and drunk it all in—the campus, awash in color, the dogwoods shading the walkways, the sweet perfume of magnolia that hung heavy in the air. But on this day, I could think only that I was leaving.

Once I left Spelman, there would be no coming back. This was 1937. People were starving. Even if I took the teaching job in the little Georgia town Miss Read had mentioned, I'd never be able to save enough to pay off my account and cover my senior year expenses. I had to live. And my family needed me.

I began walking, slowly, toward nowhere in particular, because for the first time since I'd set foot on the Spelman campus, I had nowhere to go. I walked, and I thought, and after I knew not how much time, I looked up and found myself standing in front of the brick apartment building where Miss Neptune lived.

It was ever so quiet there, and peaceful, at that early morning hour. The faculty members who lived in the apartments had gone to class, and the area was shielded from the comings and goings of students by a stand of trees. I climbed the steps of the cement stoop of the apartment building, sat down, and began to cry. I made no sound, but just sat crying silently, tears rolling down my cheeks, until I heard someone calling to me.

"Dovibus!"

There stood Miss Neptune, looking up at me in astonishment, calling me by the odd little nickname she'd given me as an alternative to "far-darting Apollo."

"What on earth are you doing here?"

I was unable to answer her, and seeing that, she reached out and led me by the hand, up the stairway and into the sitting room of her apartment. She listened intently while I explained, in a jumble, and through my tears, what Miss Read had told me. When I finished, she smiled, drew me to her in a hug, and said, with an expression I couldn't quite read, "Well, that's not the end of the world."

Much as I wanted to believe her, I could not. Even when she reported to me later that afternoon that she'd found a way, that I had some good and true friends at Spelman who were going to step forward in my behalf, I couldn't shake the sick sensation in my stomach that had overtaken me in Miss Read's office. Just what could possibly come of meeting with Phern Rockefeller, as Miss Neptune proposed, I could not imagine, and when I arrived at Miss Rockefeller's office at eight o'clock the next morning, I was even more mystified.

Miss Neptune had arrived before me, and though her face radiated a deep satisfaction, she offered no word of explanation. I watched, puzzled, as a young man I'd never seen before arrived with a sheaf of papers and was ushered immediately into Miss Rockefeller's private office, and shortly thereafter, Miss Neptune. At last, Miss Rockefeller appeared and asked me to join them. What followed was so like a strange dream that I had trouble putting it in real perspective until many years later.

Certain "arrangements" had been made to take care of my expenses at Spelman through my senior year, Miss Rockefeller told me, smiling. There was nothing I needed to do except to study and graduate.

I stared at her, incredulous, as she began to explain the two parts of that arrangement. The first part was a scholarship from the university. The second was a loan from Miss Neptune, secured by an insurance policy on my life. The insurance contract designated Miss Neptune as the sole beneficiary and it would more than cover the loan in case anything happened to me. Once I repaid my debt to her, the policy would be turned over to me and I could designate anyone as beneficiary. I need only sign the documents provided by the man sitting next to Miss Rockefeller, a gentleman she introduced as Mr. John Stanley.

Even in a state of shock, with my hands shaking as I signed the documents, I understood the magnitude of what they had done. Three white people who were no kin to me had seen fit to find money, somewhere, money that even a wealthy institution like Spelman surely needed in those hard times.

There was no explanation for any of it, really—except perhaps the one Edythe offered when I brought the papers to show her a few days later. She looked them over, questioned me closely to make sure I understood my obligations, listened as I recited them, and sat silent for a moment with an expression I can only describe as wonderment on her face.

"Dovey," she told me, "you must be God's child."

There is always someone, I am convinced, who would be the miracle maker in your life, if you but believe. Miss Neptune was that person for me.

She had made the impossible happen. It was Miss Neptune who'd approached Miss Rockefeller, who had in turn gone to President Read. She had taken on the authorities at Spelman in my behalf, at a time when scholarship funds were almost nonexistent. An elderly teacher on a modest salary, she'd used her personal savings to pay the balance of my tuition, and with precious little chance of recovering her money, given how bleak my prospects were in 1937.

Indeed, four years would pass before I was able to pay a single dollar on that loan, and another four before I presented Miss Neptune with the final installment—in a neat stack of bills, carefully folded and tucked in my bosom. Yet I knew even from the first that I could never compensate her, for what she'd given me had no price.

As I stood stammering in Miss Rockefeller's office, promising over and over again to "repay every dime and then some," Miss Neptune had shaken her head and spoken three words that amounted to a lifetime charge. Though I couldn't know how, or when, or through whom I would execute the directive she issued on that May morning, I embraced it almost as a creed.

"Pass it on, Dovibus!" she told me, looking straight at me over her spectacles and smiling as I handed the papers across the desk to Mr. Stanley. "Pass it on!"

4. MY AMERICA

Out of our indebtedness, I believe, our real selves are born. For it is when we grasp what we owe, how beholden we truly are, that we remain children no longer.

For me, that realization came in great waves, on a glorious summer morning not long after my Spelman graduation as I sat in our living room back at home, breathing in the smell of cinnamon and ginger from the kitchen, Miss Neptune on one side of me, Mama and my grandparents on the other. Now *there* was a roomful of debt to fill a ledger, and my heart was as full as the giant pitcher of iced locust beer Grandma served up in tall glasses, as she urged another helping of dessert upon Miss Neptune, who was fairly drowning in warm gingerbread, fresh from the oven, smothered in applesauce.

Right up till the moment when my grandmother actually smiled at Miss Neptune, smiled so that her cheeks dimpled, I'd been nervous about this meeting. Much as I'd raved about Miss Neptune to Grandma, I knew how deeply Grandma distrusted every white person who'd ever been born. To hear, within a few months' time, of my betrayal by Mrs. Hurley and my redemption by Miss Neptune left Grandma quiet, when I spoke to her on the phone from Edythe's about the loan Miss Neptune had arranged. Perhaps, she said, there was some catch, some trick. No, I insisted. Edythe and her lawyer had reviewed the papers. The loan was real, and so was Miss Neptune.

"Well, child, if Edythe says it's all right, then I reckon it is," Grandma had said, so slowly and uncertainly I saw that in her heart, she reckoned otherwise.

But my grandmother knew pure goodness when she saw it before her. She took one look at Miss Neptune on that summer morning of their first meeting, beaming at her and at Mama and Grandpa, and all the tightness and the worry went from her face.

"Thank you. Thank you," she said to Miss Neptune, reaching out to shake her hand. "Thank you for what you done for my child."

The fact that I was twenty-four years old was, of course, immaterial to my grandmother—and, if the truth be told, to Miss Neptune as well, who seized upon Grandma's statement as an open invitation to praise my achievements in the way one does those of a much-loved child. Mama and Grandpa, who'd been inclined to believe in Miss Neptune's genuineness from the first and, in any event, to revere without question all things associated with Spelman, sat listening proudly. It was Grandma I fastened my eyes on, relieved beyond words to see the way she leaned toward Miss Neptune, and touched her hand, and nodded in vigorous agreement with her estimation of my talents.

"Oh yes, yes indeed," she interjected every time Miss Neptune paused for breath. "Dovey Mae's smart."

This, I thought, as I sat quietly taking it all in, was my graduation—a moment even greater than the one when President Florence Read handed me my diploma in the Spelman Sisters Chapel. Bill had cheered mightily, and so had Eunice, who had come down to Atlanta on the train with her beau. But there hadn't been money enough for the rest of the family to attend. And when Mama and Grandma had the neighbors in to view my diploma the Sunday after I arrived home, Miss Neptune was not present. To have the people who'd given everything for me all in one room, and getting along so famously, exceeded anything I could have imagined. If I could have tapped into the secrets of preservation my grandmother applied to figs and pears and woodland roots, I would have frozen that moment forever. But, of course, I couldn't. Time closed in upon me in a way it never had before.

What had seemed so very possible in my rush toward graduation now eluded my grasp. Medical school was a luxury beyond contemplation, given my debts, and so, I concluded, was marriage to Bill, though if Mama and Grandma had had their way, I might well have been a bride that summer. Bill had thoroughly charmed them when he'd come to Charlotte to visit, with his courtly manners and his kind, gentle way. But though he and I had had an "understanding" of sorts since my junior year, we seemed to drift apart once he returned to Atlanta. More than any thought of marriage and children, what tugged at me was the need to help my family, as I saw—really *saw*—with the eyes of a woman, where they stood.

Perhaps I had not wanted to face, in my short trips home each summer, what a toll Grandpa's drinking had taken on him. Grandma too had aged. I looked, as if for the first time, at the broken-down furniture and worn flooring of the tiny house I so loved. I saw how hard Mama worked to hold onto it while paying tuition for Eunice at Shaw University, in Raleigh, and Rachel at Friendship College, in Rock Hill, South Carolina, and I knew that my grand dreams had to give way to earning money—now. When our pastor, the Reverend Henry Morris Moore, told me of an opening for a seventh-grade teacher in a South Carolina town not far from Charlotte, I seized upon it, glad for the salary of fifty-five dollars a month that would enable me to help my family survive.

For three years, as I sent home all but the twelve dollars I needed each month for room and board, I lived for the pupils I taught at Finley High School in Chester, South Carolina—youngsters who put me in mind of myself at their age, running and ripping every which way they could find to rip. Though I sat on them good and hard, the way Grandma had sat on me, I understood their wildness. Deep inside myself, I had every bit as much trouble sitting still as they did.

More than at any time in my life, a great restlessness took hold of me. For all the slow-moving charm of the little town of Chester, the kindness of the family with whom I lived, and the good fortune that was mine in a brand-new school building filled with young folk who lifted my heart with their eagerness, I could not shake the feeling that I belonged somewhere else. Always, I'd been a child bent on bolting past the safety of the fenced-in yard toward the forbidden creek, and Spelman, for all its splendid isolation, had made me hungrier than ever for what lay out in the greater world, no matter how dangerous and frightening.

In the fall of 1939, as I began my second year of teaching, the world was downright terrifying. On the first day of September, the Nazis invaded Poland. Thus began the war that had been coming since my earliest days at Spelman, when I'd written about Hitler's quiet movements in the Saar Basin. Every week, it seemed, the news blaring over the big radio in the main office at Finley High grew more dreadful. Denmark fell, then Norway, and late in the spring of 1940, to the horror of all the world, Germany marched into the neutral Low Countries, crushing Holland, Belgium, and Luxembourg in a matter of days.

I hated war with all my heart. The First World War had brought the influenza epidemic that had killed my father. It made lame broken men of young boys who returned to Charlotte from combat, used up great black leaders like Rayford Logan—used them up and then shut them out. I abhorred the idea that we might, finally, be drawn into Europe's bloody struggle against Hitler. And yet, with the president calling for a great defense fund after Hitler's invasion of the Lowlands and warning of the nearness of an enemy that could strike by air at any time, war seemed to be rushing toward us.

At my feet, too, the world turned upside down. That same summer, as France fell to the Nazis and Germany began its round-the-clock bombing of Great Britain, my grandfather died. Ill as he had been for so long, I found myself unprepared for his death. It was Grandpa who'd given me my love of books and an abiding hunger for things spiritual. He was the first minister I had known, and the finest, and though many years would pass before I'd walk in his footsteps to the pulpit, he planted the seed. More than anything else, Grandpa had stepped forward to take the place of the father I'd barely known. Grief filled the house that summer, not in the desperate, wrenching way it had when my papa died, but with a stillness that slowed our days and blanketed everything in quiet.

True, Grandpa had not been a breadwinner in some years, but with his gentle spirit gone, Mama and Grandma seemed so much more alone in their struggle. The thirty-eight dollars a month I sent home barely touched their needs. Perhaps, I told Mama and Grandma, the time had come for me to make a change—though not right away, of course. I assured them that for now, I'd stay close to home, in Chester, but I knew in my heart that even with a higher teacher's salary, I couldn't long remain in the cocoon of that tiny town, tucked away in my classroom while the world charged forward.

As if drawn by a magnet, I began turning my thoughts in the direction where thousands were streaming in 1940—northward, toward jobs in the big cities, where factories now turned out tanks and airplanes and weapons; northward, toward Washington, where the government had made an industry of "defense preparedness." In Washington, too, as Grandma pointed out once she saw the seriousness of my resolve, reigned the mightiest ally a young black woman could hope to fix herself to: Dr. Mary McLeod Bethune. If I must go to Washington, she insisted, then I must without question look up Dr. Bethune, whose work for black people with President Roosevelt's National Youth Administration made her something pretty close to royalty in Grandma's eyes.

Even by proxy, that great woman seemed to reach out to me when I arrived in Washington without an appointment in the summer of 1940, to find her away from her office. Whether it was because of my grandma's connection, or some quality Dr. Bethune's assistant, Arabella Denniston, divined in me, Miss Denniston took me under wing immediately when I presented myself at the offices of the National Council of Negro Women. Without doubt, she assured me, Dr. Bethune could find a place for a young woman with a Spelman degree and three years of teaching experience, should I decide to return to Washington.

History, too, conspired to pave my way northward to the nation's capital. As I shepherded another group of pupils down in Chester, the renowned black labor leader A. Philip Randolph and NAACP executive secretary Walter White were maneuvering the president into doing the unthinkable: banning race discrimination in defense industry hiring and creating a Fair Employment Practices Committee to act as watchdog. Randolph's threat of a hundred thousand Negroes marching on Washington, along with pressure from the First Lady, persuaded President Roosevelt to buck his segregationist advisers and military leaders, at least so far as defense industry hiring was concerned. To Randolph's other demand—the full integration of the armed services—the president turned a deaf ear. Still, the ban on employment discrimination and the creation of the FEPC threw wide the doors of opportunity for millions like me. When on June 25, 1941, the president issued the ban in the form of an executive order, the Negro newspapers likened it to the Emancipation Proclamation, freeing blacks from economic slavery as Lincoln had freed us from physical slavery. Both employers and labor unions with government defense contracts, the order said, must "provide for the full and equitable participation in defense industries, without discrimination because of race, creed, color or national origin."

My time had come. I packed my belongings, said goodbye to Grandma and Mama, boarded the train for Washington, and headed northward from Charlotte in search of my future.

Many years after I came to live in the nation's capital, I heard the term that some black visitor, passing through the District of Columbia in the thirties, had used to describe the shadow city that was black Washington. "The Secret City," he'd called it, writing anonymously in one of the Negro journals of the day. What he described was the web of streets and neighborhoods where "colored folk" lived and worked and traded, cut off from whites as by a great wall of stone or iron. That unnamed visitor captured something so deep, so true that the term stuck, became the title of a book on the town I would one day call home. *The Secret City.* Even now, the phrase drags at my heart, as I remember how it felt to discover for the first time the impenetrable barrier between blacks and whites in the very place that stood for freedom and democracy.

Washington straddled a queer line, with Union Station marking the division between North and South, the spot where black train passengers were required to move to Jim Crow coaches if headed south, or, if headed north, to abandon them for the white coaches. A black traveler might eat a meal in Union Station, then, but so far as I could tell, "Whites Only" was the order of the day in restaurants throughout the nation's capital. I wince, now, remembering Arabella Denniston's careful instructions for survival during my first short stay: I must report to the Phyllis Wheatley YWCA at 901 Rhode Island Avenue—the "Colored Y," they called it—and until I mastered the city, I must stay close to Dr. Bethune's office, under her protective mantle. That was the way I knew so well—the old way, the "southern way."

Washington confounded me that summer of 1940 on my first visit, and when I returned the following July, one of thousands of blacks who'd fastened their hopes for jobs on the president's antidiscrimination order, I found it no less confounding. This was a city throwing wide its doors to people of all races—at least the doors to the defense industry—and yet holding fast to all the old divisions. The greatest paradox of all for me, though, revolved around the person upon whom I'd fixed my sights—Dr. Mary McLeod Bethune. How was it that a woman with access to the president and First Lady of the United States could be consigned to "colored" water fountains and banned from white restaurants and toilets? There seemed to be no way to square "black power" of the sort Dr. Bethune wielded with the reality of the city through which I walked and rode and made my way in the summer of 1941.

Truth to tell, I wasn't sure just what to expect as I climbed the steps of the small row house at the corner of Ninth and Westminster streets, Northwest, that served as both Dr. Bethune's residence and the council's headquarters. Fifteen years, at least, had passed since I'd seen Dr. Bethune, and it had been through the eyes of a child stealing glimpses at a much-revered visitor. The woman who rose, smiling, to welcome me with outstretched hand, struck me as shorter than I'd remembered, and a little stouter. Her black skin, ever so dark in my memory, seemed darker still by contrast to her graying hair. When she greeted me, though, the change wrought by the years fell away. I doubt that anyone who ever heard Dr. Bethune speak could forget her voice—a voice so musical and cultivated that it danced over sentences in the manner of a Shakespearean actor. A story went round about that time that President Roosevelt, upon hearing her speak for five minutes at a conference, had sent word immediately to the NYA director that he wished Mrs. Bethune to head the agency's Department of Negro Affairs. No doubt it was her brilliance as much as her Victorian elocution that so impressed the president. Still, her voice alone was so arresting that even the most ordinary statement seemed clothed in finery.

"You're Rachel Graham's granddaughter," she said, rising and coming from behind her desk to take my hand in both of hers. "Turn around, child, and let me look at you!"

Her smile widened into something pretty close to a grin as I complied. And yet, homely as her welcome was, I sensed the deepest seriousness in Dr. Bethune, an intensity and deliberateness as she turned her entire attention to me—to discerning, as she put it, what I was *"about."* I daresay only a true teacher, someone in the mold of Mae Neptune or Edythe Wimbish, would have glowed as she did when I spoke of my studies at Spelman and my experiences with the children of Chester. Though her telephone rang incessantly and Miss Denniston bustled in and out, Dr. Bethune focused entirely on me. Had it not been for her warmth and her charm, I would have been in awe, so carefully did she appear to be taking my measure. She marked my every word as I told her of the medical school plans I'd had to scotch for lack of money, of the plight of my mother and grandmother after my grandfather's death, and my heavy sense of obligation toward them. At last, I wound my way to the immediate purpose of my visit: my interest in a defense industry job.

To my amazement, Dr. Bethune shook her head.

"No," she said definitively. "I have something else in mind. And in the meantime, I need you. There are things for you to do right here."

I was too intimidated at that moment to consider asking what that "something else" might be, and so overwhelmed by the swiftness with which Dr. Bethune acted that I forgot to wonder. For the next eight months, I virtually lived in her office, working sometimes from a corner of Miss Denniston's desk but more often from the floor, sitting amid the stacks of newspapers from which I clipped every word pertaining to Dr. Bethune and her projects. The *Chicago Defender*, the *Pittsburgh Courier*, the *New York Amsterdam News*—these and the other black newspapers of the day were Dr. Bethune's barometer of the mind and heart of the millions who looked to her to fight their fight. The white press carried "Negro news" in its back pages, and though Dr. Bethune tracked their perfunctory reports, she looked to the black papers for word from the trenches.

Every clip was logged into her files, as were the statistics she charged me with ferreting out and placing at her fingertips for the moment when she might need them in her fight for better schools, better housing, better lives for children. I watched her turn those cold numbers into tools, working them into letters to this or that official, citing them in phone conferences, packing them away in her briefcase for meetings at her NYA headquarters across town, slipping them into discussions with the colleagues who sought her out in the council office for support and advice.

It has been said of Dr. Bethune that she became not simply a politician, but a stateswoman in Washington. By the time I darkened her door in 1941, she had transformed the six-year-old National Council of Negro Women into such a mighty political force that all roads in black America seemed to lead to her tiny upstairs apartment at 1812 Ninth Street. The reach of the council stood in inverse proportion to the square footage of its headquarters, an impossibly tight space crammed with furniture, books, papers, files—all the paraphernalia of a thriving national organization in the confines of a living room. In the eight months I worked for Dr. Bethune in her combination residence and office, I never quite grew accustomed to how casually and constantly she met with leaders I'd seen up to that point only in the newspapers. With men like NAACP executive secretary Walter White, a longtime friend of Mrs. Roosevelt's, and the crusading newspaper columnist Lester Granger, head of the Urban League, Dr. Bethune seemed to share a particular affinity. That she headed a woman's organization was entirely irrelevant to all concerned. Dr. Bethune channeled tens of thousands of dollars in NYA funding into the black community, and her civil rights agenda was so broad that I'd hear her crossing from one issue, one agency, one project to another even within the same conference. Believing that strength lay in numbers, she built coalitions of every sort. As the lone black woman in the Roosevelt administration, she'd brought men like Mr. White and Mr. Granger together with the country's other black leaders in her home in 1936 to form the unofficial powerhouse that came to be known as the "Black Cabinet." And her years of work as director of Negro affairs in the NYA had won her readier access to the White House than most white politicians enjoyed.

I only had to hear Dr. Bethune speaking one time to Mrs. Roosevelt by phone to sense the depth of the bond between the two. Always, of course, there was a great rush and a hush when Mrs. Roosevelt's secretary, Malvina Thompson, phoned the office, but when the First Lady actually came on the line, Mrs. Bethune relaxed. She lay down the sword she wielded all day long, stopped fighting, and spoke in the way one does to a trusted ally. It was Mrs. Roosevelt who'd insisted Dr. Bethune's Black Cabinet be included in White House conferences, who'd raised funds for Bethune-Cookman College, and who joined forces with Dr. Bethune and Walter White to fight for an antilynching bill even when the president himself abandoned it for fear of losing the white southern vote.

I doubt if there was a person in America who hadn't read or heard of Mrs. Roosevelt's public slap at an Alabama law that had required her to sit apart from Mrs. Bethune in a segregated Birmingham auditorium in 1938. When the city's young police chief, Bull Connor, scoundrel that he was way back then, dispatched an order that the First Lady must move from the seat she'd taken in the colored section, she'd refused to do so. To the astonishment of the entire assembly, Mrs. Roosevelt placed her chair squarely in the center aisle between the black and white sections, despite the threat by the police that anyone defying the segregation law would be arrested. Only one other white person in my experience would have dared to do such a thing—Miss Neptune. Many a time, she'd braved curses and hateful looks as she strode past rows of whites on Atlanta's trolleys to sit beside me in the rear. As I listened to Mrs. Bethune on the phone with the First Lady, I remembered those days, and thought of what it meant to have a white ally in a world that hated you for the color of your skin.

Much has been written about the friendship between Mary McLeod Bethune and Eleanor Roosevelt, a friendship so far ahead of its time that it threatened both races, raising questions few people back then wanted to take straight on. Even today, black folk shy away from plain talk about skin tone and the way it sets us against each other in an empty quest for prestige. In the world of the thirties and forties, skin as dark as Dr. Bethune's unsettled just about everyone in the upper reaches of power: whites preferred to deal with someone they could pretend was white; many blacks—especially those avid of social status—worshipped fairness of complexion. Millions, of course, revered Dr. Bethune, who'd been called "The First Lady of the Struggle" by the Negro press. Still, there were more than a few of my race who distrusted any black who collaborated as closely as she did with whites.

Such thoughts struck me as preposterous, then and now, as did the notion some held that Dr. Bethune patronized white leaders to achieve her own ends. I cannot claim true objectivity, having fairly worshipped her from childhood onward. But I know what I saw, close up, from my vantage point in the corner of the tiny council office where she met with Mrs. Roosevelt, and of that I can speak. To my eyes theirs was a friendship between equals, grounded in respect, admiration, and yes, even love. The sight of the First Lady of the United States striding into the office at first struck me nearly speechless—so much so that on my initial meeting with Mrs. Roosevelt, sometime in the fall of 1941, I retreated to my corner in a state of awe. But no person could remain ill at ease in the presence of a woman who arrived without an entourage and sailed past ceremony as she did. After our first introduction, she greeted me by name each time I saw her and unfailingly inquired for my welfare before sinking into one of the old armchairs and getting down to business with Dr. Bethune.

The business that consumed the two of them, in the dark, terrifying months following the Japanese attack on Pearl Harbor, was the fight to bring women into the armed services. From my corner, I watched, and listened, sensing even before Dr. Bethune actually took me aside and told me, that this cause concerned me, deeply and personally. A way was being made for black women in the military, and when we entered the fight, she wanted me to be in the vanguard. This, she gave me to understand, was the "something else" she'd had in mind for me when she'd brought me into her office. Just what words I used to reply to her, I no longer remember. I'm not even certain what I thought, I was so torn. Right along with the rush of pride I felt at being chosen by a woman like Dr. Bethune came a wave of overpowering ambivalence.

It was not the war itself that divided me; I believed with every part of my being in our fight against Hitler and the brand of racism he espoused, believed in it with a completeness and a clarity that had its roots in my earliest Spelman years. No longer was the threat of fascism distant or abstract; within weeks of Germany's declaration of

war against us, their subs began sinking our ships. The day after Pearl
Harbor, the Japanese wiped out two of our airfields in the Philippines,
and by Christmas they were crushing our troops in Manila Bay. Every
young man I knew was shipping out to Europe or the Pacific. My old
college beau Bill Roundtree, whom I hadn't heard from in four years,
wrote to tell me he'd enlisted and would soon be going overseas. For all
of us, this war was a matter of life and death, a battle from which only
the rankest of cowards would run.

Yet, America did not want us—not in its armed services. That was
the bald truth of the matter, the reality that gave me pause, even as I felt
drawn to the grand challenge Dr. Bethune held out to me each day of
that winter. I listened, enthralled by the boldness of her plan for black
women, but I remained deeply uncertain, even fearful. I knew, as did
everyone who read the Negro papers, the way of things in the military
for black folk. Southern draft boards—and even some in the North—
contrived by every imaginable ruse to fill their quotas with white men.
And the old stories of Negro cowardice dating back to World War
I surfaced with greater venom than ever after Pearl Harbor. When I
heard the awful litany on some white person's lips, I cringed: the colored race was shiftless, slow-witted, childlike in its mentality. Put a
Negro in charge of troops, and you'd have chaos; put him in battle at
all, and he'd panic and run. I'd think of the black veterans I'd known
in childhood, and remember the great Rayford Logan, crippled in his
service in the trenches during World War I, and I'd sicken anew at the
lies, cited as often as not as "scientific truth."

Even the race provision in the Selective Service Act couldn't outweigh hatred that deep, nor prevail over the law of the land. The act
banned race "discrimination" in the military, but in the twisted logic of
"separate but equal," it permitted segregation. And the army enforced
it, often with an iron hand. The Negro press carried reports of southern "peace officers" shooting black soldiers, and of race riots at army
bases in the South. What place, I wondered, was there for me, a black
woman, in such an army? The more I watched and listened to the talk
between Dr. Bethune and Mrs. Roosevelt that winter, the more I began
to wonder what place there was in the service for any member of my
sex, whatever her skin color.

The country's leaders hated the idea of women in the military. When
Massachusetts congresswoman Edith Nourse Rogers introduced a
bill to create a Women's Army Auxiliary Corps in the spring of 1941,

Congress had promptly killed it. They hadn't even been willing to con-sider the notion of the quasi-military organization proposed in the bill. Only pure desperation caused them to reconsider after Pearl Harbor, when the need for troops on two fronts became so acute that Gen-eral George C. Marshall himself entered an appearance and threw the weight of the War Department behind the push to put women in the military. Every woman who served as a clerk, a teletypist, an air warn-ing supervisor, a librarian, a machinist, a pharmacist, a cook or dieti-tian, or a medical technician at an army hospital would free up one more man for combat, the general argued, and the country needed men, men to fight on two oceans and four continents. By the end of January, a new bill authorizing an auxiliary corps had reached the floor of Con-gress—this time with plenty of backers. Committee hearings opened, and inside the War Department, WAAC planning began in earnest.

Dr. Bethune seized the moment. Her demand would have amounted to madness if it hadn't been so shrewd: black women, she insisted, must be granted not merely the right to enlist, but a place in the corps' first Officer Candidate School.

Would that I had been personally present in the War Department meeting when that crafty demand was laid upon the table. If ever a group of officials squirmed, those who faced Dr. Bethune on that oc-casion must have done so, for she'd zeroed in on the one chink in the army's impenetrable wall of segregation: its officer training. True, the army refused to allow its Negro officers to command white troops, even in selected northern regiments. But they'd integrated the training of of-ficers. Perhaps because so few blacks sought such training, the Army found it convenient to mix the races in the classroom, in mess halls, in barracks. How, Dr. Bethune demanded to know, could the army depart from its *own policy* in regard to the WAAC?

With that single question—one which in any sane and rational world would have admitted of a straightforward answer—she launched a war of her own, against an adversary more formidable even than the United States Army. Dr. Bethune took on Jim Crow itself. Almost no one in the early forties—not even the pioneering NAACP lawyer Charles Hamilton Houston and his protégé Thurgood Marshall, who'd begun blasting through the state courts demanding equal pay for black teachers—dared to take the principle of "separate but equal" head on. When A. Philip Randolph had demanded the desegregation of the military in June of 1941, the president had been unrelenting.

But the war itself had exposed the hypocrisy of American democracy in a way nothing else ever had. No one could fail to see the hideous contradiction between fighting racism in Europe and practicing Jim Crow in America: so the Negro papers said, in the "Double V Campaign" they launched against "Hitler abroad and Hitlerism at home." Dr. Bethune had already made places for thousands of young black people in the defense industry, using the president's antidiscrimination order as her weapon. Now, by training her sights even more narrowly, on women in the army officers' corps, she saw her chance to strike a blow against segregation itself. And on her initial pass, she prevailed. Completely cornered by its own logic, the War Department conceded a place for black women in the WAAC's Officer Candidate School.

On the heels of that significant victory, though, came the sort of weaving and dodging I would confront so often in my courtroom battles. Simple *fairness*, the War Department told Dr. Bethune, dictated that they follow army policy in regard to the WAAC—not the policy that applied to white officers, as Mrs. Bethune had assumed, but rather the one for enlisted men. And that policy demanded segregation. They guaranteed that one in every ten women entering OCS would be black, as was the case with male servicemen in the army, but they made it clear that those women would be part of colored units. Then the knife twisted one more time. In the interest of good order, the War Department announced, they deemed it prudent to stagger the entry of the races into WAAC officers' training, with white women admitted first, and black women following sometime later. To do otherwise would invite the sort of "trouble" that might taint an enterprise as new and controversial as the WAAC.

Dr. Bethune was not a woman to show anger. But on the day she and Mrs. Roosevelt met to confer on the latest War Department pronouncement, I detected an edge in her tone that startled me. I'd arrived late on that bitter cold morning, for some reason, and as I reached the top of the staircase, the tension in the two women's voices brought me up short.

Something about the notion of simultaneous admission of the races seemed to give Mrs. Roosevelt pause; that much I divined immediately. And as I settled in with the stack of daily papers, and began to listen to the First Lady speaking of the ugly incidents at southern bases where black and white men trained together, I saw that she was truly fearful. Perhaps, she suggested, there was something to be said for waiting to bring the black women into OCS until the WAAC stood on firmer ground.

If anybody had asked me, sitting quietly in my corner, I could have told them that this would be the fight where Dr. Bethune would dig in her heels and refuse to budge. For months, I'd heard her speak of what she called "the America that *could be*," and as she sat with her hands folded, quiet, shaking her head at the First Lady, it was clear that her very vision of America was on the line—the one to which she referred in one way or another each and every day, but which I perhaps had not fully grasped until this very moment. Somewhere in her mind's eye, beyond what she called "foolish prejudices and discrimination," Dr. Bethune saw an America so perfect, so filled with possibility, that it was worth dying for. Our boys, black and white, were doing it now—in Manila Bay, in Corregidor, in Bataan. What black person dared back away from his duty—his *right*—to stand shoulder to shoulder with whites to defend the dream of American democracy, the greatest government, at least in the abstract, ever conceived by mankind? That was the call Dr. Bethune had sounded right after Pearl Harbor in a *Pittsburgh Courier* article that was being quoted all over the country: "This is America's War," she had written, "and We, Too, are Americans." If men of all races were to fight and die, women, both black and white, must stand together behind them.

Now, she leaned toward Mrs. Roosevelt, sitting in the chair across from her, and asked, "What am I going to tell my girls?"

Mrs. Roosevelt was quiet for a few moments. "Don't tell them anything yet, Mary," she said finally. "Give me some time."

I prepared myself for a wait, but it was only a few days later that the call came. It would be as Mrs. Bethune had wanted it, Mrs. Roosevelt said. She had seen to it. In the first class of 440 officer candidates, due to arrive at the army training center in Fort Des Moines, Iowa, in July, 40 black women would enter, and, although they would be segregated in their own company, they would march, train, salute together. On August 29, 1942, when the first group of officers received their commissions in the WAAC, those 40 black women would be among them. And I would be one of the 40. Watching Dr. Bethune fight so hard over so many months for a place for black women in the military, I came to the conclusion that for all my reservations and my fears, I couldn't turn away from her challenge.

Jim Crow, as it turned out, proved alive and well not only within the War Department but on the floor of Congress, which threw out the antidiscrimination amendments introduced by northern senators and backed by black leaders across the country. Modeled on the language of the Selective Service Act, which at least in principle protected black men from unequal treatment in the armed services, the amendments banned "discrimination against any person on account of race or color."

The amendments fell to the arguments of a single woman—a Georgia state legislator named Helen Douglas Mankin, who persuaded the Senate Committee on Military Affairs that the ban on race discrimination was entirely unnecessary, that the army could be trusted to use its usual good sense in regard to race, that such language would do nothing but create national disunity. Congress turned a deaf ear to the pleas of Edgar Brown, who testified for the National Negro Council, and to those of Dr. Bethune's executive director, Jeanetta Welch, whom Dr. Bethune had dispatched to act in her stead in the public battle while she herself fought behind the scenes. Even Congresswoman Rogers, no doubt fearful of losing southern votes crucial to the passage of her bill, opposed the amendment.

In the end, the bill that passed and was signed into law by President Roosevelt on May 14, 1942, was devoid of any language to protect the 40 of us who were preparing to head off to Fort Des Moines. A handwritten memo, on War Department letterhead, arrived on Dr. Bethune's desk shortly after the bill was passed. Unsigned, the note made reference to assurances by "our new commander of the WAAC," Oveta Culp Hobby of Texas, the woman who had steadfastly refused to admit blacks to War Department planning sessions until forced to do so by a strongly worded letter from Dr. Bethune to Secretary of War Stimson. The memo stated that "every care had been taken to see that equality of opportunity is given to every woman regardless of race or creed." Not even Dr. Bethune herself knew precisely what that promise was worth.

One thing was certain: if Congress trusted the army to use its "usual common sense" in regard to race, Dr. Bethune did not. Nor did the country's other black leaders, who asked that the War Department appoint Dr. Bethune assistant director of the corps, to serve right under Colonel Hobby. While army officials rejected that request on the basis that Dr. Bethune, at age sixty-seven, was too old for military service or enrollment in the corps, they appointed her civilian advisor to the WAAC, in which capacity she was to consult with the director on matters affecting black recruits. Just what occurred in her private conferences with Colonel Hobby, I, of course, do not know. But in the early weeks of that summer, as the July 22 deadline approached for the first class of WAAC officer candidates to report to Fort Des Moines, Colonel Hobby herself set out on the recruiting trail, right along with Dr. Bethune, prevailing upon graduating seniors at black colleges in the South to join a Women's Army Auxiliary Corps where equal opportunity would be theirs to claim. In the end, 39 Negro women, including me, heeded that call.

I do not believe that any of us fully understood that in so doing, we were moving straight to the front line of a race war. At least, I did not grasp it in terms quite that stark as I headed home to North Carolina to file my application at the local recruiting station. Yet I am frank to say, now, that from the time I presented myself at the Charlotte post office, papers in hand, to the moment when I separated from military service two months after the United States declared victory over Japan in 1945, I fought my own private war, a war for the right to serve an America I loved more than I knew, for all her flaws.

5. "EVERYBODY'S WAR"

No black person raised in the South ever misreads the particular kind of menace conveyed by the narrowing of a white person's eyes, the withering stare that warns you that if you value your life and your safety, you'd best keep right on walking.

Such was the look visited upon me by the white army recruiter at the Charlotte post office when I presented myself on a morning in late May to file my WAAC application. He professed to know nothing at all about any plans to let women in the army. Where on earth, he asked, had I heard such a thing?

Something told me not to mention Dr. Bethune's name, nor even Colonel Hobby's, both of whom were even at that moment urging black women to join the WAAC. I told the officer simply that I had word from "a friend in Washington" that a women's corps had opened up and was accepting applications.

"Not here, they're not," he said shortly.

The more I protested and explained, the angrier the officer became.

"Now I'm going to tell you just one more time," he said, glaring at me as I tried to hand him a copy of the enabling legislation authorizing the WAAC. His voice rose ever so slightly, enough that people waiting in line on the other side of the post office turned to look. I could feel their eyes boring into my back as I stood up and gathered my papers, hurrying to vacate the premises before I was ordered out. But the officer beat me to it.

"You get out of here," he shouted at me. "Right now. Or I'll have you arrested."

Up until that moment, Dr. Bethune's vision and my belief in her had spurred me on. Now I was angry—livid in fact—that the army for which she'd handpicked me had turned me away. How dare he tell me that I couldn't fight for America? I was an American, through and through, and I believed in the war effort. Whatever we women could do in the fight, I wanted to be a part of.

That's exactly how I put the matter to Mama and Grandma, both of whom regarded the military with fear, for all its grand connection to Dr. Bethune. And that's what I said, in more or less those very words, to the next recruiting officer I spoke to, in Richmond, where Dr. Bethune advised me to apply when I'd phoned her to report on the reception I'd gotten at the Charlotte recruitment office. Richmond, she counseled, was farther north where things were "more open," and since I had relatives there, I could wait out the process if that became necessary.

Indeed, the wait stretched over several weeks, during which time Mama's brother, Ally, and his wife, Bessie, made a place for me in their home while I battered away at the army. Banished—though politely—upon my first visit by a recruiter who took my name and phone number and then never called, and interrogated at length upon my second visit by yet another officer who seemed stunned by my educational background, I managed, finally, to enlist.

If any army recruiter has ever painted a darker picture of military life in the interest of intimidating a potential recruit than did the officer who signed me up in Richmond, I would be surprised indeed. Did I have any notion, he asked, about the toughness of military discipline, the endless drilling, the dull routine, the physical demands of army life? Had I considered how I would feel, way up north, in Iowa, far from my home and family? Homesickness did a lot of people in, he told me, as did the regimentation, if you weren't used to it. And then there was the matter of life in the barracks where you had to bunk with total strangers. No feature of military life, in the litany he recited, appeared to be anything less than purely god-awful.

Grim as his recital was, though, it paled beside what I actually encountered when at last, on the morning of July 20, 1942, I was dumped out—no other word will do—at the entrance to Fort Des Moines, the old cavalry post the army had converted in less than two months' time into the training ground for WAAC officers. I'd traveled to the base in the rear of an army truck that was shuttling the new recruits in groups all day long from the train station a few miles from the post. The only black woman in my particular group, I'd been shunted to the back of the vehicle by the driver, a noncommissioned officer who managed somehow to enforce segregation without uttering a single syllable.

His counterparts at the base enforced army policy less quietly.

"Negroes on one side!" the white officer shouted as I disembarked, waving me toward a small group of black women who stood waiting to be processed. "White women on the other!"

Only the presence of Dr. Bethune on the base made that first day bearable. She gathered her "girls" about her—the thirty-nine of the original forty who'd made it to Fort Des Moines—and reminded us of our place in history. Many a time in after years, as I've stood at the pulpit or in the courtroom, facing folk whose nerves were raw, I've thought of the way Dr. Bethune transformed the atmosphere of those uneasy hours with a few carefully chosen words. No one on the base had more on the line than she that day, yet she betrayed not a hint of fear, nor even anxiety, but only conviction about the rightness of black and white standing together.

"Here at Fort Des Moines, we have democracy in action," she said, as Colonel Hobby and the base commandant, Colonel Don Faith, hovered nearby, taking in every word. "We are seeking equal participation. We are not going to be agitators."

We did not stand alone, she told us, nor did we act in our own behalf in entering the military. We represented the blacks of America—all 14 million of them—because we were the very first to wear the uniform of the WAAC.

What she didn't say, publicly, was that she'd staked everything, all her power and influence, the entire well of trust she'd built up with Mrs. Roosevelt, on what was, in truth, an experiment in democracy. But I knew. I'd watched her orchestrate the experiment. That was the thought uppermost in my mind as Dr. Bethune made her way through the cluster of us who gathered round her as she departed for Washington, speaking to each woman individually, by name. The words she said to me, as we walked together toward her car, I took as a mandate.

"I know that you understand very clearly why you are here," she told me. "You must see to it that the others do not forget. I'm counting on you to do that."

And then she was gone.

In the sweep of my life as I contemplate it now, I find myself choosing moments that stand as turning points. Without question, watching

Dr. Bethune driving away from that army base was one of those moments for me.

Life itself, of course, isn't lived so clearly and cleanly. Change steals over you when you're looking to the right, or the left, or far out ahead at the heavens somewhere, and then, at some point, you look inward and find yourself different. So it was with my time in the army. I entered the military a girl doing the bidding of others, living out the dream of a great leader, and marching to her orders. I left it a woman grown. As powerful an ally as Dr. Bethune remained, my time in the WAAC taught me that at last, I could—and would—stand on my own.

That change began with the surge of ambivalence I felt when I entered the strange *alter* world of the military, a world that drew me in with a sense of community and shared patriotism, yet shut me out with its brutal enforcement of Jim Crow. Never have I felt so divided, so torn between pride and shame as I did in the five weeks that transformed me into a third officer, the WAAC equivalent of an army second lieutenant. Like every other woman at Fort Des Moines, black or white, I drank in the call to service Colonel Hobby sounded on the fourth day of our basic training: "From now on you are soldiers, defending a free way of life," she told us. "You are no longer individuals. You wear the uniform of the army of the United States. Respect the uniform. Respect all that it stands for."

And I did. I thrilled to the starched khaki and the spit and polish and the smart saluting of the flag. I embraced the message of the newsreels we watched, showing women in Europe carrying the banner for their men, and touting the "Four Freedoms" for which we were fighting. Freedom of speech; freedom of worship; freedom from want; freedom from fear: there was a universality in those ideals that made sense to me. Yet we watched those films in a segregated theater. And waiting, always waiting, just outside the door was the face of Jim Crow in the person of some white officer barking orders to the black women to remain apart. From the first day, we'd encountered Jim Crow in the form of "Colored" signs on the mess hall tables—signs about which the commandant professed to know nothing when I confronted him, but which, he suggested in the same breath, I must be used to, being from the South. Though the signs disappeared a few days later, we received express orders to sit separately. That was Jim Crow the army way, and it hit hard. Nothing personal could be shared: not gas masks or first aid supplies, not dining table space by day or the barracks by night, not the service club or the officers' club. And lest some dread disease pass from black to white, the commandant decreed that after the black women used the swimming pool for the hour allotted to us on Friday afternoons, the water must be not only cleaned but "purified."

If I'd ever had to watch that heinous process, I might have resigned. But I didn't. I stayed, and I discovered in those first months at Fort Des Moines a force greater than the army's attempt to divide us. That was our common belief in the war. Black and white alike, we anguished over the grim newspaper accounts of the endless string of Allied defeats in Europe, in North Africa, in Russia. When our boys began turning the tide against the Japanese at Guadalcanal in August, we celebrated together. We spoke constantly, all of us, of the fate of our troops. Every one of us knew someone stationed overseas. Though Bill Roundtree and I were no longer sweethearts, we kept in touch, and I looked for the postcards and notes, first from his stateside base, and later from Europe, that told me he was safe, and well. There were women with husbands, fiancés, brothers in the war, and all of us longed for peace, convinced we could, somehow, hasten its coming. That was what we were marching and sweating and drilling for—to fit ourselves to stand "in the place of the man behind the gun," as one WAAC newsletter put it. Powerful stuff, that—so powerful not even the army could break it.

There are, I am persuaded, places within the human heart where no system can reach. At Fort Des Moines, we found them. Nearly all of us in that first WAAC class were college graduates, driven by common backgrounds, shared ambitions, definite ideas about the shape of the future. Conversations begun in the open air had a way of spilling over into the mess hall, and with such frequency as we grew to know one another that Jim Crow became simply inconvenient. Once the mess hall signs came down, so did the invisible line, quietly enough that the commandant chose to look the other way as first one girl, and then another, broke the color line. There were, of course, white women from the South whose faces hardened when they passed us, but what grew up with astonishing speed, overall, was a camaraderie that pushed and pressed its way between the cracks of army regulations on the base. And when we went into town in groups, it spilled over freely.

Jim Crow had no place in the city of Des Moines, Iowa—not in the shops or restaurants, the banks or movie theaters. Socially, the races separated, as they did everywhere; black churches and neighborhoods thrived, as did Des Moines's black-owned newspaper, the *Iowa*

Observer, headed by a lawyer named Charles Howard, a bold activist with his own news syndicate. But in the public places, the law permitted mixing of the races, and when we assembled in one or another of the Des Moines hotels the army used for special training sessions, I could actually feel the heaviness lift. At mealtimes particularly, the laughter and the chatter seemed to my ears louder than on the base. Certainly I breathed more easily in the hotel dining halls, relieved for an hour or two to escape the watchful eye of the commandant and his subordinates, any one of whom might decide to call a halt to interracial dining.

Had I been more thoroughly schooled in the ways of the military, I would have known, then, that "official army policy" obtained wherever the army did business. But I was a neophyte—only two months commissioned—on the October evening when we filed into the dining room at the Savery Hotel in downtown Des Moines, moved through the cafeteria line in mixed groups, and began seating ourselves as we pleased, without regard to race.

Suddenly an angry command cut through the hubbub, and I knew even before I turned to see a white officer moving toward a group of black women sitting with whites, that integration in the state of Iowa had just stepped aside for the United States Army. As the black girls stood and began picking up their trays, the officer spat the hated word at them: "You darkies move those trays, and sit where you belong."

I'd heard worse. And I'd seen worse, in the South, just as Colonel Morgan had intimated when I'd spoken to him about the "Colored" mess hall signs on the base. But I had not been in uniform during my years in Charlotte and Atlanta. That made the difference. And we had come to expect better, all of us, as with each passing day we'd penetrated in a hundred small ways the wall of race. Even the quietest of the black girls fumed in the barracks that night as the group who'd witnessed the dining hall incident gathered to discuss the matter. They looked to me for guidance, and to another black officer named Irma Cayton, a brilliant young woman with connections to the Negro press through her husband, Horace Cayton, who was an influential *Pittsburgh Courier* columnist. We all agreed that if we were representing every black in America, as Dr. Bethune had told us, we could not remain silent. We were officers now, after all, with a stake in the system, and yet we felt more and more isolated with each passing week. In the nearly two months since we'd been commissioned, not a single black woman had enrolled in WAAC officer training. The word on the "Jim Crow WAAC" was out, and nearly every black organization in the country had begun sending representatives to look into conditions. Dr. Bethune personally dispatched Des Moines lawyer and newspaperman Charles Howard to conduct a full-scale investigation of race at the end of August, and post officials had appeared to cooperate with him. But they changed nothing. The time had come, we believed, to push.

The telegram to Dr. Bethune that I proposed was signed by ten women, including Irma and me, and dispatched from downtown Des Moines the next morning. We reported "unnecessary prejudice in the dining hall at the Savery Hotel," and laid out for Dr. Bethune the dozen forms of degradation, petty and egregious, to which we'd been subjected on the base from the first night in the dining hall.

When the axe fell, it fell first on Irma Cayton and me, and to our shock and horror, on Dr. Bethune herself. With stunning speed the commandant turned accusers into accused, summoning Irma and me to his office so quickly after we'd sent the telegram I knew immediately that one of the other black officers had played the stool pigeon. The army, I would learn over time, cultivated such spies, using information thus obtained to isolate, intimidate and even court-martial blacks who challenged Jim Crow. In this particular instance, the commandant employed another isolating tactic as well: he insisted that Dr. Bethune had sanctioned the segregation policy we were now challenging. We were "agitators," Colonel Morgan told us, and what we'd done in going outside military channels amounted to treason. The ludicrousness of that accusation emboldened me. We might be agitators, I told him, but we were not traitors. When we refused to submit our resignations, as he demanded, he stared at us in stony silence for a moment, then waved us out of his office.

Irma and I, as it turned out, were of only marginal interest to the army in its Jim Crow enforcement strategy. It was Dr. Bethune, with her NAACP and newspaper and White House connections, who posed the real threat. In the wake of her receipt of our telegram, the War Department moved swiftly, sending an official out to investigate even as they began driving a wedge between Dr. Bethune and the forces that fed her. Mary McLeod Bethune, they announced, had publicly endorsed segregation in the WAAC when she'd addressed the officer candidates upon their arrival at Fort Des Moines. She'd called the WAAC Officer Candidate School "democracy in action," the army said. She'd promised she was seeking only "equal participation," and she'd assured the entire assembly that she and the black officer candidates were "not going to be agitators." Every word she'd uttered in the interest of protecting us in that hostile atmosphere, they now used against her to discredit her with her black colleagues.

The War Department had conveniently chosen to ignore the antisegregation campaign Dr. Bethune had unleashed upon them from the time the WAAC bill reached Congress. But if she was forced by the army to defend herself to colleagues like Walter White and the editors of the black newspapers, I knew she had no intention of retreating from the battle. With Charles Howard's findings in hand, she had all the ammunition to bring Mrs. Roosevelt into the fray.

As for me, I became from that time forward a marked woman, a thorn in the army's side, and such a threat to discipline and good order that I was dubbed "a walking NAACP" by the commandant. Such "threats" must be neutralized when they couldn't be excised, and even before the War Department officials had completed their investigation, I received orders that placed me as far from the base as was humanly possible within the continental United States. Georgia, Florida, the Carolinas: those were the states to which my partner, Ruth Lucas, and I were assigned in the first week of November 1942, with Texas added to our orders shortly thereafter. Whether the army appreciated the supreme irony of assigning a "walking NAACP" to the task of bringing yet more black women into the corps I do not know, nor did I care, for I saw in recruiting a chance to make a real difference in the future of the WAAC before it was too late for us.

The specter of a segregated military had taken such hold in the black community that only the barest trickle of black women—not even two hundred—had enlisted by the time I set out on recruiting duty in November of 1942, and all nine classes of officer candidates who'd come and gone since my commissioning were lily white. The "First Forty"— those of us for whom Dr. Bethune had fought so hard, who'd cracked the color bar and made history—were about to become the Last Forty, a pitiful footnote in the story of the power of segregation to kill black participation.

That, I determined, would not happen—not on my watch, no matter how tough a sell I had on my hands in pitching a Jim Crow WAAC in the Deep South. Some, I well knew, believed me a fool, including more than a few of my black comrades back at Fort Des Moines, who'd become so embittered they talked privately of resigning. But I'd seen something they hadn't: I'd sat in Dr. Bethune's office and personally watched her wrangle from the War Department the promise of black participation. I'd chosen the WAAC, knowing—albeit incompletely—of its segregation policy. And I would have chosen it again, because despite all I'd endured at Fort Des Moines, I still believed in everything the WAAC stood for. I believed in the war effort, in the critical role of women in that effort, and in the right of blacks to fight alongside whites—not later, not at some distant future date when America and the army walked out into the light and abandoned Jim Crow, but now.

That was what I told the crowds of girls and women in colleges and black Y's and churches and NAACP meetings and Negro chambers of commerce all over the South. I believed it, so deeply and firmly that I was convinced I could sell other black women on the WAAC, though I knew that already the brand-new enterprise was tainted. Ugly rumors had begun circulating that women, both black and white, were being recruited for military service to serve as prostitutes for the men. Later in the war, that heinous allegation would become part of an all-out smear campaign against the WAAC, a lie invented and kept alive, I believe, by a male military establishment that hadn't wanted us in the first place. Even as early as 1942, I heard the vile gossip everywhere I went. I slammed it down as hard as I could, and I trained my sights on the only folk in the black community with the power to actually kill it: the ministers. From the time I was old enough to sit up straight in a pew, I'd known that church was where you sold whatever you were selling to the kind of people Grandma called "quality." Starting with familiar territory, in Charlotte and in Atlanta, I made a beeline for the most prominent pastors, convincing them of the fineness of the WAAC and the decency of its women and prevailing upon them to reach out to their colleagues in cities and towns all over the Carolinas and Georgia to urge them to throw their mantle of support over our efforts.

Nobody on earth, though, could smash the other "ugly rumor" about the WAAC—the one about Jim Crow—because it was true. Segregation defined every aspect of military life. This I freely acknowledged, raising the issue even before my audiences had the chance to, and taking it head on. The girls' faces fell and their jaws hardened at that bald admission coming straight from a WAAC officer, but I knew no other way to tell it. I couldn't bring myself to parrot the army line, the public whitewash with which the military cloaked its racism. I knew full well, from Dr. Bethune and my colleagues back at Fort Des Moines, that the WAAC had begun publicly declaring segregation "abolished" at those times when there were no black women—or very few—on the base, only to quietly reinstitute it the moment the numbers were sufficient to form an all-black platoon. A "variable policy," Colonel Hobby called the elaborate integration dodge in a press release she issued that fall. Only a madman could have made rational sense of such a policy, and I didn't even try. I bluntly stated what I perceived to be the truth: that a black woman entering the WAAC should prepare herself for segregated living.

But I pressed on with other truths I'd seen with my own eyes: the vibrant force of good will between black and white women at Fort Des Moines that transcended the meanness of official army policy; the chance for equal opportunity for which I'd watched Dr. Bethune and Mrs. Roosevelt give their all. Was that opportunity precisely, mathematically, documentably equal to that of whites? Probably not. But the WAAC offered a chance I believed would never come again in quite the same way: the chance to advance, to train for careers, to build the kind of future we women wanted for our children, to stand behind the men who were fighting in Europe and North Africa and the Pacific. That mattered most of all. Our boys were *dying* for freedom, I pointed out in every speech I made. What was segregation compared to that?

Thousands of black women answered that question by enlisting in the WAAC. Like me, they believed in the war with a fierceness that cannot perhaps be fully understood by the modern generation. Never at any time in my life was America more united than during World War II. Everyone, no matter of what race, felt the need to crush Japanese aggression, and black people understood with absolute certainty that if Hitler prevailed, his boot would fall hardest on the colored races. In the late fall of 1942, with our forces taking a beating in North Africa and starving in Japanese death camps in the South Pacific, the possibility of defeat was real. To shorten the war by even a day, to bring our men home and build peace for our children—these were goals where race had no meaning. Ruth Lucas and I and the twelve other black recruiters who canvassed the country in the fall of 1942 tapped into that vein of patriotism, pitching the WAAC so hard that by the winter of 1943 the army had more Negro applicants than it had imagined possible—more in fact, than it truly wanted, for all its lip service to the 10 percent quota. Even as we ratcheted up our efforts, targeting the black colleges in search of top-notch recruits, we began hearing disturbing reports of white field commanders refusing to take black women once they'd been trained. Only years later were the actual figures made public: nearly nine hundred colored women—a third of the number of blacks in the corps—were being held for weeks and even months after basic training at posts all over the country, unwanted and unassigned.

Once word of the intolerable delays leaked into the black community at large, we had yet another fight on our hands, more questions to answer—and with precious little ammunition. Still, we marched forward, taking our campaign deeper and deeper into the South, recruiting over the radio, in the local newspapers, and in every church and college and black organization willing to host us. Always, I spoke proudly and saluted smartly. But all the while, I was pitching toward a moment of reckoning with the army that was coming at me faster than I realized.

That reckoning began in a noisy, crowded Miami bus station late one night in the winter of 1943, as I stood, alone, waiting to board a bus for a Florida town farther north, where I was joining Ruth for our next campaign. I'd grown accustomed to watching my back on the recruiting trail, where the army left us unescorted and unprotected, instructing us simply to "be careful." I took particular care in riding trains and buses without Ruth, as I often did when the press of our schedule demanded that one of us go on ahead to see to arrangements in the next town while the other stayed behind to process recruits.

I sensed nothing particularly menacing about the Miami station that night. The city, a melting pot even in those days, felt more raucous and loud than it did hateful. Then, too, a crowd of soldiers and sailors streamed into the station just as I did, and there came over me that comforting sense of oneness I always felt when in the company of others in uniform.

Even when I saw the "Colored" section of the bus filling with passengers, I wasn't especially worried, as I recall, because the front remained nearly empty. I boarded, paid my fare, and moved to a seat in the "White" section. And then, suddenly, there it was: Jim Crow, hateful and insulting, shouting me down in the person of the bus driver.

"What do you think you're doing?" he called to me. "Don't you see there's somebody waiting for that seat?"

I turned to see a white soldier standing looking down at me, unsmiling. I was reduced—just as I had been by the army recruiter who'd thrown me out of the Charlotte post office when I'd tried to enlist—reduced, in the space of a single moment, to a six-year-old child, the one who'd been called a "pickaninny" so many years ago in Charlotte. And then I remembered who I was: a captain in the WAAC, a member of the United States military.

"I am traveling on army business," I told the driver, "and I have orders to depart Miami by this bus." In the way of a traveler who must justify his presence in a foreign land, I reached into my duffel bag for my itinerary.

But he'd have none of it. Like the recruiting officer in Charlotte, he seemed enraged by my pressing documentation upon him.

"Get to the end of the line out there," he ordered, motioning toward the white passengers, mostly military, standing outside the bus.

The black passengers in the rear went quiet. They knew, as I did, that this was how "incidents" started—the kind that got you killed or landed you in jail, where you could languish indefinitely, whether you were military or not. In fact, my status as a WAAC—a WAAC already branded a "walking NAACP" by my superiors—placed me in the gravest danger. For months, the Negro press had been reporting the court-martials of black troublemakers in the military. Rumor had it that black soldiers had been shot on city streets by southern "peace officers" and even lynched on the bases where they were posted for duty. The army, it was said, simply turned its back.

I looked at the driver, and at the white soldier, both silently daring me to challenge them, and I picked up my duffel bag and climbed off the bus. As I took my place in the line of white army and navy personnel, not a single one saluted, or offered a hand, or even spoke. They filed into the bus and it roared out of the station, leaving me behind.

For two or three hours, perhaps longer, I waited alone in the nearly deserted bus station, my mind screaming what I'd wanted to scream at the driver. The uniform of which I was so proud, that had set Mama and Grandma glowing as they'd walked alongside me down the streets of Charlotte, had counted for nothing. That night I wrestled with hatred deeper than I'd ever known, hatred of Jim Crow, hatred of the army that had cast me adrift in hostile territory, and most of all, hatred of these people who had treated me as an interloper in my own country.

As for what I'd been telling potential recruits for the past three months—that we had an obligation to get behind our men in their battle against oppression and tyranny—I asked myself whether it was all a lie. Whose freedom, whose America, was I asking them to fight for?

The army's answer came swiftly, in hateful waves. Even as I journeyed northward to complete my Florida mission, the War Department
handed down a brief announcement I read as a dire warning: black
recruitment had failed to meet expectation. If one believed the statistics
the army issued, fully 85 percent of the black recruits failed to pass
that most basic of all intelligence measures, the army's Mental Alertness Test. Even such tasks as filing or baking or driving a truck apparently exceeded the capacity of the majority of the Negro women
we were bringing into the corps; only years later would I learn that
white women with the same test scores were commissioned as officers.
What the army never published were the figures on the white field commanders who steadily declined to accept black recruits, no matter what
their qualifications. Like the thousands of black folk from Reconstruction days onward who'd lined up at southern polling places only to be
barred from voting by virtue of unseen "test results," a large percentage
of our recruits found themselves consigned to that shameful category of
persons with "no usable military skills." In June 1943, the army shut
down black recruitment, called all fourteen of us from the field, and
brought Ruth and me back to Fort Des Moines for urgent "personnel
work."

Even then, I held fast, celebrating the passage of the bill granting
the WAAC full military status in July, and giving my all to the task of
finding placements for the black recruits deemed acceptable by the new
Women's Army Corps. I was relieved, in one sense, to be off the recruiting trail that summer, as race riots on a scale the country had never
known exploded in more than forty cities. Just as I returned to Fort Des
Moines, reports reached us of thousands of whites marching through
Los Angeles, beating blacks and Mexicans in a horror known as the "zoot
suit riots." Barely two weeks later, violence broke out in Detroit. Like
fire in dry tinder, it spread faster than police and even federal troops
could contain it, to Harlem, St. Louis, Columbus, Indianapolis—all the
northern industrial cities where blacks had flocked for wartime production jobs and found themselves battling whites for those jobs, and
for already scarce housing as well. Through July and into August the
violence swept through dozens of overcrowded cities stretched to the
breaking point, killing blacks and whites alike, feeding on frustration I
well understood.

All summer long, as new reports of rioting surfaced daily, from
Beaumont, Texas, from Mobile, Alabama, and again up north, from

Philadelphia, I breathed deeply of the free air at Fort Des Moines, where among the officers, at least, life was colorblind. When I returned there in June, I discovered that for some months the officers on the base had been marching as one, black and white together, in a mixed-race training regiment that stood apart as something fine, the shining exception to the grotesqueness of Jim Crow that still existed among the enlisted women on our base and among all women on other bases. To me, that minute oasis of integration stood for the future that could be, the one toward which Dr. Bethune had looked when she'd fought for our inclusion. And then, the army decided to take it away.

On August 23, 1943, one week before we were to take our oath of reenlistment as officers in the Women's Army Corps, our new base commandant, Colonel Frank U. McCoskrie, issued a memorandum announcing a plan to eradicate the integrated training regiment and create in its place one regiment for white officers and another for blacks. Rumors of the conversion had been circulating for weeks, but none of the informal descriptions we heard captured the almost total isolation the plan was designed to effect. True, the colonel's plan affected only Fort Des Moines, but since the majority of officers trained there, the institution of a Jim Crow regiment had wide implications. And it reached far beyond the present: we black officers were to train other blacks, who in turn would train their black successors, thus perpetuating a Jim Crow WAC for years to come. Eight of the colored officers, including me, were directed to "understudy" the white officers and to select "suitably trained colored cadre" by September 1, the day on which we were scheduled to take our reenlistment oath.

We'd all waited for that moment for nearly a year, had anticipated with such pride the time when we'd be given full military status, with regular army ranks, full pay, and benefits. There were a handful of the black officers who clung to that even in the face of Colonel McCoskrie's announcement. They argued that an all-colored unit offered us a better chance for promotion and true leadership than did the current situation, which unquestionably favored the white women. But the vast majority of us found such rationalizations repulsive, and as the date of the meeting approached, we divided ourselves sharply into two camps. Once again, just as they had when we'd agreed to telegraph Dr. Bethune about the incident in the Savery Hotel's dining hall, the women who opposed the colonel's plan appointed me their spokesperson. As we sat up through the night of August 31, strategizing, parceling out the questions to be raised, I felt a clarity in my own mind. No oath of loyalty, no matter how soaring and noble, could be squared with an army that shut out an entire race of citizens. If the colonel persisted with his plan, I would have no choice but to resign.

In the quiet of the auditorium the next morning, I sat before the podium, flanked by the three women who'd agreed to follow my lead with questions, fixing my eyes upon the colonel's face as he began speaking of the regiment that was in his mind clearly a fait accompli. A "boomtown," he termed the isolated world he'd carved out for us, laying out the particulars with the air of a man who'd just thrown wide the gates to the Promised Land. Had he shouted the words, I could not have been more sickened at his glowing description of the opportunities for promotion and leadership open to us now that we no longer had to compete with white women. Only the details of the regiment's formation, he said, turning to the subordinate officers standing beside him, remained to be dealt with.

At that, I was on my feet.

"Sir," I began, "may I ask whether questions are in order?"

The colonel, clearly irritated, responded that the all-black unit was a reality. Before he could press forward to the instructions for transferring documents and funds to the new regiment, two of my comrades took the floor, spelling out for the colonel what he'd chosen to ignore: the fact that the majority of the black officers opposed the Jim Crow regiment. The third cut straight to the urgent question of the reenlistment oath we were scheduled to take just a few days hence. What would her status be, she inquired, if she declined to take that oath? The colonel made no response, but every woman in the room knew the answer. Our continuation in the WAC hung on our acceptance of this regiment. Behind me, I sensed the fear rising in the group. There would be those who would choose to accede to the colonel's demand. That I knew. And I understood why: to turn your back on the military, to compromise your future, to scrap all you'd accomplished was almost beyond contemplation. But I also knew that for me, it was the only possible choice. Not even my bond with Dr. Bethune changed that. The Jim Crow regiment, with its implications for the future, defiled her vision. And it defiled mine.

I stood, and, looking into the colonel's shocked face, I unpinned my captain's bars, signifying my intention to resign or accept discharge if he persisted with his plan.

"Sir, you are setting us back a hundred years," I began. "Can you actually believe that the advantages of this proposal can outweigh the damage it will cause?" In the silence I heard the echo of my own voice as I described the respect and good will that had grown up between the black and white women on the base, the sense of fellow feeling he was about to eradicate. And what of the training films we watched each week—*The Four Freedoms* and the *Why We Fight* series? If the message of those films had any meaning, I insisted, the Jim Crow regiment could not exist. It flew in the face of all that we were fighting overseas—racism, tyranny, oppression. I spoke of the Jews in Germany, of all the other nations involved in the struggle, of the resistance efforts throughout the German-held countries, of the women around the world whom we'd joined in the war effort. What were we all fighting for if not freedom, and justice and equality?

When I finished, no one said a word or stood in support of what I'd said—not even the three officers who'd helped me plan the protest. In the silence, the colonel dismissed the meeting, and quietly we returned to barracks.

My fellow officers were as quiet and subdued as they had been noisy and outraged the night before. Even the strongest of my colleagues seemed cowed, somehow, at the turn the meeting had taken, and in the hours while we awaited word from the colonel, women I'd considered allies seemed to turn from me, some subtly, some overtly.

"You ruined all our chances," one black officer told me. "They were going to give us promotions, and you cost us that."

Never had it occurred to me that my fellow blacks would feel betrayed by an attack on Jim Crow, and a sense of aloneness came over me. Yet I felt strangely free of the need for support or approbation in what I'd done. I hadn't consulted with one other person when I'd made the decision to remove my captain's bars because I hadn't needed to. What a long way I'd come, I realized, since the day I'd watched Dr. Bethune drive away from the base after her welcoming speech to us. Although I telephoned her after the meeting to brief her on what had transpired, I knew that if the army didn't change its mind, I'd resign, oath or no oath. My military service was no longer an extension of Dr. Bethune's dream, but a thing all my own.

There can be little question of Dr. Bethune's role in the ultimate disposition of the matter of the all-black regiment, of course, given that her style of "looking into" any WAC-related issue invariably involved at least a phone call to Mrs. Roosevelt, if not a personal visit. But when on September 4, 1943, four days after the meeting, Colonel McCoskrie issued a memorandum to each of the eight black officers who'd been slated to lead the Jim Crow regiment, revoking the plan in its entirety, the pride that welled up in me was intensely personal. My voice had counted. I was certain of that. Those who'd thought to take my America from me found they could not.

What a simple thing it is, this country we claim. *My America*. I owned it as surely as my own name. I'd stepped forward to take my place in the battle against Hitler and the Japanese not for some abstraction but for the shotgun houses and the clay streets of my little neighborhood in Charlotte, where fires smoked and laundry flapped in the breeze and women's voices rose in song, and my grandmother baked communion bread and pounded herbs and my mother went out to scrub floors. None of that had been consciously in my thoughts when I faced down Colonel McCoskrie. But memories of home flooded my mind in the weeks that followed, as our troops charged onto the Italian mainland from Sicily and began turning the tide against German submarines in the Atlantic. It was then that the army saw fit to send me out once again as a sort of "roving recruiter," acceding finally to the chorus of voices demanding the enrollment of more black women.

Then, too, black leaders in the cities I'd visited weighed in with letters to my superiors at Fort Des Moines, praising my efforts and urging my return to the field. Dispatched this time with two enlisted women under my command, I returned to Dallas, Texas, and from there traveled to cities and towns all over the state of Ohio. It would not be honest to say that I was entirely free of anger when I began sounding the call to black women once again. But I was deeply changed by having seen the way in which a single voice—*my* voice—could make a difference. The greatest women in my life—Grandma, Miss Neptune, and Dr. Bethune—had each in her own way told me that the idea of America was worth fighting for, however ugly its present reality. Now, finally, I had come to that myself.

Fired with that certainty, I found an eloquence for the country that had hurt me, shunted me aside, shut me out.

"World War II is not a man's war, or a woman's war, nor is it the fight of any group or race," I told the women of Ohio more than a hundred times over in the fall of 1943 and the winter of 1944. "This is everybody's war. Whatever our circumstances, whatever our past, we are all in it. We fight this day for the right to *live*. This right knows no geographical boundaries, no barriers, nor differences of sex, race, creed, or color. The war will not be won alone by guns, planes, tanks. As deadly as these may be, they mean but little if you and I lack sincere faith in a free tomorrow. A tomorrow when men live together in society to attain the highest individual and collective well-being. Whatever the past, however dark the present, your obligation, my duty to the future is not lessened. The way we participate in this global war, the way we think and work for the common good today reveals just how much we want a decent world in which to live after this conflict is ended."

Of the 90,780 women who served in the WAC during World War II, 6,500 were black. In the decades after the war, I would grapple again and again with the pain and injustice of racism, but nothing ever tempered my pride in the fact that I was one of those 6,500, and that I played a critical role in bringing into the army those women who served in impossible times, women who, like me, served out of love for the America that was ours.

6. Uneasy Peace

World War II ended on August 15, 1945, the day the United States declared victory over Japan. Peace began, for me, when I heard my mother's voice on the telephone, filled with excitement about the prospect of my homecoming—and about something else as well.

"Your young man Bill Roundtree has been calling here," she told me. "He's on his way home."

The flutter I felt surprised me. Of course, I was relieved that Bill was out of harm's way, that he'd made it home from his last posting in France, where he'd been stationed after D-Day. But something more than simple gladness at an old friend's safe return lifted me up as Mama went on to explain how intent Bill had been on finding me, that he'd called more than once and had told her he'd be calling again. There was not a doubt in my mind that he would; the Bill Roundtree who'd courted me at Spelman had meant what he said. And somehow I sensed that he meant to come courting again.

Thoughts—and feelings—resurfaced that I hadn't had in years. Heading to Charlotte by way of the army discharge center at Fort Dix, New Jersey, and my beloved sister Bea's in New York, my mind turned again and again to Bill, to our time together as college sweethearts and to the seven years since then. Shut away first in Chester, South Carolina, and then in a Jim Crow army, I'd experienced such isolation I hadn't realized until I reentered civilian life just how unnatural my existence had been. It was as though some great suffocating weight had been lifted from my chest, and I could finally breathe, and feel alive once again.

A lady never shouts, Grandma taught me—or at least she tried to, but without much success, I fear, for I was a born noisemaker. And I frankly and freely own that as I stood alongside Bea and her husband, Gene, in the crush of people lining the sidewalks of Broadway for the grand victory parade that welcomed General Jonathan Wainwright home from the South Pacific, I shouted, shouted as I never had before, shouted for the end of war and the coming of peace and the recommencement of all that was good in the world. I've known moments of pure happiness in the course of my life, but never the sort of ecstasy that shot through me for three hours on the thirteenth of September in 1945. All around me, grown men wept openly and complete strangers hugged each other. I stood a-tiptoe in my starched dress uniform, cheering and waving a flag amidst a blizzard of ticker tape so thick it obscured the edges of the shops and theater marquees and office buildings that lined both sides of the street. All along the wide boulevard, people saluted the general and I did, too, every one of us awed at the bravery that had sustained him for more than three years in a Japanese prison camp after Corregidor.

I kept on saluting all afternoon, it seemed, as up and down Broadway the soldiers and sailors I passed on the long walk back to our car saluted me. Black and white alike, it made no difference that day. This was the America Dr. Bethune had talked about to a radio audience of millions in November 1939, a few weeks after Hitler had invaded Poland.

"A dream, an ideal," she'd called American democracy, "a goal toward which our nation is marching.

"Perhaps the greatest battle is before us," she'd said, "the fight for a new America: fearless, free, united, morally rearmed, in which 12 million Negroes, shoulder to shoulder with their fellow Americans, will strive that this nation under God will have a new birth of freedom, and that government of the people, for the people and by the people shall not perish from the earth. This dream, this ideal, this aspiration, this is what American democracy means to me."

If every day could have been like the golden afternoon of that victory parade, when millions of people of every race cheered the arrival of peace, we would have fulfilled Dr. Bethune's dream. But as the euphoria of that celebration receded, a heaviness settled over me—a heaviness, as I analyze it now, that came from a sense of business unfinished, or perhaps, more accurately, of a battle not yet truly won. Everywhere about me hung the specter of segregation. The soldiers who, like Bill, had served in all-colored units overseas poured into Fort Dix and hundreds of processing stations around the country, to be divided once again, in peace, even as they were in war. The train that had brought me eastward from Iowa to New Jersey to New York had been integrated, but I knew that when it turned southward and passed through Washington, I'd move along with every other black passenger to the sooty, overcrowded Jim Crow coaches for the journey home. Even the war's great miracle—a colorblind GI Bill of Rights, with its promise of tuition payments and loans—had a dark side, underscoring as it did the doors that remained closed. The great Ivy League institutions to which veterans were already flocking by the thousands were strictly white, the GI Bill notwithstanding. As a black veteran bent on medical school, I had but two choices: Howard and Meharry. What, in the end, had the war for democracy been about, for black folk?

Even as I feasted on Bea's home cooking and our memories of the old times in Charlotte, I found my thoughts turning to those in the fight for racial equality—Dr. Bethune, of course, in Washington, and the activists I'd met on the recruiting trail, at the Kansas City home of a woman named Tommie Berry, mother of one of my finest recruits and a society hostess who entertained the most prominent black leaders in the country. Walter White and Lester Granger, whom I'd first met in Dr. Bethune's office, had called upon Mrs. Berry while I was visiting her, along with A. Philip Randolph, founder of the powerful Brotherhood of Sleeping Car Porters and orchestrator of the greatest employment boon blacks and women had ever seen, the Fair Employment Practices Committee. The FEPC had become a household word by the end of the war, and A. Philip Randolph an icon in the eyes of millions of blacks, including me. No one who met Randolph could forget him. Tall, handsome, cultivated, he was a man who changed a room simply by walking into it. The memory of our brief meeting more than a year earlier lingered in my mind, and when I phoned Mrs. Berry just before leaving Fort Des Moines, she reminded me that Randolph, overhearing me holding forth to a group of WACs about our fight for freedom at home and abroad, had made his way through the crowd of guests to talk to me. He had inquired closely on that occasion about my background and my plans, and had given me the phone number of his New York office, urging me to seek him out after the war. Mrs. Berry was certain he'd remember me.

He did indeed. He gave me an appointment within days after I called him from Bea's, and he greeted me with outstretched hand when I arrived at the Harlem office from which he was overseeing the fight to save the wartime FEPC from extinction. What a lonely fight that was.

It would take twenty years and more violence than the country had known since the Civil War to force the passage of the Civil Rights Act, which banned job discrimination in every sector and created the Equal Employment Opportunity Commission to enforce the law. In 1946, the idea of government interference in the private matter of hiring was anathema, particularly when it carried with it the possibility of black empowerment. So fierce was the opposition to such a notion that had it not been for the country's desperate need of a vast wartime work force, I doubt the FEPC would ever have come into being. It had taken the threat of a hundred thousand blacks marching on Washington to create it, and then only by executive order rather than by law. After President Roosevelt's death in April, it languished in limbo, and southern congressmen unleashed the full force of their venom against the bill that would have made it permanent. Even before the war ended in Europe, Congress slashed the committee's budget in half, forcing Randolph to shut down all but three of his sixteen regional offices even as he fought for legislation to make the committee a bona fide federal agency.

A lesser man, fighting for a program in its death throes, would have betrayed some hint of desperation. A. Philip Randolph was iron. Elegant though he was in his demeanor, his dress, the British manner of speech that belied his American birth—he'd cultivated an Oxford accent as a young Shakespearean actor—Randolph was devoid of frivolity. He was an activist in a different mold from those I'd known. While Dr. Bethune exuded warmth, he projected such formality that he'd intimidated me when I'd met him at Tommie Berry's home, and I found his socialist creed almost as alien to my thinking as his atheism. But the belief he held as a kind of religion was sacred to me as well: the right of a man, or a woman, to work. To him, it ranked alongside the right to live.

When Randolph spoke about that right, about how swiftly industry was reverting to Jim Crow hiring in peacetime, about the thousands of unemployed blacks he'd seen in his tour of the country earlier that month and the violence he felt was inevitable, his decency, his conviction, his sheer strength filled the room. This man who'd brought the powerful Pullman Company to the bargaining table with the porters' union was not about to walk away from the fight for fair hiring. On the FEPC hung the only protection against job discrimination that was available to black folk in those days. Unlike the EEOC that would follow it twenty years later, it lacked the force of law and had no power to bring suit, but it had somehow managed by means of investigation and the gentle persuasion of sanctions to break the wall of segregation in the manufacturing plants that had government contracts. Unless Congress passed legislation to make it permanent in the next session, it would die on June 30, 1946, and the herculean effort that had tripled the number of blacks in industry and in government would come to naught. Before the hour was out, Mr. Randolph had moved me to enlist in the battle to save one of the most controversial agencies in the country's history by the toughest means imaginable—softening the hearts of the public.

Lobbying Congress wouldn't carry the day, Randolph said, not when the voters eyed federal intervention in employment with such suspicion. It was going to take a grassroots campaign through hundreds of local councils across the country to pass state FEPC laws, a coalition of folk of all races, and a sustained barrage of information by people who believed so deeply in the cause that they could penetrate the public's skepticism—fast. I'd appealed to tough audiences before, in my army recruiting days, and I was certain I could do it again if that's what it took to resuscitate a dying organization on which hung the fate of millions of black people. What better use to put my time as I filed applications to medical school? That, I explained to Randolph, was where I was bound next fall, without question. And I meant it. I'd been derailed first by lack of money and then by the war. This time around, I vowed, nothing would stop me.

How wise was Shakespeare on the subject of our destinies, how eloquent his Hamlet when he spoke of the "divinity that shapes our ends, / Rough-hew them how we will—". The fact of the matter was that had I been fired from a cannon upon my exit from A. Philip Randolph's office on that autumn morning in 1945, I could not have been vaulted more definitely away from medical school. I was, from that moment, headed instead, with a directness that seems so very clear in hindsight, toward the law as the work of my life.

In the press of the moment, I was more than a little overwhelmed—first at the prospect of an assignment not in the FEPC's Washington, DC, office, as I'd expected, but in the so-called "federal cities" of San Francisco and Los Angeles. With their huge government shipbuilding and aircraft plants, the two cities had been hotbeds of FEPC investigation during the war and were fertile ground for the committee's peacetime campaign. It made perfect sense, as the FEPC's executive secretary, Anna Arnold Hedgeman, explained it when I called upon her in Washington to obtain my field assignment. But even so, the sudden, unexpected prospect of heading to the opposite coast just when I'd planned to be nearer my family and to reconnect with Bill threw me into turmoil.

Mama's face fell and Grandma grew quiet when I told them that my work, in the short term, would take me three thousand miles away. As I sat rocking with them in the autumn sunshine on the squeaky old porch swing in Charlotte, I felt myself torn in the way that was to define my life as a woman for the next sixty years. Had I "but world enough, and time," as the poet said so long ago, I could have lived all the lives I longed for, staying forever in Charlotte caring for my family, making a living for myself and providing richly for them, finding my destiny, battling injustice. As it was, I consoled myself—and my mother and grandmother—with the temporary nature of my FEPC assignment, and my intention to put down roots nearer them once I returned. I also mentioned my plans to contact Bill Roundtree before I left for the West Coast, a revelation that set them beaming, doting as they had on Bill from the moment they'd met him. Mama and Grandma would, I am convinced, have declared him their son-in-law by fiat if such a thing were humanly possible. I, on the other hand, had much to sort out after seven years of separation from the man I'd loved as a young girl, and then, too, I had a mission of the utmost seriousness to fulfill before I could phone Bill at the number he'd left with Mama, or depart for my FEPC assignment in San Francisco. I had a debt to pay, a debt to the woman whose generosity had brought me to this point. For the first time since I'd incurred it, I had the money to repay her in full, and I intended to do so in person.

We'd followed each other, Miss Neptune and I, in the seven years since my Spelman graduation. Indeed, barely a month passed that I had not sent her whatever token payment I could afford on the loan, a dollar or two when I was teaching, and once I entered the army, a bit more. Always by return mail, I'd receive a note of acknowledgment, or more often, a long letter with a clipping from the *New York Times* enclosed, commended to my attention with some remark of great pith. Though Miss Neptune never mentioned the loan in her epistles, concerning herself only with the progress of the war and my safety in traveling through the South, my indebtedness hung heavy on me. As I boarded the train in Charlotte, bound for the little town of Decatur, where Miss Neptune had moved after her retirement from

Spelman—the same place where I'd spent such painful months with Mrs. Hurley—I was filled with a sense that at last I was beholden to no one, at least not for money. With my savings and the better part of my mustering-out pay folded in an envelope next to my heart, in what my family called my "grandma's bank," I arrived at her door ready to make my final reckoning.

Her letters had not hinted at the difficulty of her retirement circumstances, and she greeted me with such exuberance that had it not been for the shabbiness of the tiny apartment I would not have been moved to wonder at her finances. Always, she'd lived modestly, sustained by her students and surrounded by her books. Even now the works of the writers she'd taught me to love—Shakespeare, Milton, Keats, Austen, Dickens—lined the walls of the tiny one-room apartment. But as I surveyed the familiar volumes my gaze wandered to the threadbare furniture, the frayed draperies and worn rugs. Never one to skirt the obvious, Miss Neptune spoke straight out about the difficulties of life on a pension that had fallen far short of what she'd anticipated. Though she'd protested, the Spelman authorities who'd succeeded Miss Read and Miss Rockefeller were unsympathetic, and she'd been left with barely enough to get by. I could not imagine why the institution for which she'd toiled so faithfully had not rewarded her efforts, nor did I ask, focusing my attention on the oatmeal cookies she brought from the oven and the steaming pot of tea she set out, and inwardly celebrating the Divine Providence that had brought me to her doorstep at this particular time with a handsome sum of money on my person.

She simply gloried in our reunion, plying me with questions in that penetrating way of hers about my military service, my plans for graduate school, the FEPC assignment I'd mentioned to her on the phone. For all of her seventy-three years, she navigated the terrain of politics and civil rights with the agility of a woman half her age, and she was as enthralled by the prospect of my FEPC work as if she herself were heading across the country to rally people to the cause of fair employment. What intrigued her most was the way in which Randolph—and I by extension—would be reaching out to people of all races, all creeds, in our campaign for a permanent FEPC. Why I should have been astonished at her familiarity with A. Philip Randolph, I don't know; she had after all been the one who'd steered me toward the lectures of W. E. B. Du Bois, Rayford Logan, and Ira Reid during my time at Spelman. Still,

I marveled at the depth of her knowledge of Randolph's work with the porters' union and the March on Washington Movement that had birthed the FEPC.

Morning had turned to late afternoon when I rose, reluctant to depart but elated at what I was about to leave behind. I reached for my cache, withdrawing the envelope that held the bills, unfolding them and laying them, one by one, on the table.

Miss Neptune looked at me, astounded.

"What on earth is this, Dovey Johnson?" she asked.

This was what I owed her and a little bit more, I told her, groping for some way to put into words the full weight of my indebtedness, the impossibility of ever repaying her legacy to me. "A sacred trust," I called it.

So she'd deemed it as well, though until I saw her pull from a drawer a sheaf of papers marked "Loan, Mary Mae Neptune to Dovey Mae Johnson," I didn't fully grasp just how deeply the loan had bound us together. Meticulously recorded in columns were the payments I'd made to her, the dollar or two I'd sent from Chester or Fort Des Moines or some other army posting, each one logged and dated.

"Paid in Full," she scrawled across the columns in her bold hand, and handed me the papers. Now, she said, I must take up the charge. I must pursue graduate school. I must write her of my progress. I must press forward with all due haste, for I held it in my power to change people's hearts, so long as I kept a weather eye on my own.

Time, they say, has no meaning where love is concerned. By the calendar, nearly eleven years had passed since the November morning in 1934 when I'd met Bill Roundtree, and four since we'd last spoken. But when I phoned him from our home in Charlotte and heard his voice on the phone, I was, suddenly, sitting on the Atlanta trolley at the Emory University stop, clutching my biology textbook and looking up at the handsomest man I had ever seen swinging himself into the seat next to me.

I don't know which of us talked faster, trying in a flood of words to close our long separation, to rush past it into the future that was opening wide for us, even as it had seemed to shut down in the months after we'd graduated. In the rush of laughter and celebration of old times, it was as though the war had not happened, as though the pain I'd felt in the WAC and the far greater pain I knew Bill had experienced, serving overseas in an all-colored regiment, had passed us by. There would be years, I told myself, to speak of those things.

Compared to the distance war had put between us, the three thousand miles between Bill's home in Atlanta and the temporary post to which I was headed in San Diego seemed but little, and Bill, with the wild optimism that had endeared him to me from the beginning, made it seem downright insignificant. He'd get himself out to California, he told me, or we'd meet somewhere in between. On terminal leave from the army until January, just as I was, Bill had a certain freedom as he mapped out his future, and he made it clear he wasn't making any plans that didn't include me.

I felt the same way. I thought of nothing but Bill as the train taking me to the West Coast moved slowly northward in the last week of October, winding its way through the mountains ablaze with autumn foliage, through the vast plains and prairies I remembered from my army tour, and then westward, and farther westward, into the snow-capped Rockies, and a world unlike anything I'd ever seen or even imagined. In that timeless time, in between the life I'd left behind and the one toward which I was headed, I sat alone with my thoughts, sifting and sorting through the welter of feelings that rolled over me as I thought of Bill. He seemed ever so much the person I remembered. But was he really? Certainly I had changed since I was a twenty-year-old girl at Spelman struggling to fit into a world of privilege and awed by my handsome "Morehouse man," who'd turned heads wherever we went.

The army had changed me, in forcing me to face its injustice, and I'd risked my career rather than swallow it. Had Bill changed, too, in his time overseas? And how? He wanted above all, he'd told me, to continue his education, just as I did, but in what direction? And how would a wife with those same ambitions fit into his plans? Would we truly be able to pick up the pieces of our relationship after seven years apart? Did he long, as I did, to have children and build a home? There were so many questions that I simply could not answer. More than anything, I remembered what a gentle person he was, how considerate of Mama and Grandma, how attentive to me, how protective, how kind.

Not a day passed once I arrived at my first posting, in San Diego, that Bill and I did not speak at least once. He'd been so enthusiastic about my FEPC assignment that I wanted to make him a part of it all, to share with him everything I could by phone while we set about figuring out some way to meet at Christmastime. He could get himself to Chicago, Bill suggested, if I could, and we'd have a few days together before I had to return to California to finish out the remaining six months of my field assignment. Hearing the excitement in his voice at that prospect, I wondered why we'd ever lost touch. That, I knew in my heart, had been my doing more than his.

All day long, as I raced from one FEPC council meeting to another in the little towns of Southern California, I found myself wondering what Bill would think, how he'd react to the "conversion speeches" I'd worked up to rally people of every race and creed to the fair employment cause. Each night, I'd wait for the phone to ring, knowing that no matter how exhausted I was, Bill would buoy me up with words of encouragement about the importance of what I was doing. The Atlanta workplace he confronted as a veteran seeking employment was ugly, closed, every bit as inhospitable to blacks as it had been before the war—perhaps more, now that jobs were scarcer. Like everyone in the cadre of impassioned folk I'd teamed up with in San Diego, and then San Francisco and Los Angeles, Bill saw the FEPC as a beacon of hope for black people.

If only the mixed race audiences who gazed upon me with such skepticism had thought as Bill did. And perhaps, as individual human beings, concerned for their own welfare in the job market, they did. But the Mexicans, the blacks, the Latinos, the whites, the Chinese, the Japanese flooding back into Los Angeles from wartime internment camps seemed to regard each other as enemies, not allies, in the fight for fairness, and there was something more than a little unsettling in the ill will I sensed just beneath the surface at the gatherings I addressed. I'd known of the unique racial mix of Southern California before I arrived, having been masterfully briefed by Randolph's assistant in Washington, Anna Arnold Hedgeman. But statistics, however carefully compiled, have no human face, nor do they speak to the irrational way in which fear and ignorance breed violence.

It would not be correct to say that I felt unsafe, as I had in Atlanta where hatred flickered so close to the surface that every trolley ride held danger. This peculiar strain of tension was not quite so raw. But it was ugly, just the same, and disquieting, particularly in Los Angeles, so recently torn by the 1943 "zoot suit riots" that had begun with an unprovoked assault on young Mexican men by white soldiers and sailors, and ended with attacks on blacks, who'd streamed into the city in such vast numbers during the war that their mere existence invited the rage of the white population. The neighborhoods through which I moved in the fall of 1945 were thick with the memory of those riots, and with fear of the Klan, which to my utter astonishment raged through Los Angeles with the same fury I'd seen in the Deep South, driving non-whites of every background out of the decent neighborhoods into filthy, overcrowded, disease-ridden ghettoes. Every day I struggled anew to find a way to reach my audiences with my conviction that unless people of every race forged a kinship, there was no hope for any of us. If one group suffered from discrimination, I pointed out, no other group was secure.

"California's peculiar social chemistry," I called it in my FEPC speeches—but the truth was, I understood that chemistry but poorly. When I spoke with Bill on the phone each evening, I'd grope for the words to describe the strange animal that was West Coast racism. When we saw each other, I promised, I'd parse out the particulars of this unsettling, alien universe into which I'd walked, a universe filled with fear, and also, strangely, with exhilaration. For even as I struggled to stay afloat, I was drinking in the intellectualism of Southern California, meeting community leaders, politicians, lawyers and law students whose thinking rocked me to my core.

I'm still waiting for the English language to acquire vocabulary sufficient to capture the phenomenon of Pauli Murray, the brilliant young lawyer who in the decades after I knew her would join forces with Betty Friedan and found the National Organization for Women, then make history as one of the first three women to be ordained to the priesthood of the Episcopal Church. Already, in the fall of 1945, when our paths crossed for one brief month in connection with the FEPC campaign, Pauli was a force in Berkeley law school's graduate program, a formidable legal scholar whose master's thesis on employment discrimination, published in the *California Law Review*, had attracted the attention of the state's attorney general. He'd been so impressed with her groundbreaking work that he'd brought her into his office immediately upon her graduation that fall as his first black deputy.

I'd heard of Pauli Murray back east, as had everyone who'd read the Negro press accounts of the bold but ill-fated war she'd waged against the University of North Carolina's graduate school in 1938 when they'd denied her admission because of her race. The tiny, fine-boned, almost waiflike person who engaged me so intently after one of my FEPC speeches bore no physical resemblance to the Colossus I'd imagined fighting single-handedly to break segregation at Chapel Hill. But Pauli was a soul on fire, and from the moment she unleashed upon me the force of her intellect, she had me in thrall. The answer for black people, she told me in one of our first conversations, lay in the law. It was the law, misapplied, twisted, disingenuously interpreted, that had generated the monstrosity known as separate but equal. And it was the law just as surely, she argued, that could—that *would*—shatter the monster. That conviction had drawn her to Howard law school in 1941. By that time the school had been transformed into an academic mecca by the great black legal scholar Charles Hamilton Houston, who'd penetrated Harvard Law School in 1919, earned advanced degrees under the mentorship of Professor Felix Frankfurter, studied law in Europe, then moved to Howard in 1929 to groom an elite army of black lawyers who would make war on Jim Crow. I had a place in that army: on that point Pauli was insistent, and unbending.

People's hard jaws softened when I spoke of justice and fairness and the right to make a decent living, Pauli told me, so often and so insistently in the brief weeks of our acquaintance that I began to wonder whether she might be right. To be sure, the fact that Howard law remained an almost entirely male institution gave me pause; I'd had my fill of outsider status as a black woman in a white man's army. But "Jane Crow"—as she termed the peculiar brand of prejudice reserved for women—had not deterred Pauli, not at Howard nor in her quest for a master's in law. When all-male Harvard Law School rejected her application for graduate work on the basis of her gender, she'd applied to Berkeley and taken the place by storm. I concluded in short order that no thinking person could turn easily from anything Pauli Murray said on any subject, and as I studied her, watched her quarterback discussions with her Berkeley colleagues, soaked up her cerebrations on the Constitution and the wrongs it could right if properly applied, I felt the power of an intellect that swallowed me up.

I also felt Pauli's pain, a racial pain unquestionably intensified by her mixed ancestry. Here was a woman just three years older than I, a lover of books and ideas as I'd been all my life, a Carolinian who for all the fairness of her complexion had suffered the worst of Jim Crow, inhabiting the no-man's-land of a white-skinned Negro who could not quite "pass," a mulatta in a world that abhorred race mixing. Perhaps the most visibly wounded soul I have ever known, Pauli Murray was, for all of her hurt, empowered. And the law had empowered her. In the law, she saw the way to real justice.

I listened to Pauli. I read her *California Law Review* article calling the right to full employment "the essence of the American tradition." I slogged through the Supreme Court opinions she gave me. And I turned my back, once and for all, on the romantic girlhood dream of medical school to which I'd clung so stubbornly for so many years. Understanding but a fraction of the dense legal material I read at Pauli's behest, I grasped enough from her informal tutorials on civil rights case law to sense a profound shift afoot in the courts, a subtle but certain return to the real meaning of the Thirteenth, Fourteenth, and Fifteenth Amendments.

Already, Pauli said, the wall had been breached. In 1938, just weeks after she'd filed her application to Chapel Hill's graduate school, Charles Hamilton Houston and his young protégé Thurgood Marshall had won a Supreme Court decision she saw as profound in its implications. Not until I actually studied law did I fully grasp the shrewdness of this cautious first pass at Jim Crow in education, wherein Houston and Marshall forced the University of Missouri School of Law to provide the full measure of equality under "separate but equal" while they prepared for a full-blown national assault on segregation itself. Their three-year fight in behalf of a young law school applicant named Lloyd Gaines had resulted in a Supreme Court ruling that affected not only Missouri but every jurisdiction that barred Negroes from its universities—sixteen in all. A state must either provide blacks a legal education equal to that of whites, the Court said, or admit them to its white law schools. Sending a black student out of state, even with tuition money, as Missouri had tried to do, in no way constituted equality under the law.

Charles Houston's campaign for enforcement of that ruling at the University of Missouri had died with the mysterious disappearance of plaintiff Gaines, and the Court's decision in *Gaines v. Canada* hadn't been far-reaching enough to win Pauli admission to Chapel Hill from her state of residence, which was New York. But *Gaines* had established an important precedent for real equality, she said, one that Houston and Marshall were invoking in their assault on the public school segregation in the South. School district by school district, they were fighting for equalization of black teachers' salaries and school facilities in an attempt to cost Jim Crow to the verge of extinction. The *Gaines* case had been the beginning, she told me, the crucial first step in an all-out war on segregation that was gaining force with each passing year. The more I processed Pauli's gospel—and a gospel it truly was—the more the law drew me like a magnet.

Precisely what Bill's reaction was when I first announced what surely must have struck him as an abrupt about-face from my medical school plans, I cannot recall. I do remember that once he sensed my conviction, he threw himself behind me, supporting me as he always had, and even, as the weeks passed and we spoke more and more certainly of our future together, voicing the possibility that law might be his course of graduate study as well. Anything was possible for us now, Bill said, sweeping me up in the last weeks of November in a campaign for marriage at Christmastime every bit as overwhelming in its way as Pauli's campaign to get me to Howard law school at the earliest feasible moment. Why put off marriage till my FEPC tour ended, Bill demanded. We'd postponed our marriage plans for too long already, allowing ourselves to drift apart for no good reason. What, really, were we waiting for at the age of thirty-one, he pressed me, with the urgency that perhaps only a man who has seen combat in wartime can feel.

Overwhelmed as I was by the desire to settle down with Bill and build a family with him, I hesitated. I understood even then, in the abstract, that in choosing the law as a vocation—and already I saw it as more than a career—I was stepping into a lonely and dangerous arena, one in which a woman, particularly a black woman, would stand out as something close to a freak. Yes, Bill supported me, or wanted to, but did he truly understand the price I'd pay for such a choice, and he along with me? On that subject Pauli had minced no words, warning me not only of the contempt white lawyers and judges would heap upon me, but also the special brand of animosity black folk reserved for their bolder fellows. How well I knew about the dangers of those blacks Pauli labeled "spineless accommodationists." I'd seen that breed in the army, I told her. I'd felt the sting of their desertion when I'd stood up to my post commandant, and I'd seen one of the finest black WAC officers I knew dishonorably discharged in 1945 on the strength of the testimony of a black stool pigeon who'd sold her soul for advancement in a white man's army. Horrified, but not in the least surprised, Pauli took in my account of the case of Captain Frances Alexander Futtrell, assessing it as yet another example of the divisions among blacks that lay like fault lines just beneath the surface, undermining the fight for justice. The unspoken, the unacknowledged, the invisible: all of it became fodder for our long talks at International House, the multiracial dormitory where Pauli lived with law students from around the globe, women apparently devoid of the prejudices she and I dissected by the hour, often late into the night.

All the while, I struggled to reconcile my newfound passion for the law with my desire to marry and rear children, to be a woman in the mold of my grandmother and my mother. Awed by Pauli's wisdom on legal and racial matters and unaware at the time of her disastrous early marriage to a boy she barely knew, I sought her counsel on the matter of Bill's proposal. Could a woman have it all, both marriage and career, I asked her, hoping for more of a response than I could express in words.

Pauli's answer was simple, devoid of all the caveats she generally appended to the statements she made on legal subjects.

"Of course you can have both," she assured me, citing the example of the FEPC's brilliant executive secretary, Anna Arnold Hedgeman, who'd been married for a number of years to a renowned musicologist and singer of black folk opera, Merritt A. Hedgeman. "She's a good example, don't you think?"

I knew no more about Mrs. Hedgeman's personal life than Pauli knew of mine. But I seized upon Pauli's answer, superficial as it was, because she told me what I so desperately wanted to hear. If it did not truly quiet the doubts that troubled me as I prepared to enter the most important of all human relationships, I made do. I pushed aside the uncertainties I felt, said yes to Bill, and reveled in the joy that flooded through me as he and I made plans to marry in Chicago over the Christmas holiday. He'd travel from Atlanta, and I from Portland, the FEPC posting where I was scheduled to report in mid-December for the final leg of my assignment.

Old-fashioned southern gentleman that he was, Bill called Mama to ask for my hand, and my WAC buddy Ruth Freeman, who lived in Chicago, proceeded to contact not only her beloved minister, Ira Hendon, when I phoned her with the news, but everyone in our circle of army friends who had the slightest prospect of making it to Chicago by 6:00 PM on Christmas Eve, the hour Bill and I had set for the ceremony in the Reverend Hendon's home. After eleven years of waiting, I suddenly found myself in a headlong rush to make ready for marriage on two weeks' notice. Never had I been one to act on impulse, yet I flew toward marriage with a man I had not seen in seven years, and he toward me. Such was the madness of the postwar world, a time when the longing for normalcy eclipsed the common sense of otherwise sane souls. Possessed by the same marriage fever that consumed hundreds of thousands of couples in the months after V-J Day, I raced about, focusing on the details that occupy every bride. There was a suitable wedding outfit to be selected, arrangements to be made for the scaled-down reception I'd insisted Ruth substitute for the elaborate affair she'd first proposed, and a semblance of a civilian wardrobe assembled if I wished to greet Bill in something other than my army uniform.

There are pockets of time in the course of our lives, I believe, where the ordinary is suspended and we occupy another universe, operate on a different plane, and for good or ill, abjure rational thought. The three and a half days Bill and I spent together in Chicago before our Christmas Eve wedding was for me one of those altered states. Had we talked more seriously about who and what each of us wanted to become, perhaps we would have pulled back at that critical point. But we were two people intent on erasing the pain and loneliness of the war, and we rushed toward marriage with blinders on.

How good it felt, in the beginning, to be with someone who made me laugh the way Bill did as we trudged through the snow the morning after my arrival to take on the clerk of the Cook County Court in the matter of our marriage license—a license, we told him, for which we were not prepared to wait past December 24, at which time friends would be gathering to see us married. No two lawyers-to-be ever talked faster in tandem than we did, persuading the clerk to issue our license in enough time that when dusk fell on Christmas Eve, we stood before Rev. Hendon with Ruth and her fiancé as witnesses, Bill in his lieutenant's uniform and I in the powder blue suit and matching hat I'd chosen with such care, to take our marriage vows.

From the moment Bill and I arrived in Portland, the city seemed to enfold us to its bosom. People we'd never met before welcomed us on the strength of Pauli's referrals, extending themselves to find temporary work for Bill while I lobbied for a state law for fair employment to support the federal legislation that would shortly be introduced in Congress. The federal bill, we all knew even before the winter was out, hung on the thinnest thread, with A. Philip Randolph staging a mass rally to save the FEPC on February 28 at Madison Square Garden and threatening a march down the streets of the nation's capital if Congress failed by June 30 to enact fair employment practice legislation. By this time, thirteen of the FEPC's regional offices had closed, and those of us in the remaining three began, reluctantly, to use the last of the committee's funds in a last-ditch campaign to get bills for fair employment on the state ballots before the money Congress had appropriated ran out completely.

Bill and I made the most of our time in Portland, a city truly made in heaven, with the beautiful Willamette River at its feet and Mount Hood rising up in all its snow-capped splendor in the background. We were, in those early weeks of our marriage, inseparable, with Bill by my side at virtually every FEPC speech I gave, applauding, encouraging, hovering, protecting. Safe and peaceful as Portland appeared to be—and indeed was in comparison with Los Angeles—Bill seemed ever fearful for my safety as he listened to me lashing out at the unfairness of current employment laws so far as blacks and other minorities were concerned. His brow furrowed the way it had in our college days when I'd hold forth in anger and in pain on the subject of racial injustice.

"You stick closer than a brother," I told him one evening, as the two of us sat in a Portland newspaper conference room, awaiting the beginning of a local FEPC council meeting.

"Of course I do. I'm your husband," Bill answered, squeezing my hand so hard my new wedding ring hurt.

It had never occurred to me that such devotion had a price, that Bill in his truest heart wanted a woman quite different from the one I'd become, that he desperately wanted to keep me to himself, to rein me in, to pull me back from the battle I so wanted to enter, the battle I had in fact signed on for back in my army years, when I'd taken on the colonel. Somewhere in the winter months in Portland, as I raced about the city finishing up my campaign for an Oregon fair employment law and Bill raced beside me, I began to sense that, much as we cared for each other, we were moving on different tracks altogether, and had been for a very long time. The more I talked of "our" law school plans as we prepared to leave Portland, the quieter he grew. At first, I pushed past the unease, filling the silences that cropped up between us with lighter things, with memories of our college years, of our time in Chicago, of our plans to visit our families in Atlanta and Charlotte as soon as we'd set up housekeeping in Washington. During our last weeks on the West Coast, though, there came a time when there was more silence than talk, and Bill, so close by my side in the early months of our marriage, chose to remain behind in the evenings while I made my rounds alone.

Once we arrived in Washington, our days were filled with the pressing matter of securing jobs. But when we faced each other across the table in the evenings, our little efficiency apartment echoed in the way a home echoes when it is truly empty. At last, there was nothing to do except admit that in our haste to marry we'd made a terrible mistake. It was late one August night when Bill told me he was not in fact interested in law school. It had been my dream, not his, he said. In that moment, I faced the truth of his silences over the past few months. He'd seen, up close, the life I wanted to lead, how consumed I was, now, by the civil rights revolution. And he had chosen a different path. When he told me that he intended to reenlist in the army, perhaps even go overseas again, the implication was clear. He was leaving.

What pain there is in the breakup of a marriage, no matter how brief or ill-advised. I know now that in separating from Bill, who'd been a part of my life for so long, I was also taking my final leave of the naïve, uncertain, overawed girl I'd been at Spelman—a girl who no longer existed. Such partings are necessary, to be sure. But oh how they hurt, for those we truly love remain always a part of us, never wholly to be set aside no matter how much we may change. It has been said that divorce is a kind of death, and I found that to be true in the year it took me to shake off the sorrow that overwhelmed me after Bill and I separated, file my application to Howard law school, and embark on the life I was destined to live.

There is, in the end, no avoiding one's destiny. And the law, with the possibilities it held for changing the world in which I'd come of age, was mine. More desperately than I can articulate, I wanted a true partner in that battle and a life mate with whom I could build the kind of home that had nurtured me. But I could not turn away from the law, once it took hold of me, any more than I could deny my own name, or my very being. I was thirty-three years old when I walked into the musty basement that housed the Howard University School of Law in September of 1947, and I was as hungry, and as certain of my course as I have ever been.

7. MAKING WAR ON A LIE:
The Assault on Plessy v. Ferguson

No lie can live forever. So said the Reverend Martin Luther King, Jr., in 1968, famously quoting Carlyle. And to the surpassing wisdom of the preacher I would append a lawyer's observation: that a lie does not die by itself, particularly not when it has been consecrated by the highest court in the land. It must be dissected, anatomized, and then attacked—not once, or twice, but a thousand times over, until at last the core of the lie is exposed for all to see, and shown to be the mockery it truly is.

A fearsome thing, the battle against separate but equal, and though sixty years have passed since the autumn when I took my place in that fight, I remark yet at the enormity of it, the duration, the grinding work involved in the layering, detail upon detail, of assaults upon the great lie. It was in the details that we battled, in the minutiae of case law and the ferreting out of buried precedents, the mastery of the particulars of torts and contracts, of property law and the constitution. All of it, our professors pressed into service in the shattering of Jim Crow. The work was exhausting, complex, at times overwhelming. But what stands most starkly in my memory was the sheer joy of it, the excitement, the exhilaration of shouldering a task whose time had come.

Still, it did not begin easily for me, nor indeed for any woman who set her sights on a degree from the ever-so-male bastion of Howard University School of Law in 1947. I'd been assured by Pauli that females, though rare at Howard law, were no longer a species unknown, as they had been when she'd entered before the war, in 1941. But in the entire crush of humanity jammed into the administration building on that first day of classes, the only women in evidence were those processing registration forms behind the counter. And I saw immediately, when I presented my military papers with a request for GI tuition benefits, that I was a creature alien to their experience.

"Are you registering for your husband or your brother?" the clerk asked me, studying my certification of honorable discharge and in particular the notation as to my rank as though the information were written in a foreign language. That a woman should have attained the rank of captain in the army seemed to confound her entirely, and her colleagues as well. One by one, they abandoned their posts at the counter and stepped over to scrutinize both me and my army papers, at which point the entire registration process ground to a halt. No, I told her, *I* was the veteran named on the documents. The honorable discharge belonged to *me*. I was claiming GI benefits on my *own* behalf. The men awaiting processing, most of them veterans themselves, stood quietly looking on as the clerk asked me once again which male relative I had come to register. Feeling almost as self-conscious as I had the day I'd presented myself for army enlistment in the Charlotte post office, I answered, once again, in the negative. I began to fear that my tuition credit would be delayed past the start of classes, and so I leaned across the counter and, pointing to the blanks on the GI benefit form, I said as gently as I could, "Do it just like you do it for the male veterans."

And through the gate I passed, my GI papers duly stamped, into the very center of a world where my gender made me as much of an oddity as my skin color had in the army. I was one of but five women in my class, and the icy waves of unbelonging hit me hard, and often, in those first days, washing over me each time a group of men broke off a conversation at my approach, or smirked or rolled their eyes at some statement I made, or cut me or one of the other women off in mid-sentence in a class without so much as a "May I—?" or a "Pardon me."

Yet there was so much that sustained me in that awkward, hurting time. Even as I struggled to make my way at Howard, I was being enfolded into the community that would become the center and ballast of my existence for the next fifty years. For so long, ever since I'd left Spelman in 1938, I'd been racing from place to place, and when I settled in Washington, I found on the east side of the Anacostia River a place so like the Charlotte of my childhood that there were times, awakening of a Sunday morning to the sound of hymn singing, that I imagined myself back in the parsonage. Garfield Heights, it was called, that web of streets that made up a close-knit black enclave in the midst of a community that was almost entirely white. It had grown out of a pre–Civil War haven for free Negroes known as Good Hope, and it was indeed for me a sanctuary and a place of solace.

Everyone should have the gift of a haven like the Garfield Heights of the early fifties, with its rolling hills and tree-lined streets rising up from the river, and the smell of barbecue and fish frying and the sound of laughter and talk over back fences, and churches aplenty, almost as many, we used to say in those days, as there were streets. The oldest among them, Allen Chapel AME, became mine. By happy circumstance, I shared a back fence with Allen Chapel's grand matriarch, Tootie Dittweiler. She allowed but one Sunday to pass before she issued me an invitation to join the congregation that packed itself into the tiny white frame structure that proudly announced its identity with a sign half the size of itself. Allen Chapel would grow, eventually, into a grand and glorious edifice called "the cathedral of Southeast." But it was so small back then you could miss it entirely unless you were on foot. Even in the Deep South, in the country, churches were larger. Only Allen's little steeple distinguished it from the houses on each side of it, but oh how that building rocked on Sundays. My mother would have deemed the choir somewhat on the half-baked side, but what it lacked in size and polish it made up for in loudness. Never in all the years since my baptism at East Stonewall AME Zion at my grandpa's hands had I wandered far from churchgoing; I'd somehow managed to find my way to a Sunday worship service in the midst of my army recruiting and my FEPC duties. It was not God's presence I'd been missing in my years away from home; it was a church to call my own. In Allen, I found it. Worshipping in a congregation named for Richard Allen, the former slave who'd founded the African Methodist Episcopal Church in 1816, made me proud. That church, and its people—Pastor James H. Mayo, the old-timers and the young professionals, the college students and the little children I began teaching in Sunday school—the faith of all those people put together kept me going in the midst of my struggle to be a lawyer, to be a woman in the law, to just simply *be*.

Howard was a tough place for anybody who aspired to meet the standards set by Charles Hamilton Houston and the formidable tribe of professors he'd recruited to teach there, men from Howard itself, of course, and Harvard and Northwestern as well. Still, there was what I call "the human thing" at work even in the midst of all that. From out of the loneliness of my early weeks emerged like-minded souls who nurtured and guided me, men and women both. Howard in that era had what no other law school in the country could claim: an Ollie Mae Cooper, turn-of-the century legal pioneer, executive secretary to the dean, administrative wizard, part-time law practitioner, and mother hen and ally-in-chief to us women students. Sixty years old when I knew her, and the very picture of matronly propriety in her dark suits and sensible shoes, Miss Cooper exuded the surety of an old pro and the warmth of a real friend—as indeed she became to every one of us women.

"Girls, don't get lost in this male-dominated profession," she told us when she gathered the five of us around her shortly after the start of classes. With that one statement, she neutralized the snide dismissiveness we'd endured at the hands of our male classmates, smoothing our ruffled feathers and bruised egos as she told us with absolute certainty, "You can do wonders to improve the practice of law. It's in need of a woman's touch."

What must it have been like for her, I wondered as I sat with my female classmates, listening to her story of entering Howard law at the end of the second decade of the twentieth century, when she was one of but two women in the class of 1921? I hear her voice now, full of wisdom and conviction and pure inspiration, as she spoke to us of the all-male world she'd negotiated back then, and of how she'd managed to strike out in 1929 with her partner, Isadora Jackson Letcher, to open a law firm in the District of Columbia—the first, I later learned, founded by any black woman in this country—and keep it running at night, while by day she ran the office of the law school dean.

"Black men with law degrees were very few and far apart back then," she told us. "But a black woman with a law degree . . . that was indeed a rarity."

Yet the times were changing, she said. True, we had a double handicap, as blacks and women, but for all of that, we could contribute mightily to the profession we'd chosen. Indeed, with persistence, she believed we could transform it. Putting me ever so much in mind of Dr. Bethune and of Pauli Murray, Miss Cooper spoke of the vital importance of "networking" in the legal profession—I believe she actually used that very modern word—and of the sorority she'd founded for women in the law, Epsilon Sigma Iota. Right then and there, she invited us into that circle of female colleagues, and she sent us back into the fray with what felt like a benediction.

"You can do it," she insisted, repeating the words she'd opened with: "Girls, don't get lost."

Her charge proved an invaluable compass in my years at Howard, particularly since Miss Cooper, without ever quite butting into our private affairs, somehow tracked our progress from her perch in the dean's office, summoning us from time to time as a group and even individually if she determined one of us needed a boost or a gentle push in a particular direction, always leaving her door open and encouraging us to take advantage of that fact.

There was, in those early months at Howard, another reason I didn't get lost. His name was Julius Winfield Robertson, and he towered literally and figuratively over just about every student of either gender on the campus at that time. No one at Howard missed Julius, an ebony-skinned giant of a man with a voice that carried round the corner and back again, and an intellect to match it. Chief judge of the prestigious student group known as the Court of Peers, Julius was everything a law student could be. From the moment he crossed my path, I admired him "something awful," as we used to say in the Charlotte of my childhood, not only for his legal brilliance but for what he'd accomplished as a family man, a husband and a father of four little children for whom he worked unceasingly. He and his wife, Nellie, and two boys and two very small girls lived in the Southeast Washington housing projects then, and Julius held down a night job at the U.S. post office to support them, while finishing his law and college degrees simultaneously.

I looked at Julius, and I envied what he'd managed to achieve at such a young age, for he was two years younger than I, barely thirty-one years old. Everything I'd dreamed of having with Bill—a career, children, a home, an understanding with a spouse who believed in me—Julius seemed to have with his family. I wasn't paralyzed then as I had been in the months immediately following my divorce, but the elusiveness of family happiness pained me, as it would all my life. The truth was that few of the prominent women I'd known up to that point had made successful marriages. And I saw little prospect of that dream for myself, given my ambitions and my single-minded, some would say obsessive, commitment to them. But I held family life as the ultimate ideal, and Julius's commitment to that, as much as the prestige he enjoyed on campus, drew me to him as a mentor and a role model.

Just what drew Julius to me remains a mystery, but our bond was powerful enough that it led us eventually to a law partnership that would bring us to places neither one of us would have ventured into on our own. In my first months at Howard I daresay I was a bundle of fear and intensity, overwork and underconfidence. But I believed in the legal assault on Jim Crow with a passion that matched Julius's, and it was he as much as any of my professors who shepherded me through Howard, marking with his insight my path through the war on segregation Charles Hamilton Houston had declared that summer.

"There is no such thing as 'separate but equal,'" Houston had announced to the Negro press in June 1947. Though the actual tactics of the revolution would divide Houston's protégés in a battle of their own, it was clear that one era had ended, and another had begun. Thurgood Marshall and his band of NAACP Legal Defense Fund lawyers had taken over the campus at the behest of Howard president Mordecai Johnson, a fire-eating Baptist minister totally committed to the cause of desegregation. The lawyers set up camp in the library, mined its materials and amassed more, and convened in our moot courtroom on the evenings preceding their oral arguments before the Supreme Court for "dry runs" of the cases. As a third-year student recruited for research by the LDF lawyers, Julius was at the very center of the assault that would climax in *Brown v. Board of Education*—the strike at the heart of the notorious case of *Plessy v. Ferguson*, the 1896 ruling in which the Supreme Court had legalized "separate but equal."

Or rather, it had *tried* to, for that which is unconstitutional can never be legal. This was the position of Professor James Madison Nabrit, Jr., the bold NAACP strategist Julius revered as the primary intellectual force behind the entire legal struggle for civil rights. James Nabrit—"Jim Reds" as we came to call him once we knew him well enough to call him something besides "professor"—shaped not only my approach to legal reasoning but, with his vision of the law as a thing of sacredness, my very identity as a lawyer. I felt as though I knew Professor Nabrit when I walked into his classroom, and in a way, I did. He was the son of the illustrious Atlanta minister I'd met through the Wimbish family in my Spelman days, the Reverend James Madison Nabrit, Sr. And though the fair-skinned Professor Nabrit, with his reddish hair and freckles, his measured, deliberate speech and his big cigars, cut quite a different figure from his fiery father, he had a whole lot of minister in him. The home from which he came was a place infused with Christianity, and though he never uttered an overtly religious word in the classroom, I felt in him a sense of the law as a ministry and of the flow of history as divinely ordained. With the rigor of his mind and the power of his spirit, he molded me and every other student who crossed his threshold, including two of Thurgood Marshall's most formidable young associates, Robert Carter and Spottswood Robinson. At the same time, in his role as adviser to the inner circle of the NAACP's Legal Defense Fund team, he quietly, almost invisibly, altered the course of the grand events that swirled around us.

We students knew what history recorded but dimly, that James Nabrit's was the uncompromising voice that pushed Thurgood Marshall toward a full-blown assault on *Plessy v. Ferguson*. It was Nabrit's argument, articulated in its most naked form, that ultimately carried the day when he and Marshall and George E. C. Hayes stood before the Supreme Court in *Brown v. Board* in 1952 and again in 1953 and took on Jim Crow in public education. And it was that same bold approach that we heard, five years before those historic oral arguments, in the classrooms of Howard. Segregation, Professor Nabrit told us, may *for the time being* have the force of law. It may *appear* to have the sanction of the courts. But it is in truth—and here his slow Atlanta drawl took on the edge of a finely honed knife blade—entirely and unqualifiedly lacking in legal validity.

Through Nabrit, I came to my earliest understanding of the Constitution, of its perversion, and of its promise. In the manner of the grand old Negro hymn that proclaims the power of love to lift us "when nothing else will do," the promise of the law *lifted* me, when so much else weighed me down. I lived in perpetual dread of drowning in the avalanche of course work. Even with Julius's guidance and the help of the study group I joined in my early weeks at Howard, I feared I would be unequal to the challenge of discerning the principles buried in the cases we students were assigned to read by the hundreds. I pushed myself so hard that my eyes, weakened by the diabetes that was to plague me all my life, sometimes gave out on me late at night. I worried about making ends meet even with two part-time jobs, about my inability to break away to visit Mama and Grandma in Charlotte or even send them money while paying rent for the tiny apartment I'd taken in Southeast Washington.

What sustained me was Julius's mentorship and the law itself, with its power to give shape and direction to the chaos of human interaction. Legal thinking—that peculiar brand of reasoning that requires the mind to move simultaneously on two parallel tracks, backward toward precedent and forward toward result—enthralled me. Then, too, I learned from extraordinary men: the venerable master of civil procedure George E. C. Hayes; labor law icons Joseph Waddy and Howard Jenkins; evidentiary authority Charles Quick; the brilliant young Harvard law graduates Herbert O. Reid and James A. Washington, later a DC superior court judge; the former FEPC lawyer Frank Reeves, who, along with Thurgood Marshall, had run the Legal Defense Fund's New York office in the early forties. These were the men who became part of the history of *Brown v. Board*, researching the case law, drafting the briefs, hammering out the strategy. Titans all, they enthralled me with their command of the law's particulars.

But James Nabrit was the one who made me a lawyer. A fearless advocate whose Texas law firm had led the charge for black voting rights in the Supreme Court in the years before the war, Nabrit had come to Howard at the invitation of Charles Houston, leaving private practice in Texas to teach law and consult with the NAACP. In time, he'd move beyond Howard's classrooms and, later, its presidency, to take his place in world affairs as an ambassador to the United Nations. Yet he remains for me ever the professor, perpetually challenging, provocative in his questions, and utterly intolerant of the rudeness of the male students toward us women. He towers in my memory for the way in which he laid upon the ragged edges of human existence the beginning words of the Fourteenth Amendment, which made the promise of the Declaration of Independence the law for all the peoples of America, in every state, whatever their race:

> All persons born or naturalized in the United States, and subject to the jurisdiction thereof, are citizens of the United States and of the state wherein they reside. No state shall make or enforce any law which shall abridge the privileges or immunities of citizens of the United States; nor shall any state deprive any person of life, liberty, or property, without due process of law; nor deny to any person within its jurisdiction the equal protection of the laws.

How, I asked myself as I listened to Nabrit parse out those two sentences, did one square the Fourteenth Amendment and its guarantee of equality with life as it had been lived by black people like me, like my grandmother and all the folk of our Carolina home, by the great Professor Nabrit in the Klan-ravaged Atlanta of his boyhood, and by the fair-skinned black man from Louisiana named Homer Adolph Plessy, the "plaintiff in error" in the matter of *Plessy v. Ferguson*?

Up from the cold text of the Supreme Court's 1896 decision, the white-skinned young black man who earned his living by making shoes rose in my imagination as a hero in the mold of my grandmother. A person of Grandma's generation, Plessy had raised his fist against the law that denied him a seat in the white section of a New Orleans train, raised it hard, and eloquently, and persistently. The Separate Car Law was unconstitutional, he said, a denial of his right to "equal protection" under the Fourteenth Amendment. Plessy had picked his moment carefully, striking out against the new Louisiana law at a pivotal moment, when those pressing for civil rights were warring with those who would gut the Thirteenth, Fourteenth, and Fifteenth Amendments. Hoping to turn the tide before it was too late, he pressed onward even when Louisiana judge John Ferguson rejected his claim, taking his case to the highest court in the land.

But the Supreme Court, too, turned its back on Homer Plessy and on the entire promise of the Fourteenth Amendment. Laws were powerless, the Court ruled, in the face of the natural tendency of humans to separate themselves by color. It was as though Reconstruction had never been, as though the horrible "Black Codes" the Fourteenth Amendment was meant to obliterate still existed, as though the Civil War had not been fought nor the black man freed from servitude. If the state provided the Negro separate facilities substantially equal to those it provided for whites, Justice Henry Billings Brown wrote for the majority, it had done its constitutional duty. And so it was, out of Homer Plessy's search for justice, that the monster of "separate but equal" was born.

Line by line, layer by layer, Dr. Nabrit ripped away the veneer of judicial authority that encased the *Plessy* decision, unmasking for us a truth that remained hidden from our privileged white counterparts at other law schools, where, in the 1940s, *Plessy* was carefully ignored. This was an era when no one—least of all conservative white Ivy League law faculties—wanted to confront that shameful decision. Nabrit alone among American law professors had dared to take it on, creating America's first civil rights law course out of whole cloth in 1939. In the pages of his massive syllabus, which would contain some two thousand cases by my third year at Howard, we traced the contours of Jim Crow's legal face. Thus began my journey into the conundrum that was to consume me for my entire life at the bar, and beyond—the distance between the law and real justice.

As Professor Nabrit untangled the web of lies upon which the Court had based that decision, the whole thirty-three years of my life under segregation took on a different cast entirely, for at last I understood how thoroughly Jim Crow rested on sand. Words cannot convey the sense of power I derived from that knowledge. The hydra-headed monster that had shadowed my existence since my first conscious moment now seemed assailable, if I could but hone the weapons Nabrit and the others were placing at my feet.

Mastering the law became the driving force of my life. I read law, I memorized it, I dug it out of casebooks, I discussed it with Julius and the members of the study group that became my second family at Howard—the five serious-minded men who gave the lie to every stereotype of the chauvinistic male law student, and Romae L. Turner, a brilliant woman who would make history as the first black female judge in the state of Georgia. To this day my passion for the law is inextricably intertwined with those dear comrades-in-arms: Marshall J. Massie; Quinton Banks; Francisco Rodriguez, who, along with our group leader, Fred Minnis, would crack the color bar in the Florida legal community; and Leroy V. Hall, a Morehouse man and friend from my Spelman years who went on to become a force for justice as an officer in the DC juvenile court.

Just how the seven of us wound up convening at my tiny Anacostia apartment on Saturday or Sunday afternoons I cannot say, except that all my life I've loved the feel of a home resounding with joyful noise, particularly when those making it are about important business. I had plenty of my grandmother in me then, and still do: no matter how tight the quarters or limited the supplies, I couldn't turn away a hungry crowd. Though I issued repeated requests that everyone see to his or her own meal, I'd find myself in the kitchen before each session ended, a textbook in one hand, a wooden spoon in the other, trying to turn cold cans of something or other into real food, and talking law while I did it.

At our loudest pitch, in the heat of the debates that punctuated our long presentations to each other, we rivaled the choir at Allen Chapel AME Church next door, but we were, all of us, deadly serious. In every realm of legal study, we sought out the way to racial justice, tracking with all-consuming intensity the changes coming down from the Supreme Court and even the White House. On July 26, 1948, President Truman, in a sweeping executive order, put an end to the horror of Jim Crow in the armed services, ending—at least on paper—the humiliation of military segregation and the lie that had fed it. I well remembered the disingenuous testimony of the southern congressmen who'd killed the anti–Jim Crow amendment to the WAAC bill in 1942 with their insistence that the army's record on race was unimpeachable, that blacks in such a fair-minded military needed no special legal protection. An era had ended, I told Fred Minnis, who'd served as a commissioned officer in the army during the war, and who had, like me, experienced the pain of segregation in uniform. Now, finally, we saw the times changing.

Yet for all that, *Plessy* stood, in all its hideousness, its fundamental premise as yet unchallenged. And no matter how wide-ranging our discussions, we circled back to that fact again and again. Ours was a unique era for legal study, a time when it can truly be said that a single case held the key. If *Plessy v. Ferguson* could be dismantled, we stood to reshape America, to return it to the ideal of its origin, in a purer form. So long as it remained intact, justice eluded us. And we looked to Dr. Nabrit for the roadmap through *Plessy* to the colorblind world we all believed lay beyond it.

Like a surgeon with his scalpel, he dissected for us the text of that twisted ruling, exposing its flawed logic and rendering it vulnerable to attack by the mind—the tool my beloved Miss Neptune had enjoined me to press into service in my Spelman days. Anger had paralyzed me then, but as I followed Nabrit's lead through the *Plessy* text, I felt the power of my own intellect rising up to engage it as an enemy.

The Supreme Court, he pointed out, had buttressed its support of "separate but equal" train accommodations in *Plessy* with a Boston school segregation case from the days of slavery. It cited a host of other decisions irrelevant to the constitutional issue at hand and one which flatly contradicted its own reasoning in *Plessy*. It declared the wildly uneven practice of segregation, disliked by bus and train companies in those days for its expense and inconvenience, to be a custom so firmly entrenched that to overturn it would be to risk wholesale chaos.

Through the Court's labyrinth of illogic and calculated omission and outright falsehood Dr. Nabrit led us to the grotesque heart of the decision. Even now, I cannot read the text of *Plessy v. Ferguson* but that I hear his voice, laden with the accents of his Georgia beginnings and moving with slow deliberation over the words that made a mockery of the founding documents:

> We consider the underlying fallacy of the plaintiff's argument to consist in the assumption that the enforced separation of the races stamps the colored race with a badge of inferiority. If this be so, it is not by reason of anything found in the act but solely because the colored race chooses to put that construction upon it . . . If one race be inferior to the other socially, the constitution of the United States cannot put them upon the same plane.

There it was: the lie that created two Americas. By leaving the matter of segregation to the states, *Plessy* created fertile ground for hundreds of Jim Crow laws that extended "separate but equal" into every corner of life in the South, consigning millions of black children in sixteen states to ramshackle schoolhouses like the one I attended. I loved poor dilapidated Meyers Street Elementary and my fellow students so dearly that the building's appalling state of decay mattered little in my child's mind.

What did cut, though, in the years of my girlhood, was the idea that books in untold numbers were forbidden to me by law. I have no memory of *not* longing for the treasures inside the all-white Charlotte Public Library—longing for them in the way one does for a beloved but inaccessible person, with a sense of exclusion which the Supreme Court of the United States, I now discovered, had dismissed as a figment of my imagination. Those blacks who read inferiority in the fact of separation had chosen, the Court said, to "put that construction upon it." Yet the feeling was real, and in some inexpressible way it pained me more deeply than my first experience on the trolley car. Somehow my grandmother's fighting words assuaged that shame. To have books designated as "Whites Only" and placed forever out of my reach—that was a sensation so crushing not even Grandma could touch it.

But the law could. *Plessy* was a creation of the law, Nabrit told us repeatedly, and it could be undone by the law, even in the most sacred preserve of segregationists—the public schools. On this point Professor Nabrit was adamant, and yet I wondered whether that day would come in my lifetime, given the seemingly bottomless power of the white segregationists to blunt every blow struck for freedom. Blacks across America had celebrated the magnificent 1946 Supreme Court ruling in behalf of the Baltimore woman named Irene Morgan, who'd refused to change her seat in deference to the Jim Crow law of the state of Virginia when she was traveling from Virginia back to her home in Maryland. When that ruling came down, I'd been applying to law school and I'd followed the case carefully, knowing that *Morgan v. Virginia* could transform the horrific experience of traveling on trains and buses. Indeed, it had seemed to promise a new era, at least for black passengers whose journeys took them across state lines.

The individual states, the Supreme Court ruled, could not impose their own segregation laws on black passengers traveling interstate. To do so was to violate the clause in the Constitution that reserves to Congress the power to regulate the conduct of business among the states—the so-called "commerce clause," meant to insure orderliness and uniformity as people moved on trains and buses from one state to another across the country. How could there be anything less than total chaos in travel among the states, the Court asked, when every state had different laws regarding segregation, when no two states agreed upon the definition of "white" and "Negro," when the implementation of the laws was left to individual conductors and drivers?

In the *Morgan* case, the Supreme Court had struck at the heart of Jim Crow in interstate travel, and it had done so on *constitutional grounds*. True, it hadn't touched the *Plessy* premise of "separate but equal," nor did it have any impact on Jim Crow travel within the individual states, but in regard to travel across state lines, its implications were enormous. It represented a watershed moment in our history, and yet, in my first year of law school I watched it turn to ashes. One by one, in rapid succession within weeks of the *Morgan* ruling, every single southern railway and bus company instituted its own Jim Crow regulations. And those regulations stood. They were the actions of private businesses, the Supreme Court said, invoking a ruling it had made back in 1910 that held carrier regulations to be outside the reach of the government. No blood had been shed, at least not in public view, and yet the white South had prevailed.

Who knew what steps southerners might take to prevent that most hated of all prospects, the integration of the schools? Blood would run in the streets, the segregationists warned, if their children were forced to "commingle" in the schoolyard with Negroes. Out of such commingling came miscegenation, a prospect so abhorrent to whites that many believed the white South would rise up and fight another Civil

War rather than see it come to pass. I'd lived in the South; I'd known its hatred. And though I longed for a new day, I dreaded the price we might pay.

Yet school integration must come, Nabrit said, as he laid out for us the target he and Marshall and the others had identified as their first line of attack: the graduate and professional schools. Feelings ran cooler in the higher realms and judges were more likely to be sympathetic. Crack *Plessy* there, the theory ran, and the public schools would follow. The NAACP had breached the wall ever so slightly in 1938 with their limited victory in Lloyd Gaines's case against the University of Missouri. In January 1948, midway through my first year at Howard, Thurgood Marshall came before the Supreme Court to take on "separate but equal" harder than he ever had before, in behalf of a brilliant young minister's daughter from Oklahoma who was, by all accounts, as tough-minded as any man. Her name was Ada Lois Sipuel, and her case riveted me, no doubt because I saw so much of myself in her. For all of her sterling academic credentials, she'd been denied admission to the all-white University of Oklahoma law school and told to wait until the state had enough black applicants to justify the building of a colored law school. Against that hollow, distant promise of "separate but equal, someday," Ada Lois had raised an outcry, demanding that Oklahoma admit her without further delay.

As Thurgood Marshall prepared to bring her case before the Supreme Court, Julius and I and my classmates watched it with the kind of wild optimism that is the province of legal neophytes. We read the brief, with the careful two-pronged argument the NAACP used as its standard approach in those days. On one hand, Marshall lashed out at segregation per se, calling it inherently evil, a perpetuation of the "slave tradition." On the other, he fell back on *Plessy*, taking great care to leave the Court a fallback position in case it was not yet ready to declare segregation unconstitutional. Even under the *Plessy* doctrine of "separate but equal," it was plain that the university wasn't giving Ada Sipuel her rights; it was, as my grandmother liked to say about all manner of blowhards and pretenders, "just fixin' to do something." How could any reasonable person see it otherwise?

When the Court's initial ruling came down in favor of Ada Sipuel just four days after Marshall argued it, my study group partners and I rocked the roof of my apartment. We took the words of Chief Justice Vinson to mean what they said: "Petitioner is entitled to the full enjoyment of her rights *now*." But when in response to the Court's demand for immediate equality, the University of Oklahoma roped off a corner of the state capitol and called it a "colored law school," the chief justice backed off his initial ruling and threw the matter back to the Oklahoma Supreme Court. The *Sipuel* case, he wrote for the majority, hadn't actually raised the question of the state's obligation in regard to the Fourteenth Amendment's "equal protection" clause and how it applied to a separate law school for blacks.

What had it raised, then? What had Marshall been talking about when he'd blasted Oklahoma's answer to the Court's mandate as a travesty? *Plessy*, so far as I could tell, stood undiminished. Apparently a state didn't really have to *provide* equality; it was sufficient under law just to *promise* it. And a separate law school, no matter how fine and well equipped, could never be truly equal. Intellectually, of course, I recognized that even a pitiful and confusing ruling like *Sipuel* was a building block, somehow or other, in the grander scheme, just as the housing covenant and interstate travel cases were. Losses, Professor Nabrit frequently reminded us, provided "windows into the mind of the Court." The legal scholar in me grasped such nuances. But I was not all scholar, then, or ever. In my heart, I sided with my neighbors—the parents and grandparents and great-grandparents in my little cocoon of a neighborhood separated from the rest of Washington by the Anacostia River, and a very different place indeed from the capital city. Like the people among whom I lived, I wondered whether change would ever come.

I didn't have answers for them when they clustered around me after services at Allen Chapel, or called to me over the back fence in the evenings, looking to me as some kind of prophet on the wing when it came to things legal. At Howard, we lived by arcane distinctions and abstract legal principles. My neighbors looked at life through a different prism, the church leaders like Tootie Dittweiler who'd hustled me into the fold at Allen Chapel and recruited me to teach Sunday school when I told her about my work with the children of Chester; the Garfield School PTA leaders Mabel Carroll and Edmund Gordon; community pillars like Hortense Washington and the elegant Amanda P. Forest, who headed the Anacostia outreach group known as the Cheerio Club. These were black folk who'd built their world from the ground up, in the way their forebears had from the time they'd settled in the Negro enclave of Anacostia just after the Civil War. What my neighbors saw on the ground was defeating.

On the other side of the river, in what people called "the real capital city," an all-out war was being waged, a war for decent black schools. And we were losing. A man named Gardner Bishop—the "U Street Barber" we called him—and his Consolidated Parents' Group, fed up with the filthy, overcrowded schools their children were forced to attend while the well-equipped white facilities stood half empty, had taken on the DC board of education with a vengeance. Represented by Charles Hamilton Houston himself, Gardner Bishop and his league of parents had begun turning the city upside down in the winter of my first year, marching on the White House, picketing, sending their children downtown to the board in taxicabs, and, finally, keeping them home from school for three months in a boycott the likes of which the country had never seen. Yet the board held firm, and when Charles Houston took the case to the DC court of appeals, the court sided with the school board, ruling that Congress had long ago sanctioned segregated schools in the District of Columbia. As for whether those separate schools were equal to the ones provided for whites, the court found them equal enough, at least for the foreseeable future.

In the midst of this weaving and dodging by the courts at every level, Professor Nabrit pointed his finger straight at the root cause as he saw it, and in so doing he took on Thurgood Marshall, the NAACP, and the entire rationale for the Legal Defense Fund's cautious, incremental strategy that sought to weaken *Plessy* by erosion. So long as the NAACP coupled its attack on segregation with a demand for equalization under the *Plessy* doctrine, the Court would take the "out"; by its very nature, it ruled on the narrowest possible grounds, addressing constitutional questions only when it had no choice. To invoke *Plessy* even as a fallback position was in Nabrit's view to be complicit in the evil, to give credence to the lie, to feed its poison. *Plessy* was wrong, he said. It was un-Christian. It was un-American. It was unconstitutional. No brief, no oral argument that came before the high Court should dilute that fact with secondary arguments that demanded equality within segregation.

Though he never raised his voice, Professor Nabrit seemed to thunder as he took on the NAACP's tempered approach, lashing out more and more strongly in the wake of the *Sipuel* case—a perfect illustration, as he analyzed it, of just how narrowly the Supreme Court ruled when it was not pressed. Now was the time to attack *Plessy* itself, he insisted in the spring of 1950, as Marshall prepared to argue two graduate school cases so outrageous in their particulars that I myself could imagine no compromise. To the black mailman named Heman Marion Sweatt, who aspired to a legal education, the University of Texas had offered three basement classrooms in an Austin office building. To elderly George McLaurin, the University of Oklahoma granted admission to its doctoral program in education, but with caveats so degrading my eyes burned when I read the particulars in the brief. First banished from the classroom and forced to listen to lectures from the hallway, then consigned to a seat behind a railing marked "Reserved for Colored" inside the lecture hall, Professor McLaurin came to symbolize everything we hated about segregation: its degradation, its humiliation, its sense of dehumanization. It was, at bottom, an assault upon the spirit. And I understood with my heart as much as my budding lawyer's mind that the evidence against such treatment was to be found not in comparisons of dollars spent or in bricks laid or in square footage of classrooms in black and white schools, but in the harm done to the black person's sense of himself.

If the *McLaurin* case did not present the argument for the evil inherent in the act of segregation itself, no case ever had. So Nabrit insisted, and so Thurgood Marshall believed, for he abhorred segregation as deeply as Nabrit. Anyone who heard him speak even for a moment knew that. But he was a pragmatist, and a leader who whether he liked it or not answered to conservative financial backers interested in funding wins. As he pushed forward, refining his approach, rehearsing it in dry run in our moot courtroom in the early part of April of my third year, he continued to hedge, if ever so slightly, and Nabrit continued to press more and more urgently for the final, clean attack on the constitutional issue.

I could not but side with Nabrit, though I respected Marshall for the inspired leader that he was. The gulf that divided them was the one that has divided black folk from the beginning of our struggle, separating those whose souls permit no compromise from those who find in restraint the better part of valor. For me, the time for waiting was over, and had been since the morning in 1943 when I'd unpinned my captain's bars, risked court martial and dishonorable discharge from the army rather than live one more hour with the ignominy of segregation.

And so that spring, even as all of Howard mourned the death of Charles Hamilton Houston on the twenty-second of April, I took comfort in Nabrit's response, in the brave and lonely path he chose to honor Houston's memory. In taking over the case Houston passed along to him in his final hours, the matter of Gardner Bishop's Consolidated Parents' Group, Nabrit framed it in the only way he could—and, I am convinced, in the way he believed Houston would have done, given the changing times. It was Houston, after all, who'd declared war on segregation three years earlier, Houston who told the world back in 1947, "There is no such thing as 'separate but equal.'" To Bishop and his colleagues Nabrit delivered an ultimatum: he would take the case they'd lost in the DC appeals court to the next level, but only as an attack on segregation per se. All pleas for equalization must be eliminated. This was the Nabrit who'd taken on the fight for the rights of American Indians in the Texas courts, the Nabrit who brooked no displays of male superiority in his classes, the Nabrit who for all his intellectualism saw the world as a minister's son, intolerant of any form of compromise. He stands forever a hero in my mind, as does the fearless plaintiff who accepted his terms: Gardner Bishop, the "U Street Barber." With everything to lose, including the tenuous backing of a parents' group grown weary of battle, he signed on for Nabrit's strategy. At that moment, one of the five cases that would make history under the caption of "*Brown v. Board*" was born. And its basis—the one that defined *Brown* in its entirety—would be that for which Nabrit had argued all along: the wrongness of segregation itself.

No one knew that, then, of course. Nor did we know, in the moment, the way in which the monumental events of that heady spring would conspire to bring Marshall and the other Legal Defense Fund lawyers into line with Nabrit's thinking, that on June 5, just thirteen days after my graduation, the Supreme Court would hand down rulings in the *Sweatt* and *McLaurin* cases that would prompt Marshall to move to the next step, to take on the constitutionality of "separate but equal." For the first time, in those two cases, the Court found that there was more to equality than mere buildings, that the intangibles counted for something—for a great deal, in fact—and that without the intangibles of fellowship and alumni influence, prestige and community standing, the essence of what constituted a postgraduate education was absent. The University of Texas must admit Heman Sweatt to its law school since its colored law school couldn't provide him equal training, the Court ruled, and if a state admitted a black student to an all-white school, as it had George McLaurin, it must treat him the same as it did the white students. The constitutionality of *Plessy* remained intact, but "separate but equal" was dealt such a crippling blow with the Court's new standard for equality that Marshall would be emboldened in its wake to forge onward to the heart of *Plessy.*

That moment lay ahead of us, existing only in possibility in the tense days of March and April 1950. Along with my classmates, I watched Marshall and his Legal Defense Fund colleagues in dress rehearsal for *Sweatt* and *McLaurin* almost as intently as if I'd been one of the principals. From my first year, I'd been spellbound by those Supreme Court "dry runs": Professor Nabrit generally at the bench, unless he wished to argue himself; Marshall and his team strutting their stuff; the faculty and even an occasional bold student firing questions at the lead attorneys, all of them anticipating the issues they thought might be raised the next day by the justices themselves. From the moment I witnessed the first of those performances, I'd set my sights on trial work. Someday, I vowed, as I soaked in Marshall's earthy brilliance, George Hayes's effortless elegance of presentation, Nabrit's flawless rhetoric, I would command a courtroom as they did, train a jury's eye on justice so inexorably they could not but see the truth.

We students thrilled to the spectacle of that army of lawyers marching shoulder to shoulder into the Supreme Court to take on the nine justices with all the combined firepower of the NAACP. But I was a maverick then, as I am now, and when a lone soldier came before the Court in the person of a black Yale law graduate named Belford Lawson, I riveted my eyes upon his case. Lawson had dared, outside the protective mantle of the NAACP, to take on *Plessy* in the very field where it had originated—railway transportation. That fact alone would have arrested my attention, but Lawson's suit held another fascination: he represented a client whose situation triggered painful memories of my own travels on segregated trains. Elmer W. Henderson, the petitioner who was challenging the Southern Railway's Jim Crow dining car policy, had been a wartime field representative for the Fair Employment Practices Committee, just as I had, only he'd had the bad fortune to travel through the Deep South, and suffer the indignities not just of Jim Crow seating but of segregated dining as well. Almost every train ride of my army recruiting stint in Georgia, Florida, and the Carolinas had been marked by that surreal experience: the wait at the entrance of the always crowded diner; the walk past the other patrons to one of the Jim Crow tables located in the back of the car by the smoky, noisy kitchen; the sight of the steward hurrying to draw the curtains that protected whites from having to watch me consuming my food. More than once, I'd seen white people react to the spectacle, seen the backs of their ears redden with embarrassment when the steward yanked the curtains closed, as though they too felt the shame of that bizarre ritual.

There'd been no shame, apparently, on the dining car of the Southern Railway train that took Elmer Henderson from Washington, DC, to an FEPC hearing in Birmingham, Alabama, on a spring evening shortly after the beginning of the war. The car had been packed with white patrons, all impatient to be served. The steward, intent on sparing them a wait, had thrown open the curtains that separated the white from the Jim Crow section and converted the two tables reserved for Negro passengers to "Whites Only." When Elmer Henderson entered the car, a chair at one of those two tables stood empty, but the steward had refused to seat him there. To do so would, of course, have violated the railroad's segregation rules. Twice in the course of the evening Henderson had returned to the crowded dining car, and each time, he'd watched whites take the seats that opened up at the erstwhile Jim Crow tables, until at last, long past the dinner hour, he gave up on the possibility of dinner that night.

But he didn't give up the fight. Back in Washington, he sought out Belford Lawson, who by that time had made a name for himself with a Supreme Court decision protecting the right to picket against job discrimination. Together, they took on the entire system of Jim Crow travel, first in the lower courts, and twice before the Interstate Commerce Commission, the federal agency that regulated the carriers and almost always sided with them in racial matters. "The Supreme Court of the Confederacy," it was called by black attorneys, and with good reason. Almost a decade before the Supreme Court handed down *Plessy*, the ICC had adopted "separate but equal" as its official policy.

When the ICC dismissed Henderson's claim for the second time, he and Lawson went to the Supreme Court of the United States, and there Lawson unleashed a three-pronged attack that took on Jim Crow in the field of transportation using every weapon available to a lawyer at that time. He invoked the Interstate Commerce Act, the law governing the carriers, and he argued that the Southern Railway's dining car segregation policy violated the language in the act forbidding "undue and unreasonable prejudice." He invoked the commerce clause of the Constitution, with its demand for systematic and orderly travel across state lines. In the *Morgan* case, he pointed out, the Court had applied that clause to the states, and forbade them from imposing their own Jim Crow laws on interstate travelers. Why should the carriers be any different? Subjecting interstate Negro passengers to the ever-changing regulations of the carriers caused at least as much chaos as subjecting them to the varying laws of each of the southern states, and it ought to be outlawed as a burden on interstate commerce.

And then Belford Lawson took his boldest swipe at Jim Crow: he invoked the Fifth and the Fourteenth Amendments, arguing that the Southern Railway had denied Elmer Henderson both due process and equal protection. Lawson was blasting the entire basis of *Plessy*, and demanding that the Court overturn it. The Interstate Commerce Act's ban on discrimination had always been interpreted within the confines of "separate but equal." But Lawson argued that the act should be interpreted as an all-out prohibition of segregation, that separateness was inherently unequal. It was a brazen position for a private attorney to take in 1950, when the Court was turning a deaf ear to the same argument Marshall and his NAACP team were making about the Fourteenth Amendment in the area of education. Still, Lawson had the support of the solicitor general himself, who weighed in with a "friend of the court" brief in the *Henderson* case that made me want to shout out hallelujahs from the Howard bell tower. "Segregation of Negroes, as practiced in this country, is universally understood as imposing on them a badge of inferiority," the solicitor general wrote. "The curtain which fences Negroes off from all other diners exposes, naked and unadorned, the caste system which segregation manifests and fosters."

Elmer Henderson's case came up for oral argument on the same day Thurgood Marshall and his team argued *Sweatt* and *McLaurin*, and Julius and I watched all three closely. I huddled with my study group and prognosticated and analyzed and speculated. I read the briefs and tracked the case law upon which the lawyers had based their arguments. And I prayed—oh, how I prayed—for justice to come down. All the while, I rushed like the "far-darting Apollo" of my Spelman years, not out of desperation as I had back then, but with joyous anticipation, toward graduation and the law practice I was planning with Julius once I passed the DC bar exam, scheduled for December.

There were arrangements for the bar review course to be attended to, the matter of final exams to be addressed, and long-overdue house-cleaning to be undertaken on a scale sweeping enough to satisfy my grandmother's strictest standards. Given the state of my paper-strewn apartment, that last task had me in something close to a frenzy, for Grandma herself was coming to Washington to see me graduate, and Mama along with her.

Never before had there been money enough for the two people I loved most to be with me at moments like this one. They'd missed my Spelman graduation, my commissioning as a WAAC officer, the awarding of my captain's bars, even my wedding, all for lack of funds. We didn't have money enough this time either, but somehow I'd scrounged it up, one dollar at time, working extra hours at my grocery-clerking job for months in advance to come up with the train fare. The Monday morning of April 4, 1950, stands in the archive of my memory not only for the fact of Thurgood Marshall and Robert Carter's historic Supreme Court appearance in *Sweatt* and *McLaurin*, and Belford Lawson's in *Henderson*, but by virtue of the proud exchange I executed at Union Station: my hard-earned dollars for two tickets for reserved seats on the Southern Railway, Charlotte to Washington and back again. Feeling like some grand official discharging state business, I mailed the tickets to Mama.

Those who love Washington as I do will know the sort of spring evening that enfolded me when I stepped out of my cab at Union Station a few minutes before 8:00 on the Thursday before my May 18 graduation to meet Mama and Grandma on the train. Not even cities in the Deep South, fragrant with blossoms as they are at that time of year, quite match the springs of Washington, when even at dusk the pink and white of dogwood is visible against the marble of the monuments, softening the edges of a city that does its business with such seriousness. I often had the sense that Jim Crow hid himself better, there, than in other places, which made his appearance, as if out of nowhere, all the more painful. In a single instant, the world could change—and in all my years under segregation, I was never quite ready for the split second when joy and contentment drained suddenly away.

The moment I spotted Mama and Grandma on the platform, I knew something was horribly wrong. Grandma was limping, and my mother, disheveled and agitated, walked alongside her, dragging the luggage and looking wildly about in all directions. I called out to them and began running down the platform, elbowing my way through the people streaming off the cars, and as I reached them I saw that my grandmother could barely walk. When I looked closely, I stopped, shocked.

She was crying. I'd only seen Grandma cry once before, when her brother died. But she'd wept quietly then, and after a few minutes she'd picked up her broom and starting sweeping.

She was quiet now, too, but I could tell by the way she staggered that she was in pain.

"Grandma, what's wrong?" I asked her. "Are you sick?"

"No, Dovey Mae," she answered, "I ain't sick."

In a rush, Mama blurted out what had happened. For ten hours—the entire length of the ride from Charlotte to Washington—they'd been forced to stand. The Jim Crow car had been packed with families, Mama said, with children on their parents' laps and luggage stacked on seats and in the aisles, and when they'd tried to make their way into the half-empty white car behind the colored coach, the conductor had shouted them back, threatening them and brushing aside the "Reserved Seat" tickets they'd presented. For hours, as they'd ridden through North Carolina and into Virginia and Maryland, they'd held onto seat edges and stood, until finally Grandma couldn't stand any more. Just outside Washington, she'd collapsed on the closed seat of the toilet in the bathroom at the front of the car, and stayed there.

She staggered as we made our way out of Union Station into a taxi-cab, and when at last I had her safely back in my apartment and saw the condition of her feet, I winced. They were bruised and bleeding, as I'd seen them so often in my girlhood when she'd worked all day—only worse. My hands trembling with a rage I hadn't known even in my army days, I picked up the phone and dialed my doctor, who upon hearing the urgency in my voice, set out for my home. And then I called Julius, newly admitted to the DC bar, because even in the midst of my frenzy I knew that this was a matter for the law. True, there'd been no permanent physical injury—my doctor quickly ruled that out—but the railroad had committed a grave wrong, a legal wrong. And that wrong must be righted. The Southern Railway, I told Grandma and Mama once we'd gotten past the night's crisis, must be held accountable for what they'd done.

Grandma grew quiet, the way she had in the weeks so long ago when she'd been wrestling with the prospect of my leaving home to attend college in Atlanta. The more I pressed, the quieter she grew.

"Ain't gonna do no good, Dovey Mae," she told me.

Yet I could not dismiss the matter, not when the Supreme Court it-self was about to rule on Elmer Henderson's claim against the very railway carrier that had abused and humiliated my family. All through the whirlwind of graduation weekend, with Mama and Grandma rallying to cheer me as I marched proudly into Howard's Rankin Chapel to claim my diploma, my mind moved endlessly over the facts of their case and my chances of winning a lawsuit in their behalf against the Southern Railway.

On June 5, 1950, just a week after Mama and Grandma had returned to Charlotte, the Supreme Court handed down its ruling in *Henderson v. United States*. The Court left untouched the constitutional questions Belford Lawson had raised, sidestepping his attack on "separate but equal." Yet the ruling had force for what it *did* say. The justices condemned the railroad for doing to Elmer Henderson in the diner precisely what it had done to my mother and grandmother in the traveling car: denying him a seat when seats were available, solely because of his race. It imposed upon him an "unreasonable disadvantage," the Court said, and it was, therefore, a clear violation of the Interstate Commerce Act. No one had really expected the Court to tie the act to the Fourteenth Amendment, as Lawson had tried to do, and rule against segregation itself. They'd stopped just short of doing that, insisting only that the railroad, operating within a segregated system, had to provide dining accommodations that were truly equal for blacks and whites. The legal basis for the Court's decision was limited, and disappointing. I took heart, though, from the tone of disgust in the Court's reference to the wooden partitions the railroad had erected in the wake of Elmer Henderson's experience to better demarcate the one Jim Crow table on its diners. Such partitions, wrote Justice Harold Burton for the majority, called attention to the race of passengers and emphasized "the artificiality of a difference in treatment."

It was as close to a condemnation of Jim Crow as we were likely to get without an out-and-out rejection of *Plessy* itself. And it cut to the heart of what had happened to Grandma and Mama. If the Southerner's refusal to seat a healthy young man like Elmer Henderson offended the Supreme Court, what would they think of subjecting a seventy-five-year-old woman with broken, crippled feet to a six-hundred-mile journey without so much as an offer of a packing crate to sit on? Were I to come before that august tribunal, I thought, with its marble-carved proclamation of "Equal Justice Under Law," what an argument I could have made for the petitioners Rachel Graham and Lela Johnson.

I wasn't going before any tribunal at all, of course, supreme or otherwise. Even if Grandma had been willing to undertake a court battle
at her advanced age, the prospect of bringing her to Washington, DC,
and subjecting her to a trial or even a hearing was unthinkable. Still, I
told Julius, perhaps the Southern Railway was assailable nevertheless.
If we framed our case narrowly, steering clear of grand constitutional
questions, and were willing to settle out of court, I thought we had
a fighting chance at a monetary damage award. The image that filled
my mind was that of Grandma and Mama's tickets: "Reserved Seat,"
the tickets had read. I'd taken great care to appear in person at Union
Station to see to it that I had precisely that type of ticket. A ticket constituted a promise of a seat—a contract, in legal terms. The Southern
Railway had breached their contract. And my grandmother and my
mother had suffered grievous harm, both physical and mental, because
of that breach. It was that simple.

Certain of my ground, I worked with Julius in drawing up the complaint, pushing past Grandma's protest that legal action would do no
good. I knew Grandma, knew why she said that. She had survived Jim
Crow by picking battles she could win and walking away from those
she couldn't. But in this matter I was playing my hand as carefully as
she ever had. And so, on a June morning several weeks after my graduation, we marched into the U.S. District Court for the District of Columbia on Constitution Avenue to file our breach-of-contract complaint. It
all seemed so clean, so logical, so reasonable, so cut-and-dried. But I
hadn't bargained on my heart.

When I learned the amount of the settlement offer made by the
Southern Railway—several hundred dollars as I recall—tears came to
my eyes, and though I bit my lip, I cried, right in front of Julius, the
defendant's attorney, and the judge who had called the settlement conference, held more than a year after the incident. I heartily disapprove
of public tears except in death, but there was something about seeing Mama and Grandma's humiliation reduced to a dollar figure that
overpowered me. Almost instantly, I controlled myself, but not before
the judge and the railroad's attorney took note of what they must have
regarded as a most unlawyerly display of emotion. Perhaps, the judge
suggested, we would like a moment to consider the matter privately.

Outside in the hallway, Julius spoke to me like the shrewd advocate
that he was, reciting the facts I already knew, the ones I myself had dug
out of the records in the Howard law library about damage awards in

comparable cases, where the plaintiffs had been able to prove they'd been abused, as Grandma and Mama had. The railroad's offer was reasonable, he told me, better in fact than he'd expected. When I didn't respond to his litany of facts and legal considerations, he shook his head and said, quietly, "You're her lawyer, D.J., not her granddaughter."

So I was. I'd been sworn into the DC bar on April 21, 1951, and I entered my appearance in the case shortly thereafter. Always a wise counselor, Julius was perhaps never wiser than on that occasion, and I was to carry with me through the years that fundamental lesson, that a lawyer must be ever watchful of her feelings, lest they cloud her judgment at the bar of justice.

Still, the settlement rang hollow for me, and I suspect for Julius as well, though he desisted from saying so for fear of riling me. I judged the relative generosity of the settlement offer to be more a function of the magic Grandma had worked on the Southern Railway's attorney, William B. Jones, than of any legal argument Julius and I made. She had served Mr. Jones homemade gingerbread and hot applesauce when he'd come to Charlotte to take her deposition. He was a kind man, she reported to me, one of those "decent white folk" for whom she made special exceptions. And he had seemed ashamed. When in later years William Jones rose to the bench and I chanced to come before him on various matters, he invariably called me forward after the proceedings to inquire after my family.

"And how is your grandmother, Mrs. Roundtree?" he'd ask, reminding me each time of the gingerbread he'd feasted upon at her kitchen table and asking that I give her his best regards.

"Indeed I shall, Your Honor," I said, taking my cue from Grandma, who needed no law degree to know that one should never confuse a client with his attorney.

And so the system that had reduced my folk to subhuman status rolled onward, untouched. And the country that permitted it, the America that had long ago breached its contract with its citizens, remained unchanged.

But there was another America out in front of me, further in the distance than I'd thought possible but clear in its outlines, the one Professor Nabrit had so often invoked even as he'd exposed the lie of *Plessy*. He'd held up to us, like a beacon, the vision of that America, laid out in 1896 in the words of the lone Supreme Court justice who'd decried *Plessy* for the mockery it was.

"In the view of the Constitution, in the eye of the law, there is in this country no superior, dominant, ruling class of citizens," Justice John Marshall Harlan had written. "There is no caste here. Our Constitution is color-blind, and neither knows nor tolerates classes among its citizens. In respect of civil rights, all citizens are equal before the law. The humblest is the peer of the most powerful. The law regards man as man, and takes no account of his surroundings or of his color when his civil rights as guaranteed by the supreme law of the land are involved."

I believed in that vision, and as I contemplated the outcome of my first matter before the bar, I was even more determined to fight for it, though Julius and I had precious little in our arsenal except our law school textbooks when we settled Mama and Grandma's case late in 1951. What we had more than anything, I think, was our pure bullheadedness—that, and our willingness to work twice as hard as anybody else for that color-blind world Justice John Marshall Harlan had spoken of in his dissent from *Plessy*. We clung as stubbornly as any two dirt-poor rookie lawyers ever did to the certainty that if we stuck it out we'd be able, somehow, some day, to win what we hadn't been able to for Mama and Grandma: real justice.

8. TAKING ON "THE SUPREME COURT OF THE CONFEDERACY"
The Case of Sarah Louise Keys

A life as long as mine is rich beyond measure in the lessons of history, of how it is shaped and fashioned and redirected by God in His good time, even as those of us laboring on the ground do battle in the day to day. It is through the prism of hindsight, a great gift of old age, that I contemplate with awe the way in which my life, so ordinary in its particulars during the first decade of my practice, was weaving itself at every turn into the tapestry of America's struggle for freedom. Julius and I fought so hard in the trenches during those early years that I dared not look upward, nor to the left or right, for fear of losing my equilibrium.

And yet, even as America was pitching forward from the NAACP's clean, cerebral courtroom victories into violence in the streets, I was moving right along with it, my fortunes intertwining with that struggle in ways I could not have imagined. If anyone had told me back in 1952 that one of my quietest battles would wind its way into the very center of the events that surrounded the Freedom Riders in 1961, that it would empower Attorney General Robert Kennedy to end forever the hideousness of segregation on buses, I would not have believed it.

Oh, I watched history, then, to be sure, watched it at least as intently as I had in my Howard years, for *Plessy v. Ferguson* was about to come under full-scale attack in the highest court in the land, and thanks to Professor Nabrit, I had a front row seat. He never did let go of me as a student, nor I of him as a teacher, and in the spring of 1952, I found myself sitting at a Howard law school convocation of two or three hundred of the country's leading black thinkers, journalists, and, of course, lawyers, all gathered to reach a consensus on the strategy for the public school cases. I had no business in that kind of company, I'd told Dr. Nabrit when I received my invitation. But he'd have none of it. And so I'd sat in that heady assembly, mesmerized, listening to him blast the leaders who were still pressing for the old equalization approach under *Plessy*. In his own school case, *Bolling v. Sharpe*, which he'd just taken to the U.S. Court of Appeals for the District of Columbia, he'd taken the hard line. Now, it seemed, he'd run out of patience with the timid souls who clung still to the safe route. More sharply than I'd ever heard him, he lashed out at what he saw as cowardice, foolishness, and utter naivete about the workings of the Supreme Court, which he believed would duck the constitutional issue as long as it was given an escape hatch.

"The attack should be waged with the most devastating forces at hand," he told the group. "Instead of worrying over the effect of compelling the Court to decide, our real concern is how we may best compel the Supreme Court to decide the question. Let the Supreme Court take the blame if it dares to say to the entire world, '*Yes*, democracy rests on a legalized caste system. Segregation of the races is legal.' Make the Court choose. Let the Court make a national and international record of this. Let the Court write this across the face of the Constitution: 'All men are equal, but white men are more equal than others.'"

I walked out of that auditorium into the April sunshine in the certain knowledge that Dr. Nabrit had finally carried the day, that America was at last approaching the reckoning that had been coming since the country began.

My own charge was, thankfully, much more humble. I needed to survive, a task that for a black lawyer in the District of Columbia in those days was a feat in itself. Banned from the DC bar association, shunned by the white attorneys and barely tolerated by most of the white judges who sat on the bench back then, Julius and I were interlopers in a legal establishment that excluded us as surely as if they'd put up ropes.

It was the old story, with a critical difference. Now I was a part of the fight, a bystander no longer. The most renowned of black attorneys walked at the margins of the judicial system in the nation's capital, men like my beloved professor George E. C. Hayes and his two partners, and Belford Lawson, who'd won the Supreme Court ban on segregated railroad car dining in behalf of Elmer Henderson. Yet they fought relentlessly and they exhorted us to fight as well in the war they were waging. Julius and I jumped at that exhortation. Within weeks of hanging out our shingle—metaphorically, of course, since we had no office building on which to hang it—we'd entered our names with the local branch of the NAACP as lawyers ready to represent any client they saw fit to send us. No Howard law graduate who'd walked in the shadow of James Nabrit or George Hayes or Charles Hamilton Houston doubted that a black lawyer had a grave and pressing duty to seek justice. To ignore that duty, as Houston famously said, was to be a "parasite on society." So Julius and I believed. Law paid the bills, to be sure—at least we hoped it would, eventually. But it was for us, more than anything, a calling.

We joined a tiny but stalwart band of attorneys who'd quietly managed to carve out a place for themselves in a city where a black lawyer had to leave the courthouse to use the bathroom or eat a meal. Let their names stand as a roll of honor alongside those the history books have preserved, men like the venerable Lindsay Cain, an institution in his own right, and the attorneys he mentored and protected: Maurice Weeks, Jesse Bedman, Wesley Williams, Jessie Lewis, and even one woman, Wilhelmina Rolark, who went on to become a force for change in Washington as a DC councilwoman.

Belford Lawson's office stood directly across the street from ours, his presence a reminder of what was possible, his counsel a source of perennial wisdom. These were the sterling souls who sustained Julius and me, who made the world within a world I was to inhabit for the rest of my professional life. We plied our trade on Eleventh Street, Northwest, in a string of narrow rowhouses set off from the street by tiny plots of grass enclosed by wrought-iron fences. That single block of Eleventh Street between U and T, with the Industrial Bank on one corner and Chisley Florist on the other, became for me sacred ground, peopled by dedicated lawyers and the block's philosopher-in-residence, Mr. Evelyn Owen Chisley, florist, poet, historian, and sage. The first person ever to address me as "Attorney Roundtree," Mr. Chisley nurtured me with his homegrown wisdom just as he did his roses, and he quickly became my consultant and sounding board for matters both large and small. I was never to turn the corner of Eleventh and U once I began full-time practice but that Mr. Chisley would call out from his flower garden, "And how's the attorney today? Any justice comin' down in that courthouse?" He was a grandfather to us all, and so was Attorney Lindsay Cain, who made a place for the youngest among us, including Julius and me. Once he saw Julius arguing and winning a small claims case, he took us under his wing, renting us a back room at 1931 Eleventh Street for next to nothing.

We took every case that came our way, provided we could do so honestly, and worked it stem to stern, researching and cross-checking each other with enough fanaticism for a half dozen lawyers. Julius maintained that anyone who stayed open twenty-four hours a day was bound to get a little business, and between the two of us we ran an almost round-the-clock operation, with Julius manning our desk by day while holding down a night job at the post office, and my taking over in the evenings after a full day's work as an attorney-adviser in the Labor Department's contracts section.

The pack of Southeast neighbors who'd watched me studying law for three years began seeking my legal assistance, and when I did my first will for the grand Anacostia matriarch Hortense Washington, I was as proud a lawyer as ever there was. People who needed wills, I reckoned, had something to pass on—what we call tangible assets. But my payment arrived at my doorstep in a basket containing eggs, collard greens, and red peppers. That night I feasted upon the peppers and greens, marked Mrs. Washington's account "Paid in Full" and assured Julius, who kept the books, that barter was a time-honored tradition, and, furthermore, that one will, especially in a tight-knit neighborhood like Anacostia, couldn't help but lead to another. He nodded, and we waited, and sure enough, within a few months we were doing wills all over Southeast.

Mostly, though, the clients who sought us out or fastened onto Julius in the courthouse hallways were people in real trouble. There were, too, I learned as Julius and I began taking on cases through the local NAACP, men and women of uncommon character who chose even in those dangerous years to take a stand. One of the greatest friendships of my life began in the NAACP referral that brought a young college student named Walter J. Leonard to my office door for the sort of representation neither one of us would have chosen but from which we couldn't turn away. Walking to the restaurant on the city's Southwest waterfront where he worked part-time as a waiter, Walter had chanced upon a scene so violent he'd stopped, horrified. A white policeman was smashing a black man up against the cement retaining wall that ran along the water, kicking him and beating him about the head and shoulders with his nightstick, beating him relentlessly, then handcuffing him and dragging him into his vehicle. Any black person who witnessed such a scene in those days and failed to walk quietly away endangered himself. Yet Walter Leonard had chosen to come forward.

He could not do otherwise, he told Julius and me in our first meeting, stunning us with his dignity and his command of the facts. A wrong had been done, he said, and without the testimony of an eyewitness, an innocent black man would be jailed, and undoubtedly convicted of a crime he'd never committed. So far as he was concerned, the NAACP's office had furnished us with all we needed to go forward: the arrest record and name of the black man who'd been jailed for assaulting a police officer and resisting arrest, and the name of the white policeman. Walter knew what he had seen. It was that simple.

By the time Walter and Julius and I arrived at the courthouse to take on the white policeman, I knew I had in Walter the sort of witness lawyers pray for. Eloquent, unflappable, and every inch his own man, he'd enlisted in the Coast Guard at age fifteen and served for two years at the end of the war. He'd founded an NAACP chapter at Savannah State College, and when the administration failed to support him in his protest of segregated buses in Savannah, he'd left the school. Now, in Washington with his new bride, working three jobs and attending college classes at night, he had set his sights on law school. This, I told Julius, was someone so far above the common run of men that his testimony was sure to carry great weight.

We walked into court ready for a brawl. But for all the policeman's menacing looks in our direction, he backed down on the witness stand, giving such a benign account of the black man's behavior and his reason for arresting him—"I told him to move off the sidewalk and he asked me why he should"—that the court dropped the charges. Walter never was called to testify, but I maintained that his powers of observation had carried the day nevertheless: he'd overheard the lawyers for the other side conferring outside the courtroom about a phony "witness" they'd scrounged up to back the policeman, and then he'd passed along to Julius and me their plans for fabricated testimony in a whisper I'm quite certain they heard. Like many a bold-faced liar, the policeman ran for cover, hurrying through his testimony, hurrying the district attorney out of court, hurrying past us in the hallway. We hurried, too, following the dictum we'd learned from Professor Hayes and Professor Nabrit: *When you get what you want in the courtroom, get out.* It was, thankfully, a little case, and yet stunning in its human dimensions, putting in my path in the person of Walter Leonard a protégé, a friend, a peerless comrade in the civil rights battle unfolding before us.

With a peculiar intensity I felt the threads of my life coming together in that first year of my law practice, heard the voices of the great men and women who'd shaped me rising up in chorus now that I was actually in a position to live Miss Neptune's charge: "Pass it on." She hovered ever so near, in those early months, having personally delivered to me two weeks after my Howard graduation the monogrammed leather briefcase that was to see me through five decades at the bar. Her visit had been a weeklong intellectual fest, filled with long talks about civil rights, about my role in the fight, about the importance of my lawsuit in behalf of my grandmother. I'd summoned to my home every Spelman woman of my era I could find, and every Morehouse man as well, for she'd mentored many of us "on both sides of the street," male and female alike, before her retirement in 1948. What a time we'd had, gathered around Miss Neptune in my apartment, remembering the college years she had so entirely defined that in the minds of the women at least, she was synonymous with them.

As for Dr. Bethune, I felt I'd never really left her, even during my frenetic law school years, during which time she'd moved the headquarters of the National Council of Negro Women from her tiny apartment on Ninth Street to a grand three-story Victorian she purchased at 1318 Vermont Avenue. In the decade that had passed since I'd sat at her feet clipping newspaper articles and soaking up her wisdom, she'd transformed the council into a vast umbrella, a force for political change so potent it rolled forward on its own momentum upon her retirement, passing smoothly in 1949 into the hands of her successor, the renowned activist and physician Dr. Dorothy Ferebee. Right up until 1954, when she moved home to Florida, Dr. Bethune presided over the council's activities from her apartment on the building's third floor, and as I climbed the grand staircase to the paneled board room where she received her most distinguished visitors, I felt very much as I had when I'd called upon Miss Neptune with a pack of hundred-dollar bills in my bosom. It was time, high time, that I began to pay her back, I told Dr. Bethune, laying out the offer that would become the basis for one of my longest professional associations: pro bono legal services, for the rest of my life, to the council. It was, in my mind, the least I could do by way of paying her back. She'd brought me into an army that for all its discrimination had given me a voice and a role in shaping history. I no longer recall whether she and I discussed the army on that particular occasion, but given Dr. Bethune's propensity for focusing on the future rather than the past, I doubt it. Whether we spoke of it or not, the military experience was at the center of my relationship to her, the basis for my gratitude. It had altered me so deeply that it was perhaps inevitable that at some point it would rise up to marshal me forward. When I took my leave of Dr. Bethune, I did not imagine how quickly, and how powerfully, that would happen.

Nine years had passed since the terrifying night in Miami during my army recruiting years when I'd been thrown off a bus by a driver who'd forced me to yield my seat to a white marine, then left me standing in the station at midnight, to wait for hours until the next bus came. Such was the power of that memory, though, that those nine years fell away in a single moment as I sat with Julius on a sweltering September afternoon in 1952, listening to a painfully shy young WAC private named Sarah Louise Keys tell her story. She'd been referred to us, with her father, David, by the head of Washington's NAACP office, my old professor Frank Reeves, who saw in our shared army connection what he called "a perfect match" of client and attorney.

On the surface, Sarah Keys was as different from me as a woman could be. Only twenty-two years old, she struck Julius and me as impossibly young to be taking on a southern bus carrier in a court of law, as her father proposed that she do. She was no Rosa Parks, whose defiance of the Montgomery, Alabama, city bus system three years later would spark the civil rights movement in the streets of America. For the first few minutes of our meeting, she didn't say a word, but simply sat stiff and upright in her starched WAC uniform and cap, nodding quietly as her father spoke of the wrong, the terrible wrong that had been done to her by a driver who had put her off the bus in the middle of the night and left her to fend for herself in a little North Carolina town in the middle of nowhere.

David Keys was a large, handsome man, a farmer who pieced out a living for Sarah and her six brothers and sisters by doing masonry work wherever he could find it, he said, and he was now working at Quantico Marine Base in Virginia and living temporarily in Washington. He was well dressed and well spoken, and so enraged at the humiliation his daughter had suffered that I worried that perhaps this was his case more than it was Sarah's. That would not do. David Keys could not walk this path for his daughter, nor could he buffer her from the ugliness of a trial, in the way he'd so obviously sheltered her all her life. He'd sent her to a local Catholic school the Sisters of Mercy ran for black children in Washington, North Carolina, a school he'd help found. He had wanted nothing but the best for his daughter, and he'd protected her as best he could. And when this awful thing had happened to Sarah—"to *my child*," he said—he'd engaged an NAACP attorney to fight the disorderly conduct charge the local police had levied upon her. The appeal in the Roanoke Rapids Recorder's Court had failed, and so he had contacted a friend in Washington, DC, with connections to the NAACP office here. Mr. Keys was, without question, a father on a mission. But it was Sarah who'd be grilled on the witness stand, Sarah's motives that would be questioned, her account of the night's events that would be challenged, her character that would be impugned. I watched her closely, taking her measure, weighing her fragile demeanor against the power of the story she had to tell.

She'd left her WAC post at Fort Dix early on the morning of August 1 on a Safeway Trails bus for her first furlough since she'd enlisted in 1951, she told us, in a voice so low Julius and I had to lean forward, at first, to hear her. As Sarah spoke about her military service, though, she seemed to summon herself. She had two brothers stationed in Korea, she told us, and she was ever so proud to be serving in the army. Even though she wasn't traveling on military business, she chose to wear her uniform for her trip home.

All had been quiet as the bus headed southward, stopping in Washington, DC, where, Sarah said, she'd transferred without incident to a Carolina Trailways bus that would take her to the "other Washington" that was her final destination: her hometown of Washington, North Carolina. She'd taken the fifth seat from the front upon boarding the second vehicle, settled in for the journey homeward, and somewhere along the way, she'd fallen asleep. What jolted her awake was the voice of the driver, asking for her ticket. He was not the same person who'd taken the wheel in Washington, DC, and he spoke sharply. When she handed him her ticket, he demanded that she move to the back and give up her seat to a white marine who'd been in the Jim Crow section.

"I told him I preferred to stay where I was," Sarah said, her voice thickening. "He got off the bus and was gone a little while. When he came back, he returned my ticket and he told everybody sitting there, 'All passengers get off the bus except the lady who refused to move.'"

It was as though I sat looking in a mirror, so strong was my sense of having walked where Sarah Keys had walked. The bus company's treatment of her, as she'd described it up to that point, could have been mine, even down to the coincidence of a white marine standing ready to displace a woman traveling in uniform. What made it all the more appalling was the realization of how little had changed in nine years' time, despite the Supreme Court's 1946 ruling in *Morgan v. Virginia*, which in principle should have placed Sarah and me in different worlds altogether. The *Morgan* bus desegregation case had been hailed as a landmark, a turning point for black travelers all across the South, because it had forbidden the individual states from imposing their Jim Crow laws on bus passengers whose journeys took them across state lines. But Sarah's experience reminded me of just how effectively the carriers had circumvented that ruling, how completely they'd managed to impose their own regulations upon black passengers in the wake of *Morgan*. Because they were private companies, they'd managed to dodge interference from federal and state courts. And so the humiliation and the upheaval and the degradation continued, unabated, across the South, where the individual bus drivers and train conductors remained, for all practical purposes, the law of the land. And Sarah Keys, like millions of her fellow travelers, had the bad fortune to encounter a driver of the worst type.

When she'd refused to back down, exiting the bus along with all the white passengers and walking with them to another bus that stood waiting on the platform, he had the motor already running. And when she approached the door, he slammed it in her face. At that point she'd become frantic, she told Julius and me. It was late, sometime between midnight and one in the morning. She had no idea when another bus might come, or whether she'd be allowed to get on, and she ran into the station, looking for someone who might help her. The dispatcher ignored her, and so did the woman behind the ticket counter. She then prevailed upon a police officer. And that was when things turned ugly.

"I showed him my ticket and explained I needed to get home," she said, "and he told me, 'You shut up before we have to take you down and lock you up.' I heard someone say to him, 'Get her out of here tonight.' The next thing I knew, he was shoving me into his car, shouting at me that I was under arrest for disorderly conduct. He told me, 'If you say one more word, I'll slap you across the face.'"

Even before Sarah had finished her account of the night she'd spent, incommunicado, in the Roanoke Rapids jail and the kangaroo court hearing where the mayor had praised the vigilance of the local police force and found her guilty of disorderly conduct, I had made up my mind we were going to take this case. So had Julius. He and I read each other so accurately that I knew without asking how impressed he was with our client. She was tiny, frail, almost childlike in her person. But she was tough. She could have chosen the safe, easy route and moved to the back of the bus. Instead, she'd stood up to the driver, not out of naivete, I judged, but out of a sense of indignation. She did not flinch when Julius and I began laying out the risks, the discomfort, the time, and even the danger that went along with any serious assault upon the Jim Crow rules of a train or bus company. The statute that regulated the carriers, the Interstate Commerce Act, had always been read as permitting separate accommodations so long as they were substantially equal. It might be years before Sarah won satisfaction, monetary or otherwise. And there remained the chance that we might win nothing at all. We believed in her case, and in her cause, Julius and I assured her. But we could make no guarantees.

Sarah was undaunted. She'd come this far, she told us. She wasn't going to back down now. She lacked the eloquence of Walter Leonard and the imposing presence of her father, but Private First Class Sarah Louise Keys saw herself as a woman wronged, and she spoke with the surety I believe God gives to persons who are telling the truth.

That September afternoon of 1952 was the last day Julius and I passed like the proverbial "ships in the night," consulting by phone and elaborate notes left on the stack of files for the other to sort through upon arrival. I didn't quit my day job—I couldn't, I told Julius, until we had a steadier stream of clients—nor did Julius give up his night work at the post office. But we began setting aside hours at the edges, in the early mornings and late afternoons, to map out the basis of our suit, beginning with the simplest claim of all: breach of contract. The northern carrier, Safeway Trails, had sold Sarah Keys what was known as a "through-line" ticket guaranteeing her uninterrupted passage over its various connecting bus lines from Trenton, New Jersey, to Washington, North Carolina. And they had broken their contract. That, of course, was precisely what the Southern Railway had done to Mama and Grandma two years earlier.

That pained me, on one hand, but it drove me, too, as I seized upon the chance to right the wrong I'd been so powerless against just two years earlier. Julius and I were ready, now, to unleash an attack on segregation in the field of bus travel using the same weapon Belford Lawson had employed when he'd argued Elmer Henderson's case before the ICC and the Supreme Court: the Interstate Commerce Act, with its prohibition of "undue and unreasonable prejudice." Those words held a world of justice in their bosom, if only they could be tapped. It was time, we believed, to go after the carriers, and close the loophole left by the *Morgan* ruling.

As Sarah Keys departed for Fort Dix and her father returned to North Carolina and left Julius and me to our strategizing, the Supreme Court was docketing the public school cases that would force the Court to confront, once and for all, the underlying premise of segregation and overturn it. Not a single one of the five cases collectively known as *Brown v. Board* even raised the issue of whether the black schools were equal to the white schools. That was now immaterial. The entire NAACP Legal Defense Fund team was preparing to argue what Nabrit had argued all along: it was segregation that was wrong, demeaning, damaging to the self-esteem of the black children, detrimental to their ability to learn, and a violation of their right to "equal protection" under the Fourteenth Amendment. What the Supreme Court would say about that argument, no one knew. Just about every lawyer in America was trying to second-guess Chief Justice Fred Vinson and his eight colleagues as we edged toward the opening of the Court's October 1952 term, but the truth was that not even King Solomon himself could have read the minds of the men who were about to confront that fundamental question.

Still, *they were considering it.* For the first time since the *Plessy* ruling had come down in 1896, there existed the possibility that the Fourteenth Amendment might be restored to its original vigor, that its "equal protection" clause might be lifted up out of the mire of "separate but equal" and be understood as a guarantee of true equality, the kind that could only be realized in an integrated society. And if the Fourteenth Amendment were so construed, the Interstate Commerce Act would follow.

That was no idle dream on our part. The Supreme Court itself had opened the door to that line of thinking in a 1941 railway segregation case known as *Mitchell v. United States*, in which it had tied the Fourteenth Amendment and the Interstate Commerce Act tightly together. What the one did in the realm of state action, the Court had said, the other did for the motor carriers of America. In 1941, of course, both were understood to permit segregation. But the key, for us, was that the connection between the two had been plainly laid out.

It was a connection so central to our own argument that Julius and I scrutinized every word of the *Mitchell* decision, which fascinated me in particular for its personal echoes. The truth is I have yet to encounter a petitioner in the lines of any Supreme Court civil rights decision who doesn't rise up out of the text and reach out to shake my hand in the way of a trusted ally accompanying me into battle, and *Mitchell v. United States* was no different. I felt as if I'd actually met the powerful black Chicago congressman named Arthur Mitchell who'd filed the case, so closely did his political life and fortunes parallel those of the distinguished older brother of my childhood mentor Edythe Wimbish. Like Christopher C. Wimbish, Jr., Arthur Mitchell had migrated to Chicago from the Deep South and been catapulted to political power by the votes of the thousands of blacks who'd poured into Chicago along with him during the Great Migration of the 1920s. A Democratic party wheel and a prosperous lawyer, Congressman Mitchell wasn't one to take the insults of segregation lightly. When an Arkansas train conductor evicted him from a Pullman car on the strength of the state's segregation law and forced him to move to the Jim Crow coach despite his first-class ticket, Mitchell filed a complaint not only with an Illinois court but with the Interstate Commerce Commission as well. He alleged that the railroad's treatment of him violated the nondiscrimination clause of the Interstate Commerce Act, which the commission was charged with enforcing.

And he and his attorney went one step further: they cited the Fourteenth Amendment, and they argued that the railroad had denied Mitchell "equal protection" of the law. The commission, to no one's surprise, would have none of it; true to their racist history, they held that the railroad was well within its rights in enforcing state Jim Crow laws. Given the infinitesimal number of Negro passengers traveling first class, the commissioners told the congressman, it was unfair to expect any railroad to go to the trouble and expense of creating Pullman accommodations just for them.

The Supreme Court came down hard against the ICC's point of view, ruling that Arthur Mitchell's first-class ticket had without question entitled him to Pullman accommodations equivalent in every way to those it provided white passengers. Equality, the Court said, mattered a great deal. And it mattered for every single individual, regardless of whether his situation was utterly unique or representative of the plight of thousands. The *Mitchell* case was, in its language, a magnificent ruling, yet it was so limited in its practical effects that it had barely raised a whisper when it came down in 1941. It helped so few blacks and threatened so few southern whites that no one except Arthur Mitchell and his lawyer and a handful of constitutional law professors paid much attention to it. Yet the quietest case can bellow when it is resurrected in its proper time, I discovered. The Court had linked the Interstate Commerce Act to the Fourteenth Amendment, and in so doing it had given Julius and me a foundation upon which to build, now that the Fourteenth Amendment stood to be purged, at last, of the "separate but equal" concept. And every court in America would have to attend to that, including the one where we filed Sarah Keys's claim.

Just which court that would be, Julius and I were not sure. For all the merits of Sarah's claim, the question of jurisdiction was such a thorny one that it consumed us, initially, more than the outline of the case itself. To go south—presumably to North Carolina, where the incident had occurred and the Carolina Trailways line was based—was to face certain loss. I knew that even before I got a look at the transcript of the preliminary hearing in Roanoke Rapids and saw the testimony of the white policeman, the bus dispatcher, and the female ticket agent, all painting our client as a cursing, wailing rabble-rouser who so threatened the citizenry of Roanoke Rapids that she needed to be hauled off to jail and incarcerated overnight. I'd lived in the South such "witnesses" inhabited, and so had Julius, who hailed from a little Georgia town outside Atlanta and had grown up in Tennessee. We'd be lucky to get out of North Carolina alive, much less with an equitable ruling. But in the District of Columbia, the location where Sarah had transferred from her northern to her southern bus line, we confronted a challenge of another sort: neither carrier was based in Washington, but only ran their buses into and out of the city's main terminal. That ought to qualify as "doing business" by any reasonable definition, Julius maintained, but still, knowing how ripe the situation was for buck passing, we gave the matter close scrutiny. And we discovered that in one respect, at least, Sarah had perhaps been fortunate. She'd been traveling north to south, a fact that in the strange and ever-shifting world of 1952 race relations gave her a slight advantage.

From the beginning of time—which is to say, within my grandmother's memory—northern carriers, in the interest of "peace and good order," had segregated black passengers boarding railroad cars and buses in the North to avoid the necessity of seat changes as the vehicles crossed into Jim Crow states. But in 1949, that picture had begun, very quietly, to change. The Pennsylvania Railroad stopped cooperating with Jim

Crow, allowing its black passengers to sit where they pleased when they boarded in the North and guaranteeing that they would not be forced to move to the Jim Crow coach when they crossed into Dixie. The Southern Railway had, miraculously, chosen to honor the original seat assignments made in the North when black passengers transferred to its lines from the Pennsylvania Railroad. It was true that no court had mandated that change in policy; it had resulted from pressure by the NAACP and the Congress of Racial Equality. Still, the practice was suggestive—or at least we hoped it would be in a court of law—of responsibility on the part of a northern carrier for what happened to its passengers as they transferred to Dixie lines in Jim Crow states. We could with reasonable justification, we concluded, sue both the carriers that had transported Sarah Keys. Both had wronged her—the northern line for selling her a ticket and failing to deliver her safely to her destination, the southern line for evicting her and having her arrested without cause. The two lines connected in Washington, DC. Therein lay our argument for jurisdiction in the federal district court in the District of Columbia.

Once we established that, we moved fast, and we moved aggressively, demanding a jury trial and hitting the bus companies on four counts, at ten thousand dollars per count. We sued for breach of contract of interstate passage; for violation of the Interstate Commerce Act's ban on "unreasonable prejudice"; for the false arrest that had violated Sarah's right to equal treatment under the Fourteenth Amendment; and for the mental anguish she'd suffered as a result of her exposure to "ridicule, contempt . . . and grievous indignities."

And then, having served papers on both bus carriers at the Safeway Trails DC office, we contacted the press. It was a bold move for a couple of nobodies like Julius and me, a move I doubt I would have made if I'd been left to my own devices. But Julius never would let me just *be*, even at the beginning of our practice, and he pushed, hard: *now* was the time, he said, to raise our profile, to put the word out, to let the entire black community know what we were taking on. The winds were blowing our way, up in the Supreme Court, and we must take advantage—or rather, *I* must, since I was the one with the "connections." On that score, he was right; everything about the case seemed to circle back, one way or another, to my army career, and I did in fact have a contact, through my WAC colleague Irma Cayton, to the *Pittsburgh Courier*, where her husband, Horace, had long held a prominent editorial position. It was Horace Cayton's presence at the *Courier*, the country's premiere black paper, that I believed had been so persuasive to the army authorities when Irma and I telegraphed Dr. Bethune about the segregated dining at Fort Des Moines. I had no intention of trying Sarah Keys's case in the press, I told Horace, but I did have a matter I thought would interest him.

Indeed, it did. "Jailed WAC Sues: $40,000 Damages Against Bus Firms," read the headline of the *Courier* article that ran the day after we'd served papers on Safeway Trails and Carolina Trailways. Over the years, the *Courier* had trumpeted dozens of such claims. And yet ours, I believed, was different—not in its particulars, which were all too common, but in its timing, coming into being as it did at almost precisely the same moment as *Brown v. Board of Education.*

Ever since our graduation from Howard, Julius and I had tracked every move, every shift, every communication from or about the high Court through Professor Nabrit and Professor Hayes, both of whom were on the legal team arguing the public school cases. One by one, as summer rolled into fall, those cases were docketed for hearing in the Supreme Court: *Brown v. Board of Education*, the case from Topeka, Kansas, in behalf of the plaintiff Oliver Brown, whose name would become synonymous with the entire cause of desegregation; *Briggs v. Elliott*, the case from Clarendon County, South Carolina; *Davis v. County School Board of Prince Edward County*, the case from Virginia. They'd finally emerged from the shadows of the lower courts, along with the one I'd tracked most closely, the District of Columbia case Professor Nabrit had taken from Charles Houston upon Houston's death in 1950 and shepherded to its final incarnation as *Bolling v. Sharpe*, with a new group of plaintiffs. Chief Justice Vinson himself had requested that Professor Nabrit bypass the U.S. court of appeals, where *Bolling* was pending in the fall of 1952, and petition the high Court to hear it along with the school cases from the states. Nabrit did so, and in the same week in November that Julius and I filed our claim in behalf of Sarah Keys, the Court accepted his petition. Immediately thereafter, the justices took the case from Delaware, *Belton v. Gebhart*, and scheduled oral argument in all five cases to begin on Tuesday, December 9, 1952.

I'd watched that day coming toward us since my first hour in Professor Nabrit's classroom back in 1947. As the *Bolling* case solidified in the months after my graduation, I'd quietly cheered as Nabrit vaulted out ahead of the other lawyers on the public school cases with his unadorned assault on segregation. He'd jettisoned all the old equalization arguments as he moved *Bolling v. Sharpe* through the lower courts, laying the burden of proof upon the government of the District of Columbia to demonstrate that there was any reasonable justification whatsoever for segregation. He'd quoted the Supreme Court's language in the Japanese wartime internment cases damning racial distinctions as tolerable only under conditions that posed a threat to national security. To deprive black children of their right to an education was to punish them as though they were criminals for the mere accident of their birth, Nabrit had argued, taking a position no other lawyer I knew would have dared to espouse. It was *the federal government itself* which had committed the criminal act of punishing innocent citizens, he told the court, the federal government which had denied the black children of the District of Columbia their right to due process under the Fifth Amendment, in the same way that the Jim Crow states were robbing them of equal protection under the Fourteenth.

While Marshall and the rest of the Legal Defense Fund team continued to hedge their arguments almost to the moment they went before the Supreme Court in December of 1952, Nabrit pressed forward alone. And because he'd mounted his case right in my section of Anacostia, I took in every detail. It was at the historic Campbell AME Church, formed as an offshoot of my own Allen Chapel AME, where the families involved in *Bolling v. Sharpe* had begun in the fall of 1950 to hold their strategy sessions. There, Dr. Nabrit had teamed up with Campbell's pastor, the Reverend Samuel Everett Guiles, and together they'd mapped out their moves in behalf of the lead plaintiff, Spottswood Bolling, the child whose name headed the list of the black pupils refused admission to the brand-new all-white Sousa Junior High School. All of Anacostia—from my teenage Sunday school pupils at Allen Chapel to the greyest great-grandparent—had thrown themselves into the fight, but I daresay no one regarded it in quite the same way I did as I watched the professor I so revered leading my neighbors and their minister to the Supreme Court.

Now, as the *Bolling* case took its place on the Court's calendar along with the four state cases, Dr. Nabrit reached out like the teacher that he was, favoring Julius and me with two "day passes" to the Court for the ninth of December, when Thurgood Marshall was scheduled to argue the South Carolina case. Nabrit was well aware of the fight I'd launched in the matter of Sarah Keys, with its intimate connection to the issues before the Supreme Court in the five school cases. When he offered Julius and me an invitation to watch Thurgood Marshall's oral argument as his special guest, I could not bring myself to protest, nor to question why he'd deemed Marshall's argument more important for me to hear than his own. I just gave thanks for my extraordinary good fortune in securing two of the coveted tickets as well as a ride to the Supreme Court, courtesy of Walter Leonard. Walter drove a taxi, in those years, in addition to his two or three other part-time jobs and college night courses, and his offer to Julius and me on that historic occasion was to guarantee us delivery to the Court's main entrance opposite the Capitol, in plenty of time to take our seats in the gallery before Marshall took the floor in the South Carolina case, *Briggs v. Elliott*. Given the crowds of lawyers, reporters, law students, tourists, onlookers, and gawkers outside the Court that day, front-door service was a bonus indeed.

Only the Divine Hand could have made a parking space anywhere near One First Street, Northeast—the address of the Supreme Court—on December 9, 1952. Miraculously, Walter found an open spot behind the Court, and we pulled in. With that kind of luck, I told him, we might make a pass at having him seated in the gallery.

"He's with me," I told the guard checking visitors into the gallery, handing over to Walter the briefcase that had been my graduation gift from Miss Neptune. Miraculously, the guard waved us through, and we took our seats with the two or three hundred others fortunate enough to have gained entrance to the proceedings. It was a moment Walter Leonard and I would relish many times in the years following, as he rose to become a law professor and eventually assistant dean of Harvard Law School. That day provided him a series of small miracles relative to *Brown*, Walter liked to say, chief among which was the distractedness of the guard who took two tickets from three visitors and in so doing provided a would-be lawyer with an hour that would inspire him for a lifetime. I, of course, watched with a lawyer's eye—a lawyer trained by the men seated alongside Marshall or directly behind him, a lawyer who'd lived all thirty- eight years of her life under Jim Crow and now looked analytically at the mechanics of its impending demolition, a lawyer who had a specific and immediate stake in the proceedings because at that precise moment she herself had a case at bar whose outcome hung upon the decision that would emanate from this oral argument.

But I must confess to a simpler perspective as I watched the nine robed justices emerge from behind the velvet curtain and take their places at the bench, heard Chief Justice Fred Vinson read out the full caption of the South Carolina case, followed Thurgood Marshall's movements as he rose from counsel table (all six feet two inches of him) and strode forward toward the bench. I watched this, I frankly own, with the eye of a child, and a young one at that, with all the awe that frame of mind implies.

There are those, I know, who may find that perspective naïve, given the history of the Court which now confronted the question of segregation's inherent wrongness. I was, of course, thoroughly acquainted with that history. But I was also the granddaughter of Rachel Graham, and along with my grandmother's rage and indignation at racial oppression, I'd breathed in her faith in the possibility of justice. Perhaps because Grandma was to me the law incarnate, I was forever to regard every courtroom, and certainly the highest court of the United States, with something bordering on reverence, not for what it was, but for what it stood for and might become.

Marshall, too, moved and gestured and spoke like a man who expected the full measure of justice the United States Constitution owed him and every other black person in America, and he wasn't going to leave the Court till he got it. From the moment he started to speak, he dominated the chamber, dominated it with his voice and the largeness of his person and his absolute certainty about his mission. As with a scythe, he cut away any lingering notion on the part of the justices that he might possibly have come before them, this day, to press as he had in the past for the mere equalization of facilities. Let there be no doubt, he told them, about what he now demanded for the children of School District 22 of Clarendon County, South Carolina, and by extension for their fellows across America: equal protection of the laws, now denied them by segregation. That was their right—their "personal and present right," he said—under the Fourteenth Amendment, and to deny them that right was to harm them irreparably, permanently, unconstitutionally. Not even the appellees, he told the justices, had tried to deny that segregation was injurious to a child's mind. For the Court to approve it was to act in direct opposition to the Fourteenth Amendment, to its intent, the reason for its passage, its very purpose as a shield for individuals against the vicissitudes of the states.

Again and again, Marshall returned to that theme, to his fundamental premise, laying the amendment's equal protection clause over the facts of the situation that obtained in the Clarendon County public schools, laying it on with deftness and surety. How simple it all seemed, in his expert hands, that laying on of the law, in a way that put me in mind of my mother, down on her knees with her old dress patterns, smoothing them out over a bolt of wool or crepe or cambric, pinning them in place over the shapeless goods spread out before her, in the certain knowledge that with care and precision they would yield up something altogether new, and perfect.

So Marshall did with the words of the amendment, and he did not deviate from his position, even after Justice Frankfurter began grilling him on the particulars, whirling in his chair and firing with each whirl yet another question, pushing and probing and pressing. If anything, Marshall drove harder under the bombardment from the bench, engaging Frankfurter in a parry and thrust that was like a dance—the short little justice, feisty dog that he was, raising every imaginable pitfall to Court-mandated desegregation, and the tall, lanky attorney, direct and plainspoken and downright friendly, for all the profound seriousness of the matter before the Court, answering him.

No, Marshall told Frankfurter in response to his question on whose problem this was, the integration of the schools was *not* a matter for the state legislature. It was a matter for this Court, because it concerned the rights of individual persons, something the Court had upheld over and over again. And no, it was not relevant to the issue at hand that southern school districts might try, as Frankfurter suggested, to evade a Court mandate by "tricks" like gerrymandering. There was but one question before the justices, Marshall said, and that was the one he'd raised at the beginning of the hour: could the Supreme Court, the place to which men looked for the protection of their individual rights, now turn from that fact and leave the matter of education to the southern legislatures? They could not, he told them. Yes, undoing decades of segregation was a tough problem. But it was one that had to be faced.

Would that I could have returned to the Court the next day to hear Marshall deliver the rebuttal that would go down in the history books as one of his finest speeches before the Court. Even in print, it made me want to stand and shout right along with him the challenge he laid before the justices on the morning of the tenth of December: this was their problem, he told them. He had come for justice to the place that was obligated to deliver it to him and to every other individual seeking his rights: the Supreme Court of the United States. They were the ultimate authority.

My maternal grandmother, Rachel Bryant Graham, as a young woman, circa 1895.

"Grandma Rachel," circa 1925, as I remember her from my girlhood years.

My mother, Lela Bryant Johnson, whose vision set me on my way to Spelman College, circa 1940.

The father I barely knew but whose life inspired me always: James Eliot Johnson, shortly before his death in 1919 in the influenza epidemic, when I was five years old.

On the occasion of my baptism in July 1914 by my grandfather, the Reverend Clyde L. Graham, pastor of East Stonewall AME Zion Church in Charlotte, North Carolina, the church in whose bosom I was reared and to which I returned in my retirement in 1996.

My Spelman College professor and mentor, Mary Mae Neptune, as I remember her from my college years, 1934–1938. In her final letter to her students, she spoke of a world "where every child would always have justice among his fellows."

Proudly serving as an army recruiter in Ohio during World War II, as one of the first forty black women selected by Dr. Mary McLeod Bethune for officer training in the newly created Women's Army Auxiliary Corps.

With Dr. Bethune at a WAAC luncheon, circa 1944. Credit: Photographs and Prints Division, Schomburg Center for Research in Black Culture, The New York Public Library, Astor, Lenox and Tilden Foundations.

On the occasion of my graduation from Howard University School of Law, May 1950, by which time I had already undertaken my first case, a civil action against the Southern Railway for racial discrimination against my mother and grandmother.

On the steps of the Supreme Court of the United States in October 1955, after my admission to the Court, with my first law partner and role model, Julius Winfield Robertson (standing behind me), and Miss Mary Emma Pipes and her friend.

In Washington, DC, circa 1963, not long before I took on the greatest criminal case of my career, the *United States v. Raymond Crump, Jr.*, in which I won acquittal for the little man accused of the murder of Washington socialite Mary Pinchot Meyer.

With the Reverend James A. Williamson, on the steps of my beloved Allen Chapel AME Church shortly after the completion of the structure we proudly call "the cathedral of Southeast Washington." Allen Chapel was my home from the time I arrived in Washington in 1947, and I served as an associate pastor there from my ordination in 1961 to my retirement in 1996.

Outside the U.S. District Court for the District of Columbia, circa 1985.

Yet those nine faces remained inscrutable—even Frankfurter's, for all his questioning. No one knew—and Lord knows Julius and I entertained Walter with extensive speculation on our cab ride back to the office—just what lay behind Frankfurter's barrage of questions. Certainly he was intensely interested; I'd known that ever since my third year at Howard, when he'd sent his law clerk, William T. Coleman, to the LDF's dry runs of the graduate school cases in our moot courtroom. What Frankfurter himself actually felt was uncertain. I wanted to believe, and so argued to Julius and Walter, that Justice Frankfurter was forcing out into the open every conceivable objection his brethren on the Court might be quietly harboring, in order to give Marshall a chance to answer those objections. There was no doubt that Marshall had brought the Court to a point of reckoning, and from that simple fact, I derived a large measure of hope. But none of us really knew what reservations, what concerns, what prejudices lay behind the unreadable masks the justices wore in the Court.

What was painfully clear, however, upon our return to the office that evening was the downward turn our fortunes had taken in the matter of Sarah Keys. The papers from the Court awaited us as we walked in the door: Carolina Trailways, Sarah Keys's southern carrier, had refused the summons we'd served upon them at the DC office of Safeway Trails. They were a Virginia corporation, their affidavit stated, with principal offices in North Carolina, and they had no relationship to Safeway Trails. Our service of summons within the District of Columbia had, therefore, been improper. We'd hoped that a common-sense definition of "doing business" in the District of Columbia would prevail. Clearly, it hadn't, at least so far as the Dixie carrier was concerned.

How we scrambled, then, Julius and I, in those weeks before Christmas, holing up in the Howard law library on weekends in search of precedents we could use to weave a net around the northern bus line. Neither of us had the time for that kind of legal research, but we filed for an extension and we made the time, splitting the job between us, trying to make up for the gaping hole that remained now that the bus line whose driver had personally committed the wrongdoing had disappeared from the case. The bus company's humiliating treatment of Sarah had been the basis upon which we'd hoped to appeal to the sympathy of a jury. Absent the human question, the fine points involved in the application of the Interstate Commerce Act were unlikely to carry the day with twelve ordinary citizens unschooled in transportation law.

As it turned out, we never had the chance to find out what a jury would or would not have done. Citing the language on the ticket itself, as well as their own "public tariff" provision, the northern bus line washed its hands of the entire matter. Their tariff, they argued, approved by the Interstate Commerce Commission, plainly indicated they bore no responsibility beyond their own lines for anything except baggage. Whatever happened to a passenger on a connecting line was the passenger's problem. The U.S. district court agreed with Safeway Trails, declared Sarah's complaint outside their jurisdiction, and on February 23, 1953, they dismissed the case.

It is one thing to understand, as a lawyer, the basis for an adverse ruling on jurisdictional grounds. It is quite another to explain it to the client, to whom the entire matter is ever so personal. When Julius and I phoned Sarah with the news, she was crushed. She spoke quietly, just as she had in our first meeting, but her voice shook with anger. And though I tried mightily to calm her rage, I understood it. She'd been cheated—cheated of her seat, cheated of her right to due process in being jailed, cheated of her twenty-five dollars in being forced to pay a fine for a crime she hadn't committed. And now, having brought her case before a federal court, she'd been cheated by what she saw as a legal trick.

For Julius and me, the district court's ruling hit with a different sort of force. It robbed us of any prospect of satisfaction in the court system, and left us with an option no black attorney would ever have chosen to present to a black client: the Interstate Commerce Commission.

Since law school, I'd known about its unyielding position on segregation, and now that every other choice had dropped away, the particulars rose up to declare themselves with great specificity. In the sixty-six years of its existence as the federal enforcer of the Interstate Commerce Act, the commission had ruled so consistently against black travelers when they'd protested Jim Crow that it had become known as "the Supreme Court of the Confederacy." Even with a client as totally committed as Sarah Keys, the odds were overwhelmingly against us.

But Julius and I couldn't walk away, any more than we could turn our backs on the dozens of smaller wars we'd been waging every day since we'd set out in practice, wars that many of our colleagues saw as doomed. It was said, back then, that no black client stood a chance with a black attorney in a personal injury matter before the white judges of Washington, DC, but Julius chose to plunge ahead anyway, quitting his night job at the post office in the winter of 1953 and throwing himself into trial work. It was time for me to do the same, he urged, time for me to get into the courtroom with him, to do what he said I was born to do.

Somehow, Julius saw in me talents and gifts I couldn't see in myself, saw me as the lawyer I could become as opposed to the greenhorn that I was. He was a mentor among mentors, a man with the rare ability to relate to a woman as an equal. I well knew that there were those who regarded our unusual partnership with a skeptical eye, and some few who believed there was more between us than a professional bond. Those whispers of romantic involvement stung, but they were so far from the truth that I gave them little thought. Julius had no patience for small-minded courthouse gossip of any type, and he never dignified the idle talk with a response. Always, he was concerned that I be accorded equal status right along with him among our colleagues. "What *difference* does it make that you're a woman, D.J.?" he'd ask me whenever he saw me reacting to an innuendo by some colleague suggesting that perhaps I had no business at the bar. "You're a damned good lawyer!"

I took to heart that vote of confidence coming from someone I considered a master advocate, and concluded it was indeed high time I joined him in full-time practice and quit the Labor Department. The first chance Julius got, he pushed me forward before judges and juries to try cases. He cast a long shadow, but I was eager, too, and when an aggressive developer named Waverly Taylor set about to seize the land upon which stood the historic Garfield Junior High in my own beloved Anacostia, I was the one to take him on. No one touched my neighborhood with impunity, I told Julius. I was pretty nearly irrational on the subject of Anacostia, and even after I moved across the river to be nearer the courts and my office, I continued to worship at Allen Chapel AME Church, and to teach Sunday school there. Allen Chapel had pulled me into a network of religious folk so wide that a weekend seldom passed that I wasn't invited to speak at one church gathering or another.

As for the schools, I looked upon them as would a woman who had fifty children, and when the overcrowded and understaffed Garfield school looked like it might go under, I'd headed up an emergency brigade of parent volunteers to work alongside the teachers. I wasn't about to let the entire school property slip into the hands of a builder who'd break it up into tiny parcels and sell it off, as Mr. Waverly Taylor

intended to do. Just as the DC board of education was about to ca-
pitulate to Mr. Taylor, I managed to halt his scheme with an injunction
from the court. From that case came dozens of others, at such a rate
that by the spring Julius was able to combine our partnership profits
with his own funds to acquire a building through his great friend and
real estate investment colleague Ernest Eiland. What a proud day that
was, when we hung out our shingle at Julius's building at 1808 Eleventh Street, Northwest. After two years of working almost around the
clock on cases, we were positioned to throw ourselves into the cause of
taking Sarah Keys's case before the ICC.

Julius and I set out, in the matter entitled *Sarah Keys v. Carolina
Coach Company*, to force the ICC to look with a new eye at the act
it was charged with implementing. This was a fight entirely unlike our
daily skirmishes in the DC courtrooms. It was an intellectual battle
with a federal administrative body over the meaning of four words in a
statute—a statute which regulated the lives of hundreds of thousands of
black travelers, and which had, up until now, humiliated and degraded
them. It was time, we believed, to subject the act's language forbidding "undue and unreasonable prejudice" to the same kind of intense
analysis the Supreme Court was bringing to bear upon the Fourteenth
Amendment's "equal protection" clause.

The same month that Julius and I set out to frame our case in behalf
of Sarah Keys, the Supreme Court trained the microscope more closely
upon the Fourteenth Amendment than it ever had before. Or, to be absolutely precise about the matter, the high Court demanded that Marshall and his Legal Defense Fund team train *their* microscope upon the
amendment. On June 8, the Court announced it was postponing judgment in *Brown* until it could hear a second round of oral argument on
certain questions concerning the original intent of the Congress that had
passed the Fourteenth Amendment and the state legislatures that had
ratified it. Had they understood it as a guarantee of integrated schools?
And if that question yielded no definitive answer—public education
was after all in a rudimentary state at the time of the amendment's passage—what then had the Congress and the states taken it to mean?

From all around the country, Marshall recruited historians and Fourteenth Amendment scholars for the epic research task upon which the
Brown ruling was, as it now appeared, going to rise or fall. He also
telegraphed an urgent request for money to every NAACP office in the
country: the Legal Defense Fund had exhausted its resources, he said,

and required donations on an urgent basis, lest the entire *Brown* effort be forced to fold. Upon our receipt of that notification from Frank Reeves, who headed Washington's NAACP office, Julius instituted a fund-raising program right at 1808 Eleventh Street. Robertson and Roundtree, he announced to each client who appeared at our door, was mounting a drive to help fund the public school segregation cases, and every client would be assessed one dollar. Knowing Julius's flair for the dramatic, I shouldn't have been surprised to see a photographer from the Washington bureau of the *Afro-American* show up at the office to shoot pictures of the kickoff of our fund-raising drive—a kickoff we staged on the spot at Julius's desk, with Julius and me and our secretary, Mr. Haywood Johnson, all ceremoniously dropping bills into the collection box, flanked by a group of clients. It was the sort of display that would inspire people when they saw it in their newspaper, Julius said—shame them even—and when it came to the matter of integrated schools for his four children, Julius was not above shaming the rest of the community into digging deep into their pockets.

And so, while a veritable army of scholars convened at the New York headquarters of the Legal Defense Fund, a fund now perhaps a hundred dollars richer for the efforts of Robertson and Roundtree, Julius and I embarked on a research journey of our own, into the history and the thinking of the Interstate Commerce Commission. If we could somehow manage to wrest from them a ruling on Jim Crow in bus travel, the effect would be far-reaching, given the agency's powers. It was not only the watchdog over interstate travel, but the enforcer as well, and once it issued a decision, it generally followed up with specific regulations to make sure that the carrier in question complied with that decision.

Yet we nearly despaired at the world of hardened prejudice inside the vast stone edifice on the corner of Twelfth Street and Constitution Avenue that housed the ICC's headquarters. There had never been a complaint about Jim Crow in bus travel, but the dockets we studied on the matter of train travel painted a grim picture. No black plaintiff had ever managed to find anything close to real justice before the ICC, not even citizens as prominent and well represented as Congressman Arthur Mitchell, with his 1937 complaint against Jim Crow seating for first-class Pullman passengers, or FEPC representative Elmer Henderson, when he'd protested the Southern Railway's dining car segregation policy five years later. Mitchell and Henderson had been forced to go to the Supreme Court for the limited satisfaction they finally won.

I'd paid more attention, earlier on, to the high Court's handling of those two cases, but now, in anticipation of taking on the ICC, I dug deeper into the commission's rulings, at the actual language that had supported their denial of claims that seemed to have such merit. Individual rights, at least for black passengers, had counted for nothing when the commission evaluated Arthur Mitchell's complaint. It acknowledged that he'd been discriminated against, as a first-class ticket holder forced into a Jim Crow coach, but it ruled that such discrimination didn't matter. So few blacks traveled first class that the railroads couldn't reasonably be expected to provide equality for them.

Not even Supreme Court rulings—with the exception of *Plessy v. Ferguson*, which the commission relied on consistently—appeared to carry much weight with the ICC. When Elmer Henderson came before the commissioners for the second time in 1946, citing the high Court's ruling in *Mitchell*, they brushed it aside as irrelevant. They also turned their backs on the Supreme Court's decision in *Morgan v. Virginia*, which held Jim Crow laws an undue burden on interstate commerce, and therefore unconstitutional, because of the constant seat-changing those laws necessitated for black travelers moving in and out of southern states. Again, the ICC sided with the carriers. They declared that *Morgan* pertained only to *state* Jim Crow laws, not railway segregation rules, which were the actions of private businesses and thus beyond the reach of the federal government.

They'd even opposed the solicitor general of the United States when he entered an appearance on Elmer Henderson's behalf in the high Court. And when the Court finally overturned the ICC's decisions, the commissioners continued to dodge, construing the Court's decisions in *Mitchell* and *Morgan* so narrowly that in practical terms, almost nothing changed for black travelers. Against such an agency, we stood no chance at all, standing alone.

But we were not alone. The presence of *Brown* before the Supreme Court made our fight before the ICC worth every hour of our time, and Sarah's. The public school cases, grounded upon the same premise Julius and I were advocating, stood to transform our complaint about a single bus incident into a case the ICC would be forced to regard with the utmost seriousness. From September 1, 1953, when Sarah Keys became the first black petitioner ever to bring a cause of action before the commission on a bus travel matter, we marched in step with *Brown*. In December, we followed the second round of oral arguments in the school cases with *Keys* uppermost in our minds. And in May, when we went before the ICC for our evidentiary hearing, it was the clarity of those oral arguments, and the one we'd heard Marshall deliver a year earlier, that steadied us amid the welter of vitriol and inconsequential detail that swirled around us in the hearing chamber when the bus company's chief witness—the driver M. E. Taylor—took the stand.

Mr. Taylor argued loudly, and at some length, that Sarah had been occupying not the fifth seat from the front as she contended, but the third, and on the other side of the bus to boot. It was, of course, a matter of complete indifference to everyone but him, since both seats were in the white section, but he pressed the point with hearing examiner Isadore Freidson as though his very life depended upon the examiner's accepting his version of the facts. Carolina Trailways' attorney, Frank F. Roberson, of the prestigious Washington law firm of Hogan and Hartson, grilled Sarah, hard, under cross-examination about how she'd behaved when she was barred from boarding the second bus. Hadn't she, in fact, cursed? Hadn't she shouted, as the driver and dispatcher contended? Hadn't she threatened to make a test case of her situation? Sarah, calm and exquisitely polite and ever so military in her WAC dress uniform, quietly made a mockery of the bus company's characterization of her, as much by her manner as by the content of her answers. She made me proud that day—proud to be a WAC, representing another WAC who took the uniform and her service as seriously as I myself had.

But the truth was that Sarah's reaction to the driver's conduct had no bearing on our case. It was segregation we were attacking. Only three facts were relevant to that attack, and no one disputed them: Carolina Trailways had a Jim Crow rule that governed the seating of passengers; their drivers were authorized to impose it; Sarah had been directed to move to the back of the bus solely because she was a Negro. Had Sarah complied with the bus driver's order to change seats, he told the hearing examiner, "everybody would have been happy and we would have went on our journey."

Everybody, of course, but Sarah. Her happiness was immaterial in the bus company's scheme of things, grounded as it was on a set of assumptions at once twisted and dehumanizing. Carolina Trailways' Jim Crow rule and the hundreds of carrier rules just like it rested on the lie that segregation did not constitute discrimination, that the notion of inferiority was a delusion, that the law was powerless to guarantee true equality. That was the lie we sought to destroy in *Sarah Keys v. Carolina*

Coach Company, and five days after our evidentiary hearing before the ICC, the Supreme Court of the United States empowered us to do so.

There are times when the world, after interminable waiting, changes in a single moment. Monday, May 17, 1954, was one of those times. When the Supreme Court's new chief justice, Earl Warren, began reading the decisions in *Brown v. Board of Education* and the DC case of *Bolling v. Sharpe* a few minutes before 1:00 PM that Monday afternoon, "separate but equal" was the law of the land. When he finished reading a few minutes after 1:00, it had been obliterated. All the agony that followed in the wake of that historic ruling, including the agony of our present-day struggle to fulfill its promise, has not diminished what the Court did that day. Justice showed its face in that half hour of time, and those of us who sat in the court chamber listening to Warren reading the words of the *Brown* decision recognized it for what it was: the truth, uttered unapologetically, putting to rest at last the lie of *Plessy*.

Warren's voice, deep and husky and filled with authority, held me fast as I sat with Julius and Walter, honored guests once again of Professor Nabrit, waiting, watching, just as he and Thurgood Marshall and Professor Hayes were, for an outcome none of us could predict. Nothing in Warren's methodical march through the history of the Fourteenth Amendment betrayed the direction of his thinking on the case, and I remember feeling scared, just plain scared to death, that the Court, having been cornered in precisely the way we had wanted for so long, might in the end choose to uphold *Plessy*, and in so doing, strengthen it.

Through the list of hideous rulings birthed by *Plessy* Justice Warren moved, and then onward to the graduate school cases of my law school years, *Sipuel* and *Sweatt* and *McLaurin*, which had dealt with inequality but had not required the Court to address the premise of *Plessy* directly. Now it was being asked to do just that, he said, and as he came to the essential question before the Court, the already hushed chamber grew absolutely still. "Does segregation of children in public schools solely on the basis of race, even though the physical facilities and other 'tangible' factors may be equal, deprive the children of the minority group of equal education opportunities?" the chief justice asked. And then, after a pause, he answered, "We believe that it does."

A very quiet but audible sigh rippled through the rows of listeners. I, too, sighed, and closed my eyes. A great heaviness lifted from me at that moment. As Warren moved forward to take *Plessy* head on, I felt the ugliness that had shadowed my life from childhood draining away. The cuts and the hurts and the signs, the words of the trolley car driver in Charlotte, the shouts of army officers separating me from my fellow officers, the terror of the night in the Miami bus station—all of it evaporated. I felt as though I was being born again. I *was* being born again, and so was every other black person in America. The chief justice of the Supreme Court of the United States, speaking with all the authority of his station, was overturning *Plessy*. The wrong of segregation, Warren proclaimed, lay in what it did to the *spirit* of black children, to their sense of themselves, to the feeling of inferiority it created in them. That feeling was not, as *Plessy* had held, a mere creation of the black psyche. It was real. And it did grave and permanent harm to Negro children. "To separate them from others of similar age and qualifications solely because of their race," he said, "generates a feeling of inferiority as to their status in the community that may affect their hearts and minds in a way unlikely ever to be undone."

Their hearts and minds. Who would have thought to hear such language in a court of law? And yet the chief justice used it, supporting it with the testimony of the Topeka, Kansas, case, and sweeping onward to the legal ramifications of that psychological reality. Rejecting the language in *Plessy* that contradicted the conclusions he'd just set forth, Warren announced that he and his eight brethren—*the entire court*—were banishing the legal underpinning of segregation as unconstitutional. "We conclude unanimously," he declared, "that in the field of public education the doctrine of 'separate but equal' has no place." Somewhere behind me, I heard muffled sobbing, but it might just as well have been cheering, for the joy it betokened. None of us had dared to hope for a unanimous ruling on this, the most controversial of all cases, and the implications of the Court speaking with one voice on a decision of this magnitude were stunning. "Separate educational facilities are inherently unequal," Warren said. "Therefore, we hold that the plaintiffs and others similarly situated for whom the actions have been brought are, by reason of the segregation complained of, deprived of the equal protection of the laws guaranteed by the Fourteenth Amendment."

He came, then, to the case that in my mind would always be first: Professor Nabrit's District of Columbia case, *Bolling v. Sharpe*, which had paved the way for the four state cases with the antisegregation argument the other lawyers had avoided making right up until they went before the Court in December 1952. Grounded in the Fifth Amendment rather than the Fourteenth as the state cases were, it required the Court to issue a separate ruling. Would that I'd been able to see Professor Nabrit's face, instead of the back of his head, as the chief justice spoke of liberty, of what it really meant, of its reach beyond "mere freedom from bodily restraint." Quickly, but pointedly, Warren touched on the Japanese wartime internment cases Nabrit had invoked in his brief, and then, at last, he swept up *Bolling* in the same stream of logic he'd applied to the four state cases, declaring it "unthinkable" that the Constitution would impose a lesser duty on the federal government than it did on the states. What was intolerable in the states under the Fourteenth Amendment's equal protection clause was equally intolerable in the District of Columbia under the Fifth Amendment's guarantee of due process. Segregation was an "arbitrary deprivation of liberty," he concluded, and therefore unacceptable under law.

The Court had chosen. What they had written across the face of the Constitution was not a reiteration of the *Plessy* doctrine that said *"all men are equal, but white men are more equal than others."* Instead, with a single unanimous voice, they'd declared that the words of the founding documents meant what they said. Before the law, *all men* were equal.

No one could fail to understand that simple, unequivocal declaration. Certainly the southern states instantly grasped its import, roaring back at the Court with disgust and contempt and threats of noncompliance in the days following the announcement of the ruling. It would be more than a year before the Court took on the overwhelming question of how *Brown* would be implemented, how millions of white and black children in the segregating states would actually be commingled, how the dual school systems that had coexisted for decades would be merged and the custom of two centuries erased without bloodshed. The matter of "implementation"—a task that requires the changing of hearts and minds—tears us asunder even now. But on the matter of the law, there was clarity. The Court saw to that. Lest anyone mistake its legal intention, the high Court roared again, one week after *Brown*, nullifying segregation in a series of unanimous decrees that extended the school decision to golf courses, public housing, and amusement parks. At least, those decisions sounded like a roar to my ears, attuned as I was to all matters that potentially touched upon the case of Sarah Keys. Taken together with *Brown*, those rulings amounted to what Julius and

I saw as a mandate—a mandate the Interstate Commerce Commission couldn't afford to ignore, as it had so many other Supreme Court rulings. *Brown* had restored the equal protection clause of the Fourteenth Amendment to its original meaning, reducing to ashes the notion of "separate but equal" that had for so long crippled it. The Fourteenth Amendment, of course, did not govern the Interstate Commerce Act directly. But the Court had wedded the meaning of the act so tightly to the amendment in the *Mitchell* and *Henderson* rulings that there could be no doubt, now, of the interpretation of the nondiscrimination language in the act: it must be taken as a ban on segregation. So Julius and I argued in the brief we filed with the ICC on June 17, just a month after *Brown*. It could "no longer be doubted," we said, invoking the school segregation cases as our primary authority, "that any regulation requiring segregation of passengers in interstate commerce on the basis of race is not only unreasonable but unlawful."

When the Interstate Commerce Commission speaks, as it did in the matter of Sarah Keys on the last day of September 1954, it does so very quietly. No crowds gather in the hallways, as they do on the occasion of great Supreme Court cases, to await the issuance of decisions, nor in fact does anyone actually report to the hearing chamber at all. The ICC's rulings arrive by mail, to be perused and digested by the lawyers and their clients in the peace of their offices or homes. It had not occurred to me until Julius and I ripped open the envelope containing the decision of hearing examiner Isadore Freidson in the case of *Sarah Keys v. Carolina Coach* and saw its first paragraph that privacy is on certain occasions a gift from on high. To have heard Mr. Freidson's words read aloud in open court, or even in an examiner's chambers, would have stung too hard.

"The examiner finds that Carolina Coach Company, a motor common carrier of passengers, in interstate commerce, has not subjected complainant, a passenger on its line, en route from Trenton, N.J., to Washington, N.C., to any unjust discrimination or undue and unreasonable prejudice or disadvantage, in violation of the Interstate Commerce Act, and that the complaint should be dismissed."

What followed in the six pages of justification for the decision stunned Julius and me almost as much as the ruling itself, with the ICC's reliance on its own findings, its own body of precedents, its own conclusions dating back to its beginnings in 1887. As I made my way through the tangled web of Freidson's argument, I felt as I had when I first read *Plessy*. The decree was devoid of logic, and the only truth it recognized was that of long-standing tradition. "From the beginning, the Commission has interpreted the Interstate Commerce Act as not prohibiting carriers . . . from requiring separation of white and Negro passengers," Mr. Freidson wrote, buttressing his argument with nineteenth-century ICC decisions that predated *Plessy*, and even by the commission's 1947 ruling in *Henderson*. The fact that the Supreme Court had overturned the ICC in *Henderson* three years later was something the hearing examiner chose to ignore. When he did invoke the high Court, in the *Morgan* case, he construed its finding in such a way that it supported, rather than undermined, the carriers' right to impose Jim Crow upon its Negro passengers. *Morgan* applied only to the states, he said, adding that until Congress passed a new law outlawing segregation in interstate transportation, "carriers are free to adopt reasonable rules and regulations for the conduct of their businesses, including those relating to the seating of white and colored passengers." Carolina Coach Company's segregation requirement was, he asserted, "entirely reasonable," a statement which made me grateful that Sarah Keys was not at that moment sitting in the office with Julius and me. That phrase insulted her intelligence, and ours. But more than anything else in Mr. Freidson's proclamation, the most devastating was the position he took on *Brown*.

Brown didn't matter, he said. It was irrelevant to the instant case. "The segregation which the Supreme Court has condemned in the *Brown* and companion cases concerns only the field of *public education*, a State activity," he wrote. "Such decision does not preclude segregation insofar as the conduct of a *private business* is concerned, as, for example, a carrier engaged in the for-hire transportation of passengers. Thus, the recent rejection by the Supreme Court, in respect to the issue of public education, of the doctrine that the races may lawfully be separated, if substantially equal facilities and privileges are afforded Negroes and white persons, in no way affects or prohibits separation or segregation of the Negro and white races insofar as transportation is concerned."

What stood, untouched and untouchable, were the bus company rules reserving to Carolina Coach Company "full control and discretion as to seating of passengers," and empowering it to enforce Jim Crow seating. "White passengers will occupy space nearest the front of the bus," the rule read, "and colored passengers will occupy space nearest the rear of the bus." These rules, Mr. Freidson noted, had been "followed continuously" since the time of their passage, invoking them as if they were Holy Writ.

To every young lawyer who foolishly regards justice as a foregone conclusion, there comes sooner or later a moment of chastening. Mine came on the day we received Isadore Freidson's ruling, and forever after I took nothing for granted before a judge or jury or hearing examiner, no matter how overwhelmingly meritorious I believed my claim to be. I learned then what the great lawyers who argued *Brown* had understood even in the midst of their joy at the Court's ruling, that the words of *Brown* standing alone were in the end simply words, until they were pressed into service.

In my anger, I sought out Professor Nabrit, who told me that I *should* be angry, that the ICC's ruling was in fact personal to me, inasmuch as the Constitution applied to each person individually. "But you have to move past your anger," he counseled, "or it will consume you."

I was not able to do that, until much later. I managed in the short term, however, to turn my entire attention to the urgent task at hand. Unless Julius and I filed exceptions within twenty days, one man's opinion would become a decree that would freeze Jim Crow in interstate travel for the foreseeable future—and not only in bus travel. Railway segregation, too, was under review by the ICC. Three months after we'd filed our complaint in *Keys*, the NAACP had come before the commission seeking a blanket order that would outlaw segregation on thirteen southern railway lines and in the waiting rooms and terminals that serviced them. They'd fared no better than we had at Mr. Freidson's hands. As Julius and I rushed to meet our deadline for submission of our exceptions, I reached out for help from Sarah's congressional representative, Adam Clayton Powell, through my Spelman sister Dr. Grace Hewell, who was a long-time member of the church Powell pastored in New York City. The congressman was so outraged by Freidson's indifference to the *Brown* ruling that he telegraphed ICC Chairman Richard F. Mitchell and demanded Freidson's removal. But even if Chairman Mitchell took Powell's demand seriously, Isadore Freidson was only a hearing examiner. Our case would be made to the eleven commissioners.

For all our uncertainty and our sense of isolation, we weren't without resource. No lawyer ever is, provided he can elucidate the precedents that help his cause and discredit those that work against it. Julius and I had spent the better part of two years digging through transportation law, and now the time had come to deploy everything we'd unearthed and meld it with *Brown*. Our primary weapons were the Interstate Commerce Act and the commerce clause of the Constitution,

either one of which had the potency to carry the day if we had anything remotely resembling a fair hearing. The act had taken on an entirely new meaning in the wake of *Brown*. We'd said that before, of
course, but we would say it again to all eleven commissioners, this time
more explicitly, citing *Mitchell* and *Henderson*, which had linked
the interpretation of the act's ban on "undue prejudice" so closely to the
Fourteenth Amendment's guarantee of "equal protection." As for the
commerce clause, it reached into places Mr. Freidson had failed to acknowledge in his reading of the *Morgan* case, which he saw as pertinent only to the states. The clause spoke to all manner of burdens upon
interstate commerce, we believed, and we had unearthed a 1949 circuit
court case that said so. *Whiteside v. Southern Bus Lines*, it was called,
after the black Kentucky woman named Elizabeth Whiteside who'd refused to obey a driver's order to move to the back of the bus taking her
homeward from Missouri and sought redress when the driver evicted
her. The three judges of the sixth circuit court where she'd brought her
complaint found that such a seat change, imposed by a private carrier,
was as much a burden on commerce as a state Jim Crow law. It was
true that the ruling extended only to the four states in the sixth circuit,
but its logic added clarity and power to our argument.

Our brief spoke with the combined force of every voice we summoned
up in our litany of citations. The "Exceptions to Proposed Report and
Order" that we filed on October 19, one day before the deadline, put
the ICC on notice that Sarah Keys and the four million other black
citizens who'd been shoved to and fro and evicted from buses across
America now demanded the full measure of justice due them under an
Interstate Commerce Act that could be understood in no other way than
as a ban on "separate but equal."

We began at the beginning, with the Jim Crow regulation that examiner Freidson had cited as inviolable. It was a law that robbed Sarah
Keys of her right as a passenger in interstate commerce to proceed to
her destination undisturbed, a right the *Mitchell* and *Henderson* cases
had established for each person individually. Carolina Coach's rule and
the hundreds like it engendered a state of complete disorder in the conduct of travel across the forty-eight states. The repeated seat changes,
the arbitrariness of enforcement, the disruption of travel, the impossibility of determining by mere skin tone who was a Negro and who was
not: these were the things that had so offended the Supreme Court that
it had banned the states from imposing their laws on interstate travelers

in *Morgan*. In the weeks after the *Morgan* ruling, every Dixie carrier had rushed to enact its own rules to insure that segregation continued undisturbed. It was time, Julius and I argued, for logic and consistency to prevail. If the Constitution's commerce clause was offended by the chaos resulting from the imposition of state Jim Crow laws upon interstate travel, it was equally offended by the chaos carrier rules produced. "Can the regulation and rules of a carrier have more potency than a law of a sovereign state?" we demanded. "We think not."

We turned, then, to the matter of segregation itself, to the wrong that had been done to Sarah by the act of singling her out solely because of her race. Even before *Brown*, the Supreme Court had condemned such conduct in the cases involving the internment of Japanese citizens during World War II. It had found racial distinctions of the sort the United States government had imposed upon the Japanese to be acceptable only at times of extreme emergency, when the country's safety and security were at stake. These cases had held pride of place in the argument Professor Nabrit had made before the Supreme Court in *Bolling*, and Julius and I invoked one of them now, quoting the words of the justices in *Hirabayashi v. United States*: "Distinctions between citizens solely because of their ancestry are by their very nature odious to a free people, whose institutions are founded upon equality," the Court had said. "For that reason legislative classification or discrimination based on race alone has often been held to be a denial of equal protection."

And so it should be now, we said. Now, in *Brown*, the Supreme Court had spoken without equivocation, condemning racial discrimination per se, so plainly and so forcefully that there could be no mistake about the meaning of the Fourteenth Amendment with regard to race, and thus, of the Interstate Commerce Act.

Lest any one of the eleven commissioners mistake *Brown*'s essence in the way Mr. Freidson had, we took it upon ourselves to spell it out, to shine the light upon the words of the decision in a way that clarified its reach. It had to do with a fundamental constitutional principle, and that principle extended far beyond the single area of public school education into every area of public life in America.

"It is submitted that what the Supreme Court did say in the 'segregation cases' was that enforced separation generates a feeling of inferiority, stigmatizes those persons segregated and calls attention to their inferior status . . . In any reasonable interpretation, it is logical to assert that the Supreme Court has decided that segregation per se in fields affected with a public interest subjects the person segregated to an unreasonable and constitutionally forbidden discrimination." No longer was it possible to construe the Interstate Commerce Act as had been done under *Plessy*, we maintained; the Supreme Court had "specifically relegated the doctrine of 'separate but equal' to limbo" and so now must the ICC.

With that, we rested our case. We were demanding that the commission do what they'd resisted doing for the sixty-six years of their existence. They must, we asserted, protect the rights of travelers as much as they did the rights of the conveyances upon which they traveled. They must condemn the conduct of drivers who isolated and bullied passengers for no other reason than the color of their skin. They must declare that segregation, standing alone, amounted to unjust discrimination and unreasonable prejudice against Sarah Keys and members of her race, and that such discrimination and prejudice worked to the disadvantage of any Negro traveler.

That the commission saw fit, on November 7, 1955, to do precisely that, to condemn "separate but equal" in the very field where it had begun, made me proud beyond the telling. One year after Julius and I filed our exceptions, the ICC ruled in the matter of *Sarah Keys v. Carolina Coach Company* and in the companion case the NAACP had brought against segregation on railroads and in terminal waiting rooms, *NAACP v. St. Louis–San Francisco Railway Company*. In both rulings, they interpreted the Interstate Commerce Act as a prohibition upon segregation itself, and stated in *Keys*:

> We conclude that the assignment of seats in interstate buses, so designated as to imply the inherent inferiority of a traveler solely because of race or color, must be regarded as subjecting the traveler to unjust discrimination, and undue and unreasonable prejudice and disadvantage. In addition to the discrimination, prejudice and disadvantage resulting from the mere fact of segregation, additional disadvantage to the passenger is always potentially present because the traveler is entitled to be free from the annoyances which inevitably accompany segregation and the variety and unevenness of the methods of its enforcement.
>
> We find that the practice of defendant requiring that Negro interstate passengers occupy space or seats in specified portions of its buses, subjects such passengers to unjust discrimination, and undue and unreasonable prejudice and disadvantage, in violation of Section 216 (d) of the [Interstate Com-

merce Act], and is therefore unlawful. An order will be entered prohibiting the continuation of such a practice.

The commission went further still, extending their ruling beyond the vehicles themselves into the area southerners regarded as private ground—the bus and train stations and the waiting rooms therein. Julius and I were astonished; we had not, after all, demanded an order of that reach. But the NAACP had. In its railway case, it had taken the position that the terminals functioned as such an integral part of the interstate transportation system serviced by the railroads as to be inseparable from them for legal purposes. The ICC had agreed, and when it joined our case with the NAACP's, it made it clear that its reasoning extended to *Keys* in every particular. In so doing, the ICC had reached beyond the matter of seating on vehicles into the heart of every southern town and village and outpost. Wherever an interstate bus or train stopped to discharge or pick up passengers, white and black must be permitted to share the same space, to sit alongside each other on the same benches, to wait in the same lines, to use the same restrooms. The ruling, of course, did not affect travel *within* each of the southern states; that realm would remain untouched until Rosa Parks defied the Jim Crow laws of the city of Montgomery, Alabama. The *Keys* and *NAACP* rulings also exempted restaurants in the bus and train terminals from their desegregation orders, since they were privately owned businesses. But its potential impact on the vast interconnected web of interstate travel was enormous.

The ICC had also done what the Supreme Court had declined to do five months earlier when it issued its open-ended ruling regarding the implementation of *Brown*: it had set a firm deadline, and a short one. There was no indulgence of the sort the Court had shown the southern states with its suggestion that they proceed "with all deliberate speed" to effect school desegregation "as soon as practicable." The segregating states had six weeks from the publication of the decree on November 25, 1955, to comply with the *Keys* and *NAACP* rulings. By January 10, 1956, the ICC ordered, all Jim Crow seating on interstate buses and trains must cease, and all signs separating waiting rooms into "Colored" and "White" sections in the terminals serving those buses and trains must be removed.

Newspapers around the country hailed the ruling as a legal breakthrough. "ICC Orders End of Segregation on Trains, Buses—Deadline January 10," the *New York Times* announced. *Newsweek* called the

Keys case "a history-making ruling," and Sarah herself, in a piece in one of the New York papers on Thanksgiving weekend, spoke of the ruling as "the greatest thing for me and my people."

More than any other single statement, the words of the renowned *New York Post* columnist Max Lerner touched me most deeply. Dismissing the "blustering" of the diehard politicians from the Deep South who'd begun threatening litigation or flat-out noncompliance, Mr. Lerner spoke of what he felt, as a white person, in the wake of the ICC rulings:

> The Negro traveler will now have the freedom to ride (on train or bus) and the freedom to wait (in waiting rooms and at stations) as a human being along with other human beings. These freedoms are now added to the slowly-accumulating list of other hard-won freedoms.
>
> Together these victories, won and still to be won, add up to the greatest issue of freedom and the greatest challenge to conscience in our generation. I don't mean that the struggle for labor rights, or for religious freedom, or for freedom of the press and speech are unimportant. They are a part of an indivisible web. But in our time the fight for Negro rights has engaged the bitterest resistance and hostilities, and has become the great test for the nation. That is why I light a candle in my heart with the knowledge that white and black alike, we can now ride together across the state lines of 48 states. The name of Sarah Keys is now added . . . as a symbol of a movement that cannot be held back.

And yet, that movement *was* held back, by forces and individuals none of us could have imagined as we celebrated the triumph of *Keys v. Carolina Coach Company.* How could Julius and I have known that the seventy-seven-year-old South Carolina Democrat J. Monroe Johnson, who'd been the lone dissenter in the *Keys* ruling, would shortly advance to the chairmanship of the ICC and do everything in his power to prolong its segregationist tradition? Julius and I were, after all, only lawyers, not prophets, and even if we'd been aware of the intentions of Mr. J. Monroe Johnson, we would have been powerless to neutralize them. And there were thousands of J. Monroe Johnsons across the South, then, more than I had been willing to acknowledge. America, in truth, was not yet ready to bury *Plessy.*

Six years would pass before the Interstate Commerce Commission acted upon the promise of *Keys,* and in those six years, the country would see violence on a scale none of us thought possible in 1955. It would require the singular courage of Rosa Parks, refusing to obey a Montgomery bus ordinance one week after the *Keys* decision was made public, the birth of a nationwide civil rights movement led by the Reverend Martin Luther King, Jr., two more rulings by the Supreme Court in the field of bus travel, an invasion of the Deep South by the students who called themselves the Freedom Riders, and the intervention of the Department of Justice and the attorney general of the United States to bring about the change we believed we had won before the ICC on November 7, 1955.

9. AT THE THRESHOLD OF JUSTICE

It was in the end not simply bloodshed or mass protest or fear that brought the promise of *Keys* to fulfillment. It was shame. The whole world looked on, and was horrified, at the image of the Freedom Riders' bus bursting into flames on a highway outside a little Alabama town called Anniston on May 14, 1961. And the whole world—at least the world that was reached by television—saw the young men and women, black and white, stepping out onto bus platforms in Birmingham and being met by mobs of cursing Klansmen armed with clubs and chains, being beaten and bloodied long before they even reached the restaurants and soda fountains they were bent on integrating. It seemed to me there wasn't a politician in the North who didn't raise an outcry, nor a preacher, anywhere, who didn't join the Reverend Martin Luther King, Jr., in condemning the violence.

Attorney General Robert F. Kennedy confronted the ICC, cited *Keys*, and pressed them to deliver on it. For six years, the commission had dodged the enforcement of its own ruling, but there was no dodging the Department of Justice. The ICC capitulated, issued regulations banning Jim Crow from buses, trains, and stations, and began enforcing them. And so it ended—not the hatred, nor the violence, but the fact of segregation on the buses and in the terminals and restrooms and eating places that serviced them.

In the six years that separated *Keys* from the day in September 1961 when the ICC finally acted in accordance with the order it had issued in 1955, I walked a path far removed from the firebombs of Anniston and the bloodied platforms of bus stations, and I became a different person, a different sort of lawyer, in fact, from the one who'd battled the ICC. I am not sure that I chose that path, so much as it chose me.

People chose me, people in real pain. And there were hundreds of them in the District of Columbia, more than I'd ever imagined until I started practicing law. The Anacostia River separated my home and my place of worship from the section of Northwest Washington where my office was located, but Southeast folk sought me out in such numbers I sometimes felt that 1808 Eleventh Street, Northwest, stood squarely in the middle of my old neighborhood of Garfield Heights. The clients came at first from Allen Chapel, and then, over time, from churches throughout the greater Southeast community, where I'd begun speaking to parents' associations and women's groups and all manner of gatherings, generally at the behest of one minister or another. Julius had a reach of a different sort, with his overpowering courtroom presence and his influence in the black community through the magazine he founded not long after we won the *Keys* case. *Stride,* he called it, and he wove his articles on politics and business and law with a kind of social gospel that put me in mind of my grandpa's sermons.

In his direct and pragmatic way, Julius was saying through his magazine what I was telling my audiences in the churches: that black folk were on the march forward to a new era. So Dr. Bethune had said right up until the time of her death in 1955, but now, in the wake of the Montgomery bus boycott that had followed the *Keys* decision, there came the voice of Martin Luther King, and with it, a force for goodness that promised real transformation. The Supreme Court had acknowledged the "hearts and minds" of little children in *Brown,* but it was powerless against the vitriol of the white southerners who were fighting school integration. King spoke directly to that, preaching a gospel of peace and nonviolence that moved me so deeply that his thinking, and even his words, wound their way into my own speeches. I'd begin by talking about the law, but before I finished I'd find myself speaking in a different vein, about education, and opportunity, about parenthood and its sacredness. I reached out to people, and they felt it.

To our doorstep came clients who were hurting in every way human beings can hurt—mothers fighting for their children, fathers fighting for their jobs, teenagers who'd been preyed upon by the adults charged with their care, husbands and wives in bitter child custody battles, victims of violent crimes, like twenty-one-year-old Barbara Vanison, whose husband had broken out of St. Elizabeths Hospital, a federal psychiatric facility in Anacostia, and come after her with a hatchet. He had fractured her skull in such a way that she'd suffered brain damage, the full ramifications of which remained unclear. That made the mishandling of the matter at St. Elizabeths all the more appalling, in our view. Their psychiatrists had determined that Barbara's husband was of unsound mind upon his admission to the facility in 1954. They'd been well aware that he'd threatened his wife and mother-in-law, and yet they'd moved him from a maximum to a minimum security ward. When he'd escaped, they hadn't notified police or made any effort to apprehend him.

For all the assistant U.S. attorney's efforts to minimize the negligence at St. Elizabeths, the facts carried the day with federal judge Ross Rizley, who awarded Barbara Vanison twenty-five thousand dollars in damages. Ten times that amount would have been insufficient in our view, but it was the maximum allowable in the District of Columbia under the Federal Tort Claims Act at that time, and the verdict gave people hope—not only clients, who saw that Robertson and Roundtree would fight negligence cases themselves instead of referring them "uptown," but our fellow attorneys as well. We'd proven something every black lawyer had wanted to believe, and now could: that we had a fair shot at winning damage awards before white judges, if we worked the cases expertly enough. Our colleagues began phoning for advice, and Julius and I began holding after-hours seminars on personal injury law. The office became, in the wake of the Vanison verdict, a hub for a new generation of black lawyers eager to prove the old way wrong.

I reveled in the teaching of law, and even more in the mentoring of younger lawyers who looked to me for guidance. How, I asked myself, had I moved out from under the wing of giants like Professor Nabrit and Professor Hayes to imagine I could coach any attorney about anything? At the age of forty-five, I hardly felt the "senior" lawyer, but I discovered to my deep satisfaction that Julius and I had accumulated enough know-how, at least in the area of personal injury law, to begin that greatest of all tasks: passing it on. The teaching stretched us, but it also fed our spirits as we fought to do justice to the clients whose problems often overwhelmed us. We had journeyed ever so far from the mountaintop of civil rights law, where statutory and constitutional principles governed the fray, to a place much closer to the ground. I often had the sense that the two of us had tapped into some deep well of hurt to which no one had paid much attention, and having touched it, watched it burst forth with an unimagined force.

The clients Julius and I faced, day to day, were men and women at the extremes of the human condition, not only victims like Barbara Vanison, but those on the wrong side of the law, people who'd committed terrible crimes—assault, arson, and even murder. Each time such a client sought our help, Julius and I confronted a reckoning with ourselves and our belief in a legal system whose greatness lay in the right it granted each person to a fair trial. I believed in punishment for crime; this was the legacy of my childhood, of my grandmother, of my religious faith, and I was never to wander far from that conviction. Yet I also believed in the possibility of redemption, even for persons whose actions I found reprehensible. Again and again, I found myself struggling to reconcile my duty with my faith, my legal perspective with my heart. On matters involving a client's mental state, I looked to the expertise of Howard psychiatrist Alyse Gullattee. My new pastor at Allen, the Reverend A. J. Hayman, became a touchstone of wisdom for me in the thicket of criminal defense work, as did the formidable Dr. Charles W. Green of Pilgrim Baptist Church, where I often spoke. Julius, with his unerring moral compass and his abundant common sense, had a way of clarifying even the most complex situations, and when he and I turned away a client for ethical reasons, we did so together.

Still, I wrestled constantly with a feeling of insufficiency, and nowhere more than in what the romanticists call "matters of the heart." The Barbara Vanison case had seasoned me in a way no young attorney would wish to be seasoned, with the knowledge of the very worst that is possible when an unstable situation goes unwatched. True, Barbara's husband was of unsound mind, but even in the most seemingly "ordinary" divorce, I observed that hatred and love were twin passions, with all the volatility attendant thereto. I trained myself in the art—and it is unquestionably more art than science—of taking what I call a client's "vital signs," in the way a doctor would upon first seeing a patient. I learned to listen to what I *sensed* from husbands and wives embroiled in divorce and child custody fights, as much as to what I saw and heard, and hoped in that way to stave off disaster. But there was no remedy, legal or otherwise, for the ravages suffered by the little children who were the pawns when parents warred. To watch children ripped apart, wounded, abandoned, as I did so often in my practice, left me with a bitter sense of helplessness. I grew ever more agile in the courtroom, more adept in my legal machinations, but what overtook me more and more often was my powerlessness to fix what was truly broken.

In those last months of 1958, I longed for peace, and a little rest. I was ill, as ill as I'd ever been in adulthood, even during the brief periods when my diabetes had spiraled out of control. My doctor had diagnosed a fibroid tumor earlier that year, and with each passing month the symptoms worsened. I was thin and anemic, but once I learned the tumor was benign, I clung to that as an excuse to ignore the situation.

"I don't have time to be sick," I told my doctor each time he pressed me to undergo a hysterectomy. I refused even to contemplate postponing all my pending court matters and dumping my case load on Julius, who worked far too hard for his own good as it was, in my judgment. I sometimes wondered if he ever slept, given his court schedule, his *Stride* magazine production, and his family, whom he adored. Even after he managed to move them from the housing projects of Southeast into a lovely home on upper Sixteenth Street in Northwest Washington, he refused to cut back his schedule. I knew Julius worried terribly about his wife, Nellie, who suffered from epilepsy. He was constantly in search of better doctors, better treatments, new medications that might help her, and all that required money, as did the nursing and household help necessitated by her condition. Almost obsessed with Nellie's medical needs and his ambitions for the children, Julius drove himself to the point that I worried about his own health. No one in my experience except my grandmother worked that hard, and even she'd rested occasionally.

There was nothing for me to do as his partner but push forward and shoulder my share of the work, but the exhaustion nearly leveled me, sometimes right in the middle of a trial or a hearing, when my blood sugar would drop so low I'd have to excuse myself and leave Julius to finish. Reluctantly, I sought permission from the judges to carry a thermos of orange juice with me into the courtroom, and though most of them were kind and understanding, I shrank from having to request such an accommodation. I was a woman, after all, and though Julius maintained that my gender was irrelevant, I abhorred having to reveal any weakness to the white male lawyers whose respect I was still fighting to win. But diabetes is a relentless adversary, one I discovered was impervious to my stubbornness. I struggled daily with the worsening fatigue and the wild swings in my sugar levels, exacerbated, I was certain, by my gynecological trouble and my constant worry over one client or another.

I survived those months in the only way any of us ever survives such times: through prayer, and the goodness of friends. My circle was not vast, but it was filled with people of faith, and I kept them close. I'd moved across the Anacostia River to be nearer my office and the court-houses, and bought a cozy old Tudor house at the edge of Rock Creek Park with one of my neighbors from Garfield Heights, Gwen Heygood, and her mother, Mrs. Winslow. My home, so enshrouded in trees that it seemed a part of the park itself, was my haven during the week, and after church services on Sundays when the weather was fine we threw wide the front and back screen porches and the yard and held open house, generally with one of Gwen's musical relatives at the piano, and always with vast quantities of home-cooked food spread out on the dining room table. Cooking was then and still is my therapy, as sooth-ing for me as any medicinal balm. No matter how overwhelmed I was with my weekday troubles, I generally managed to beat them back over the stove, at least temporarily. Of course, the folk who filled my home fed me as surely as I did them—the Allen Chapel friends who made the trip "over the river" after services, my Allen pastor Rev. Hayman, and Dr. Charles W. Green of Pilgrim Baptist, who'd mentored and sup-ported me from the first time I'd addressed his church group. These wise and prayerful friends became mainstays for me, along with Gwen's family and my dearest colleague, Dr. Dorothy Height, with whom I'd begun working hand in hand as legal counsel when she took over the presidency of the National Council of Negro Women two years after Dr. Bethune's death. From such company I drew great sustenance.

Still, neither my closest friends nor my family knew how burdened I really was. I discussed my most worrisome cases with Julius and Dr. Gullattee, and my illness with Gwen and her mother when it became so grave I couldn't hide it any longer. But there was a deeper sense of unease I could share with no one, because I didn't understand it myself. I had experienced periods of nagging restlessness in my life, particularly after the war, when I was casting about for some way to enter the fight for civil rights and didn't know how or with whom to do it. This was restlessness of a different sort altogether. I could not put a name to the feeling, nor assign it a cause. Even in church, even in private prayer, even as I read scripture, I could not find that place so beautifully de-scribed in one of my favorite hymns:

When peace, like a river, attendeth my way,
When sorrows like sea billows roll;
Whatever my lot, Thou hast taught me to say,
It is well, it is well with my soul.

At no point in my adulthood had I been more involved in religious life; in fact, I was in one church or another whenever I wasn't in the office or in court. But peace did not attend my way, and all was not well with my soul.

So I kept rushing. That had been my answer to nearly every major crisis of my life, from my junior year at Spelman when my money was running out to my days at Howard when I'd despaired of mastering the law in the hours allotted to me. Racing came as naturally to me as breathing, and in the early months of 1959 I had every reason to race: Julius was overworked, our client load seemed to double weekly, our court calendar was booked with trials back to back, my church needed me, and so did the dozens of others across the city who were calling upon me to speak. I ran out of habit, partly, but also out of fear of that sensation that would not let go of me, that dogged me everywhere I went. Amid the noise of my life, the buzz of the office and the intensity of trial work, the ringing of phones and the voices of people perpetually crowding round me for help of one kind or another, I thought to drown out whatever it was that wouldn't let go of me.

But there are times, I know now, when God would have us be quiet, in order that we might hear what the Bible calls His "still small voice." That quiet came for me, at last, in the spring of that year, as I lay in Freedman's Hospital, forced by my illness to a complete halt. I'd begun hemorrhaging so badly the night before that Gwen and her mother had called an ambulance, and I was too terrified to protest. Not for one more hour, my internist Dr. Purcell told me, could I postpone the hysterectomy he'd been urging upon me for close to two years. Beside him at the foot of my bed stood surgeon Randolph Kelly Brown, his kind face filled with concern and frustration over the mess I'd made for myself, and for him, by refusing to take my illness seriously. My blood sugar was spiking, and then plunging; my heartbeat was arrhythmic; I was anemic and weak.

Would that I had the medical training to fully appreciate the miracle those magnificent physicians performed in bringing me through the surgery under such complicated circumstances, and straightening me out afterwards. For the two weeks I spent in Freedman's Hospital, Dr. Brown and Dr. Purcell hovered as close as my sister Beatrice, who arrived from New York on the night of the surgery and refused to leave my side. But brilliant as the doctors' ministrations were in healing me physically, in stabilizing my insulin levels and building up my iron-depleted blood, they couldn't minister to my overwrought mind. No one could. Bea had from my earliest childhood been able to divine my thoughts, but neither her voice nor Mama's and Grandma's on the phone penetrated the odd, unsettling restlessness that enervated me. Everywhere about me, there was noise. The hospital was filled with its own kind of din—the doctors' directives, the consultations, the evaluations with endocrinologists, the visitors who gathered round me, full of questions and concern, their presence a constant reminder of the work and the obligations that awaited me.

It required silence, silence without and silence within, for me to turn inward at last, and then having done so, to speak to someone about what troubled me. Precisely why I chose to discharge my mind to the Reverend Charles Green when he called upon me shortly after my hospital discharge to bless my recovery, I do not know. There are certain people, I believe, in whom we sense acceptance of our deepest selves, and Rev. Green was for me one of those people. Then, too, there are moments at which we simply have a readiness to reach out. There, in my study, with the warm breeze from the windows that opened onto Rock Creek Park working its cure upon me, and Gwen and her mother busy elsewhere about the house, the reverend and I chatted about church projects, about various members of his congregation at Pilgrim Baptist, about all manner of everyday matters, until at last I touched upon the heavy thing that had lain for so many months upon my heart.

"Rev. Green," I began, "I have something on my mind."

I paused, and he waited—a good long while, as I recollect, and with an expression of puzzlement at my hesitation, no doubt because it was my custom to speak rapidly and without groping for words. I pushed forward once again, still uncertain of my direction.

"It seems to me that the law is not enough for me," I said, "that there is something else . . ."

"Something else you ought to be doing?"

"Yes, but I don't know what it is. Once I wanted to study medicine, but it's too late now," I told him. "I wouldn't want to turn myself around like that."

Confused, I retreated from that line of thought, insisting that in point of fact I loved the law, that my partner and I had more clients than we knew what to do with, that no lawyer could hope for a more successful practice. And then abruptly, I blurted out, "What would you say if I told you I wanted to become a minister?"

My own words astonished me. In an instant, that which had been amorphous felt suddenly very near, very tangible, despite the fact that in the spring of 1959, full ministerial status in the African Methodist Episcopal Church was an impossibility for me or any other woman. There were hundreds of female preachers in AME congregations all over the country, but they had no standing beyond their local churches, and they were strictly limited in their authority even there. The bishops had not yet seen fit to grant women the right to be part of the AME's "itinerant ministry," to assume permanent positions in well-established churches, to pastor, to bless and administer communion and officiate at funerals and weddings. Each year, though, the push for full ordination grew stronger and louder nationwide, and many of the Allen congregation, including our pastor, believed it was an idea whose time had come.

My mind was not on church politics at that moment, however. Having articulated my soul's longing to Rev. Green, I now saw the ministry as something I wanted to pursue, at whatever level was open to me once I completed my training. And so apparently did he. Rev. Green was a man in the mold of Julius, of Professor Nabrit, and of my own pastor, Rev. Hayman; like them, he rose above small-mindedness and jealously and looked to the essence of people and ideas and movements. What I had said touched him deeply, I could see.

"Oh, I've been *following* you," he told me. "All this time you've been speaking, you've been preaching. You know that, don't you?" And he began to talk about how I'd touched people, people I hadn't even known, about the way his own congregation at Pilgrim Baptist flocked round after my speeches, how they felt lifted up. He spoke with such joy and such confidence and such enthusiasm about what he'd observed in me that although he seemed to be describing an entirely different person from the one in whose skin I lived, I felt emboldened to push onward.

I was frightened, I told him straight out, scared to death that people would laugh at me, the way I had laughed as a little girl at a woman in Grandpa's East Stonewall congregation who had taken it upon herself, with Grandpa's uncertain blessing, to mount the pulpit one Sunday and preach. Poor Miss Viola Davis had cut such a poor figure with her high, squeaky voice that my sisters and I snickered aloud until Grandma reached over and whacked us into silence.

Rev. Green listened with the utmost seriousness.

"Well," he said, "I don't laugh at you. And neither does anyone else."

Still, he acknowledged, it would not be without pain, this road I meant to walk. Great student of human nature that he was, Rev. Green cut straight to the difficulty I would face in undertaking the path to ordination.

"People will not readily accept this lawyer who is a preacher, this preacher who is a lawyer," he said. "People are not like that. They'll wonder, '*What does she want? What is she after?*' You must prepare yourself for that, and understand that this will be no easy thing, not for you, nor for the people you love. You must think further, and pray. And if, then, you are determined to go forward, I am in it with you, all the way. We'll go over to Howard, to the divinity school, I'll have you to meet all the great folk I know over there, and we'll get this going."

And with that, he stood up and reached out to touch my forehead and give me his blessing. I slept that night as I had not slept in a year or more, without the heaviness of spirit that I feared would never lift. In the morning, my thoughts turned, as they had at every crossroads of my life, toward home.

I would wish for each person the gift of a place in the world where the aching soul can rest, where the burdens of life fall away, where God is ever so near. The home of my childhood was such a place for me. My walk to the ministry had begun in Charlotte, in Grandpa's church, where Mama had sung in the choir and Grandma had baked the communion bread and starched the altar linens, and only with Mama and Grandma's blessing did I feel able to proceed. My mother, I knew, would support whatever I determined to do, but I was less certain of Grandma's approbation, given the reservations I knew she had about women preachers. What I hadn't told the Reverend Green about Miss Viola Davis was that my grandmother, in the privacy of the kitchen but well within range of my "little pitcher's ears," had said to Mama and Grandpa after church on the occasion of Miss Viola's foray into preaching, "Viola Davis is a good woman, but she's got no business in the pulpit." Even as a child, I sensed Grandma's objection had to do with more than Miss Viola's squeaky voice.

I let two days pass before broaching the subject of my ministry to her, during which time she hovered and fussed over me as she had during my childhood illnesses. Even at the age of eighty-five, she insisted on turning out hot food all day long, particularly when she had sick folk on the premises. The aroma of her cooking filled the entire house when I arrived, even the screen porch out back, which is where, on the third day of my visit, I finally spoke up.

"Grandma," I said, "I want to tell you something."

"Are you all right, Dovey Mae?" she demanded, turning to me. "Are you really getting well?"

"The doctor says I'm doing fine," I answered. "He wouldn't have let me come down here if I weren't."

That seemed to satisfy her, and I pressed on, posing the same question I'd put to Rev. Green.

"Grandma, what would you say if I told you I want to go into the ministry?"

She stopped so still that there was almost a sound in the stillness. We looked at each other in that loud silence for a long moment.

"Well, child," she said finally, "if you *don't* preach, you will die."

She turned abruptly and, without another word, she left the porch.

It would be years before I fully grasped the depth of her wisdom. In the moment, I was crushed. In fact, I cried afterward, standing alone there, I was so stung by her abruptness. I had wanted, in my naivete, an outburst of enthusiastic support, a hug, a few words of encouragement. But Grandma had understood as I had not, then, that any display of emotion would have belittled what God had ordained, and that when we tread on sacred ground, we gravely imperil ourselves.

Still, when I left Charlotte, I knew all was well. Though Grandma did not mention the subject of my ministry any further after our moment together on the porch, she spoke to Mama about it, and in so doing, gave her approval.

"Grandma told me something good about you," Mama said the next day, her face radiating joy. "Remember, you've been preaching for years. All you need to do now is what God wants, and not worry about what other people may say."

Thrice blessed, by Mama, Grandma, and Rev. Green, I embarked on what was unquestionably the most important journey I was ever to undertake, a journey that would profoundly transform me and the way I practiced law. Impatient as I am by temperament, I was nevertheless content simply to groom myself for the ministry, confident that in due course the AME Church would take the final step in granting women full rights as clergy and that when it did so, I'd be ready. In my evening classes at the Howard University Divinity School, where I enrolled immediately upon my return to Washington, the great professors who were carrying on the ninety-two-year-old tradition of that venerable institution poured their wisdom into me. I reveled in the study of scripture, of systematic theology, of homiletics and ethics and philosophy as one who had at long last found herself, her course, her mission. And among my closest friends, I found affirmation and support for the unconventional path I'd chosen—from Julius, from Gwen, from Dr. Dorothy Height, from the small circle of Allen folk in whom I confided, from my pastor, who astonished me by calling me up to the altar to preach even before I finished my first term at Howard, catapulting me forward on my path to ordination with a resounding vote of confidence.

I had no thought of darkness, that summer, despite the fact that much of what had propelled me toward the ministry was the terrible human pain I confronted on a daily basis. All was celebration, and peace, and tranquility as June rolled into July, July into August. Yet even as I gloried in my new vocation, I was moving toward a case that would challenge me to my very core spiritually and force me to a reckoning with my own limitations.

When first I met the client named John Pledger on an August afternoon at the close of that joyful summer of 1959, I sensed nothing of tragic proportions. I saw only a man in pain. For all the enormity of his person—John stood six feet tall and must have weighed nearly three hundred pounds—he struck me as fragile, like some small broken thing rather than the great hulking bear of a man that he was. I'd represented women so shattered by the dissolution of their marriages they were almost incoherent, but I'd never encountered a man quite so distraught as John Pledger was on that occasion. He spoke poetically of the love he had for his young wife, Zelma, and he impressed me with his determination to preserve their marriage and the home they'd made together. They had children to raise, he told me, their little boy, Vincent, two years old, and Peggy, his teenage daughter by a prior marriage. He'd met Zelma after his first wife died and had fallen madly in love with her. Her demand for a separation after only three years of marriage was something he simply refused to accept, something he felt he had to fight by every means available to him. He had come to me for legal help, he said, because one of his co-workers had told him I was "a lawyer who cared."

Many a client had said those words to me, and many would say it afterwards. I did care, probably too much for my own good, as Julius unfailingly pointed out to me whenever I reached out to some poor tormented soul whose legal prospects were dim and whose human prospects were dimmer still.

"Where do you *find* these cases, D.J.?" he'd ask me. What he really meant, of course, was "Why do you *take* them?" and to that I had no ready answer, except that if I believed I had it in my power to help a client, I couldn't turn him away. At the same time, I'd learned to be watchful in situations where emotions were as ragged as John Pledger's, particularly when I had facts before me, or even allegations, to suggest that all was not as it seemed. Zelma Pledger had claimed in her petition for separation that John had threatened her during one of their quarrels, and the record showed that twice in one night she'd been frightened enough to phone the police, who had arrested John for disorderly conduct, then released him. A mere charge of disorderly conduct did not necessarily bespeak danger, but the Barbara Vanison tragedy had forever colored my approach to every divorce matter involving the remotest hint of violence, and I pressed John hard, and repeatedly. Had he ever harmed his wife? Had he even threatened to hurt her? Had he ever said anything she might have construed as a threat?

He answered each of my questions in the negative. That his wife made him angry, even furious, he readily admitted. She had shamed him, he said, with her infidelity, and with more than one man. Why then, I asked him as gently as I could, did he wish to remain in a marriage with a woman he trusted so little? Would it not perhaps be better to accede to her request for separation, and build a family with someone else? He recoiled at that suggestion, insisting that Zelma, for all her flirtatiousness, was just young and unthinking. Men trailed after her because she was so young, and so beautiful, he explained, and she responded all too quickly. He was certain she'd come to her senses, given enough time.

"Lady," he said, "I love her. I love the ground where she walks. Will you help me?"

I could not turn away such a plea. If ever a person needed guidance through the thicket of divorce proceedings, it was John Pledger, and as I shook his hand and agreed to represent him, I took comfort in the calmness that seemed to have come over him during the hour or so we'd spent talking. I can't pinpoint the day when I first sensed that there was inside this tormented man something more than the pain of a wronged spouse, more than the insecurity I'd seen so often in middle-aged husbands struggling to hold the affection of much younger wives.

In the beginning, I reached out with all my heart to John, whom I saw as a man of great decency and honesty. I continued to urge him as I had in our first meeting to look long and hard at the relationship, to seek marital counseling, to weigh what was best for himself and his children. There was something pitiful about his naïve campaign to regain his estranged wife's affections, and I winced each time he arrived at the office lugging bags of gifts for her, peace offerings of expensive clothing and perfume I was certain were well beyond his means as a government security guard. That a mature person should behave in such adolescent fashion gave me pause. Yet he spoke so articulately and calmly about his twelve-year-old daughter, Peggy, and his little son, Vincent, conducted himself with such deference, such clarity and intelligence that it was not until we began preparing in earnest for the court hearing in December that I felt the first flicker of real unease.

Something far beyond ordinary pain and anger emanated from John when he touched upon the subject of his wife's infidelity, as he did with increasing intensity in our consultations that fall. The tender proclamations of love that had touched me in our first meeting became mixed with wild declarations of hatred—real hatred, of the kind that blotted out reason. Absent any firm proof, John insisted that Zelma had sought an abortion that summer when she'd become pregnant with their second child. The U.S. attorney's office had investigated the matter when he'd filed a complaint against the doctor in question, and had found no grounds for prosecution. But that carried no weight with John; he was utterly convinced that his wife had not, as she claimed, had a miscarriage, but rather that she'd ended her pregnancy in order to hurt him. He believed, too, that she had committed adultery with many men, men of all types, even taking up with her lawyer, he said. The more John railed about his wife, the wilder he became, and I began to fear that by the mere act of listening, I somehow fed his obsessive rage. Yet there was no pulling back, for me. Having entered my appearance as his attorney in a matter involving a court hearing, I had an obligation to continue to represent him. To have abandoned him would have placed him at a severe disadvantage. So I told Julius, when he broached the possibility of my withdrawing from the case as he observed John growing increasingly agitated that fall. John had not behaved toward me in any way that could remotely be construed as dangerous, nor had he deceived me, I pointed out to Julius, and absent those conditions, I was obligated to continue my representation of him.

That was true; I had a clear legal obligation in the case. But it was also true that I'd chosen to go well beyond my role as a lawyer with respect to John Pledger. He'd moved me so deeply that I'd bound myself to him as a human being, a friend, an adviser, a crutch, an ally and comforter, and in so doing I'd opened myself up to all the pain and turmoil of his poisoned relationship in a way that utterly drained and exhausted me. Such is the tendency of the novice counselor, to believe in one's power not only to help people, but to save them. This I attempted to do, ministering to John with all the fervor of my new vocation and addressing what I perceived was a spiritual question. No human being in the world, I told him, could control the mind and heart of another person, as he so clearly wished to do with his wife. Other people were not ours to own, and to try to swallow up a spouse in this way was wrong, unhealthy, destructive. On and on I went in that vein, and when he sat before me in my office John appeared to be paying the strictest attention to my counsel. It was when he left that the trouble started. He'd begin courting Zelma once again, reconcile with her, and pitch again into the poisonous cycle that tore him to shreds. I saw John's situation with great clarity: the mad possessiveness grounded in the insecurity of his age, the manipulative quality of the wife, the poisoned chemistry between them that drove John to a state of complete irrationality. Of this there could be no question, and sometime in the course of that winter, I began to understand that when it came to his wife, John Pledger was truly delusional. This was far worse than simple dishonesty; had I believed John lied to me about his treatment of his wife, I would have dismissed him, as I had other clients who'd misrepresented the facts. John was a deeply honest person, but he inhabited a world of wild imaginings about his wife, and in the grip of those imaginings, I believed he might in fact be capable of violence.

That was a dark winter, a time when I felt burdened not only by the Pledger situation but also by what I saw happening to Julius. He kept a schedule that no human being could maintain, and I worried constantly he would break down. There'd been no avoiding the burden he'd shouldered during my illness, but it seemed to me when I returned that he was pushing the limits even further. Despite the fact that Julius was the senior partner of our enterprise, I looked upon him as a younger brother, and treated him in just that way when I saw him acting against his own best interests. He needed to think of his own health, I urged, particularly in view of Nellie's medical condition. I prevailed upon him to consider what the children would do if anything happened to him; incessantly I urged balance, reasonableness, and moderation. It was so plain to me he was exceeding his limitations.

Yet such was my stubbornness that I couldn't see that same failing in myself, when it came to my emotional involvement in the Pledger matter. I rationalized that I had no choice, that given John's refusal to seek the psychiatric help he so clearly needed, I was all that stood between him and disaster. When at the December court hearing Zelma Pledger's attorney, Halcott Bradley, took the stand and testified that John had phoned him at home, accused him of adultery with his wife, and threatened to kill him, I shuddered. I knew Halcott Bradley to be a circumspect individual, a former policeman not given to exaggeration, and his testimony corroborated my worst fears: John was indeed capable of violence, not only toward his wife but also toward any man he believed was romantically involved with her, whether or not there was any factual basis for such a belief. I had no fear for my own safety, despite the fact that Dr. Gullattee warned me that John might in a fit of agitation turn on me. Rather, I clung to the belief that I represented a ballast for John, a calming influence, a voice of rationality as his world collapsed on him in the wake of the court's ruling in January granting Zelma her petition for separation and awarding her custody of little Vincent. Indeed, the court itself saw me in that light, and when Judge Frank Myers summoned me to his chambers, I felt the full weight of my obligation settling over me.

"Attorney Roundtree," he said to me, "you must keep careful watch over your client. That is your duty."

"Rest assured, Your Honor, that I am fully aware of Mr. Pledger's state of mind," I responded, "and I am talking constantly to him."

I never stopped talking to John, in fact, as he sank into despondency in the weeks following the ruling that was issued early in January. He had lost everything he loved except his daughter, Peggy, and I feared for his sanity. My task at that point, as I saw it, was to pull him back into the world, if I possibly could, to stand by him as a friend and bring him to an acceptance of the fact that his marriage to Zelma, so poisonous and destructive to his very being, was over. But John grieved in such an all-consuming way, and alternated so wildly between rage and quiet that I lived in outright terror. He began phoning me late at night, his voice always ragged with emotion, and although I dreaded the calls, I took them and stayed on the line for as long as John continued to talk, constantly attempting to soothe him, reason with him, guide him toward that well of rationality that I still discerned in him. Two or three times in the months following the issuance of the separation decree, he and Zelma reconciled, an eventuality I came to dread as much as I did their fighting, believing as I did that the two of them so inflamed each other that nothing but heartbreak could result from their living together. Still, when John called me a few days before Christmas to tell me that they'd reached a real understanding, that they'd arranged to go to New York together over the holidays and spend some time together without the children, I sensed a calmness about him I hadn't seen since our very first meeting. As I spoke with John that day, I wondered whether perhaps, at last, he and Zelma had somehow found a way to live in harmony together. I'm not sure that I actually held out any concrete hope for their long-term happiness, so much as I felt that I'd reached the end of my usefulness in the matter. This was a couple bound to each other in some way I could not fathom, and I felt there was nothing left for me to do but pray for them.

For the first time in more than a year, I felt a lightening of the ominous feeling that had shadowed me for so long where John was concerned. It was, I think, the reasonableness in his voice on the phone that quieted me during the holidays. At home with Mama and Grandma over Christmas, and then with Bea and her husband, Gene, in New York over New Year's Eve, my thoughts turned for the first time in ever so long upon joyful things, and with my family I celebrated the decision the AME bishops had made in May to grant full ministerial rights to women. Once I completed my two years of required preparation in the fall of 1961, I'd be eligible for ordination as an itinerant deacon, and two years thence, if all went well with my training and performance at Allen Chapel, I could advance to the status of itinerant elder, the highest level of clerical orders in the AME Church. Preoccupied as I'd been throughout the year with the Pledger matter, I had not paused to relish the historicity of the bishops' vote that stood to place me and thousands of other women in the ranks of the leadership of the AME Church. It was a breakthrough that capped decades of struggle by women who'd refused to settle for partial status in the church, and one at which Mama and Grandma and Bea rejoiced when I shared it with them.

Such was the rush of business and the start of the spring term at Howard when I returned to Washington after the holidays that I thought but fleetingly of John Pledger. John had promised to phone me upon his return from New York, and he'd always been perfectly punctual about such matters, so I had no doubt I'd hear from him in due course. Julius and I were moving at full tilt, as usual, after the quiet period of the holidays, and the two of us were scrambling so hard on our own cases that by the second week of January we hadn't yet found time to consult on several upcoming trials we were handling as a team. Given our tight schedule, Julius's proposal that I ride with him to the circuit court in Upper Marlboro, Maryland, when he picked me up on the morning of January 11 made perfect sense to me. He needed to access a property record at the courthouse, and he thought the drive would give us a chance to hammer out strategies in the peace and quiet of the car ride without the constant interruptions we had in the office. Accustomed as I was to Julius's method of meticulous analysis, I thought it odd that he jumped from one topic to another, fumbling and losing his train of thought. Julius was one to race from one thing to another, and when I saw how he dallied at the clerk's desk, it came to me that he was deliberately stalling for time.

It was late afternoon, perhaps 3:00 or so, by the time we arrived back at the office, and as we walked into the waiting room, a crowd of reporters converged upon us, firing questions at me about John Pledger. They had been told I represented him in a domestic dispute, they said, and they wanted to interview me. Julius took me by the arm and led me upstairs to our conference room, sat me down, closed the door, and began to talk to me.

At 9:00 that morning, he said, John Pledger had gone on a killing rampage. He had driven from his job at the Government Services Administration to the temporary building in the Main Navy yard where Zelma worked, and he'd killed her. Then he'd driven across town to the office of the doctor he believed had performed the abortion upon Zelma, and had shot the man to death. He'd also shot two men who worked in Zelma Pledger's office, and both were in the hospital at that moment. The news of the murders had come over the car radio, Julius explained, as he was on his way to pick me up, and he'd been trying to keep me out of the city as long as he could, lest John come after me.

"There's no telling what he might have done, D.J.," he told me. "Or will yet do."

I believe that I shrieked aloud at that point, although memory has so obscured that moment that it is possible I shrieked only silently, in the way we do when our horror is too great to find voice. I have no idea what I said to Julius, nor he to me, as the two of us sat across from each other at the conference table struggling to summon the presence of mind to face the reporters. At some point I began to weep, and at some point I stopped weeping, whereupon Julius stood, opened the door, and walked downstairs with me into the waiting room. Before I could say a word to the reporters, one of them told me the final horrible fact that had not been broadcast on the first radio reports Julius had heard that morning: that John Pledger, after having murdered his wife and her doctor, had shot himself to death. Did I have any comment upon the murders, the reporters wanted to know. Had I anticipated this? Had I known John Pledger to be violent?

From some icy part of my being where my purely legal self dwelt came the careful answer I gave to the reporters. Yes, I told them, I had represented John Pledger in the matter of his divorce. I had not seen nor spoken with him since before the holidays and had no explanation for his behavior. Domestic relations cases were filled with emotion, and violence was possible at any time. I expressed my profound regret, and then I turned, retreated to the conference room, and left the reporters to their task.

In a matter of hours, all of Washington knew the details of what the *Washington Post* called John Pledger's "three-stop death tour," the murderous rampage that had begun at 9:15 am with John's murder of Zelma and then her doctor, and ended at 10:05 when John shot himself just as police were closing in on him in a vacant lot near the home of the woman who cared for his daughter, Peggy. Reduced in the press reports to a monster "crazed by jealousy," John became not so much a real person as a character in some horror movie, a deranged maniac devoid of humanity. Yet I grieved for him in death even as I had grieved during his lifetime that he had not been able to find peace, and each time I read the details, I grieved again for the human being who had so entirely lost his way in the morass of that twisted relationship that he had snapped. I grieved for Zelma Pledger and for the two orphaned children, children John had loved better than life. All of that destruction had happened on my watch, and what I grieved for more than anything was my own appalling insufficiency.

Sooner or later, each of us is confronted with that reality. Indeed, the acceptance of our powerlessness as human beings is in my view the ultimate spiritual challenge, and one I wrestled with for a very long time. In the beginning, the minute details consumed me. Every one of my conversations with John over the past sixteen months replayed itself in my mind in the weeks after the tragedy, and I wondered what I'd missed, what I might have said to him, what I might have left unsaid that would have made a difference. Had I been foolish, naïve, even arrogant, in believing I could help John? Would he have been better served by another lawyer? Should I have been more skeptical of the calm he manifested in our last phone conversation just prior to Christmas? When all was said and done, I'd been inadequate to the task I'd taken on. Eventually, over a period of many years, I would come to an understanding that for all my stubborn belief in my own abilities as counselor, friend, and lawyer, John's fate, like the destiny of all human beings, rested in God's hands, not mine.

What shattered me most in the moment was the aloneness of John's two children. Mercifully, little Vincent was taken by Zelma Pledger's sister, but fourteen-year-old Peggy was truly orphaned. The fine woman who'd looked after her from the time her mother died years ago was too elderly to assume total responsibility for a teenage girl. I worried that her grandfather Pledger was also, but because he was the only family member left standing in the wake of the tragedy, the court appointed him guardian of his granddaughter. He was a good man, but he was advanced in years, and clearly overwhelmed by the task of rearing a child as bereft and shattered as Peggy. My powerlessness overwhelmed me, just as it had with her father. I was, after all, only her father's lawyer.

It was in my legal capacity that I found help for Peggy—or the beginning of help. Peggy, as it turned out, had suffered a legal wrong at the hands of a publication called *Sepia Magazine*. The magazine's editors had somehow obtained a photograph of her with her father and stepmother at their wedding, and had run it with an article about the murders, without obtaining the required permission. I was outraged by the blatant invasion of the child's privacy, so much so that I refused to let the matter pass. The magazine's liability was manifest, and whatever monetary award a court might make would be well used for Peggy's education.

The sum I won, in combination with the survivor benefits due Peggy from the federal government, covered not only the tuition at the North Carolina boarding school her grandfather and I selected for her, but it also created a handsome nest egg for her college education. The money did not touch her pain, her loneliness, the anger she wore so plainly on her sleeve. But it was a start.

That is all the law can give us, in the end. And that counts for something, that chance, that hope, that open door. There's a gloriousness in the law, in its ability to bring us to the threshold of justice. But if we are to cross that threshold, we must find it in ourselves, in our own hearts and minds, to live out the rulings and decrees and mandates of the courts. Such were my thoughts in the spring of 1961, as I confronted my own limitations as a lawyer, and watched in horror and in awe at America battling its way toward the fulfillment of what Julius and I had won in the *Sarah Keys* case.

I thought often that spring of Professor Nabrit, of Thurgood Marshall, of George E. C. Hayes, of Belford Lawson, and of all the other lawyers who'd inspired Julius and me six years earlier to take on the cause of civil rights in the courts. I thought, too, of the soaring words columnist Max Lerner had written the week after the *Keys* ruling had come down: "I light a candle in my heart," he'd said, "with the knowledge that black and white alike, we can now ride together across the state lines of the 48 states."

There was no lighting of candles in Birmingham, Alabama, on Sunday, the fourteenth of May, as the Freedom Riders rolled into the city's bus station to test the Supreme Court's ruling in the most recent travel desegregation case, *Boynton v. Virginia*, which had banned Jim Crow in the restaurants and soda fountains located in the bus terminals of the southern states. In so doing, it went one step further than had the ICC in the *Keys* decision, which had banned segregation on the buses themselves and in the station waiting rooms, but had not touched upon the eating facilities therein. The *Boynton* ruling had come down in January of 1960, the same month that John Pledger had sunk into despondency at the separation decree the court had granted Zelma, and for the next twelve months I'd lived in terror of what he might do. In that state of mind I hadn't tracked the particulars of the Supreme Court's doings with my customary intensity. But thousands of others had paid the closest attention. Young men and women, both black and white, had seized upon the *Boynton* decision as the test case for which they'd been waiting, and in May they'd boarded buses on an integrated basis in the North and begun riding into the heart of Dixie to demand an end to Jim Crow in every aspect of bus travel—on the vehicles themselves, in the stations, in the restaurants, the waiting rooms and restrooms.

I watched the mobs in Birmingham, the beatings, the violence spewing forth as the Freedom Riders pressed their cause, and I watched too the majesty with which the Reverend Martin Luther King, Jr., led fifteen hundred protesters in prayer and singing through the long night of the Montgomery Freedom Ride, as federal marshals, the Alabama National Guard, and a mob of Klansmen fought each other. As the mob threw bottles through the stained glass windows of First Baptist Church of Montgomery, King stood at the pulpit and waited. All night long, the newspaper accounts said, King kept praying and waiting and urging the protesters to pray with him until finally, around dawn, the mob outside grew tired and went home. King had won, by outwaiting the enemy.

What a lesson he taught us all, about the kind of unflinching bravery and calculated patience and perspective required to prevail in any great fight for justice. Waiting is a hard, hard thing, and Julius and I had almost despaired, at times, that the words of the *Keys* ruling would take effect. Never had we imagined that the attorney general of the United States would be the one to invoke them, as Robert F. Kennedy did on May 29, 1961, in an extraordinary legal communication with the Interstate Commerce Commission. Pressed by Martin Luther King to end the violence against the Freedom Riders, supported by Secretary of State Dean Rusk, who told him that segregation was an international embarrassment, and goaded by clergymen and politicians of all stripes, the attorney general issued a "petition" to the Interstate Commerce Commission which confronted them with the words they themselves had written six years earlier in *Keys*.

There it was, for the entire country to see on May 29, 1961, in the pages of the *New York Times*: the petition containing the text of the decision for which we'd fought so hard, and which had for so long lain dormant: "We conclude that the assignment of seats in interstate buses, so designated as to imply the inherent inferiority of a traveler solely because of race or color, must be regarded as subjecting the traveler to undue and unreasonable prejudice and disadvantage." Now, cited by the attorney general of the United States along with the Supreme Court's ruling in *Boynton*, *Keys* could no longer be ignored. Quietly, Julius and I celebrated as we watched the ICC begin closing the many loopholes they'd left open to segregation in the wake of *Keys*. By September 22, the commission had admitted that the case-by-case method of resolving individual complaints of race discrimination wasn't good enough, and issued a set of clear, comprehensive regulations. They barred interstate motor vehicles from segregating passengers on buses, including those that were traveling *within* the states; they mandated that bus companies post signs aboard the buses prohibiting Jim Crow seating; they prohibited the bus lines from utilizing or supporting segregated stations; they demanded that bus companies report violations to the ICC within fifteen days. And they set a six-week deadline for compliance. This time, the compliance was real. By Wednesday, November 1, 1961, signs were to be posted in every bus and train in America, and in the terminals that serviced them. The ICC had, at last, done what it said it was going to do.

It was a great thing to come to that moment, as a lawyer, to reap the reward of battle in such tangible terms. But I could no longer regard mere legal victories in the same light that I had as a beginning lawyer. Along with everyone else in America, I'd seen the tidal wave of violence as the white South fought the *Brown* decision, and I'd despaired at the "white flight" from the District of Columbia that had created all-black schools in Washington and left *Brown* ringing hollow. The practice of law had shown me how truly powerless I was in the face of certain kinds of human pain. My reach to the ministry had been in part an acknowledgment of that fact. More than any other experience, the Pledger case had changed me, and was changing me more and more with each day that passed, as I contemplated on one hand my own insufficiency and on the other the price I'd paid, emotionally, for the kind of investment I'd made. It had nearly broken me, and I was more acutely aware than ever that none of us is invulnerable, or inexhaustible. This, I told Julius with more than gentle insistence, was a lesson he needed to learn.

Reining him in became for me a campaign that fall, even as I myself rushed from the office to Howard to Allen Chapel, preparing for my ordination at the end of November. I'd tried coaxing Julius to slow down, and that hadn't worked, so I began prevailing upon him to take on an associate or two and perhaps a law clerk. It was inhuman to work the way he did, I argued; he could refuse to acknowledge his limitations, but he was liable to wind up, just as I had, good and sick.

I didn't actually believe that, given Julius's superb health and stamina, but I wasn't altogether surprised that he'd had to go briefly into the hospital in November after experiencing chest pains in court. This, I thought, would furnish me with sufficient ammunition to penetrate his hard head and persuade him at last to hire help, delegate routine matters, and perhaps even refer out some portion of our work. I was so bent on implementing my plans that I had to fight down the urge to start working on him when I stopped by his house the evening of his hospital stay to check on him. I visited with him just long enough to satisfy myself he'd had nothing more than a good scare, and I made sure Nellie wasn't in need of any help. I'd give Julius the weekend to rest, I figured, but I made up my mind that first thing Monday I'd sit him down for a good long talk.

At 8:00 the next morning, I got a phone call. Julius was dead.

10. OUT OF THE DARKNESS

There is no preparing for death, not even when it comes at the end of a long life, or mercifully intervenes amid terrible illness. But when someone young and vital is wrenched from your midst without warning, all is shock and horror and dismay. Faith, to be sure, gives meaning to death, deep and abiding meaning. But it does not free us from the pain of losing someone we love. Julius was far more to me than a law partner. He was a faithful ally, a steadfast colleague, a brother.

Every day for the ten years of our practice, he'd picked me up at home and driven either to the courthouse or the office, and so, when I stepped from the bus on the corner of Eleventh and U Streets into the biting November air on the morning after his funeral, I felt lost. A bare two and a half blocks lay between the bus stop and the office, but it was one of the longest walks I ever took. My feet were heavy. My legs were heavy. My head was heavy, so much so that I must have been looking down, for as I passed Chisley Florist, Mrs. Chisley called out to me from the doorway.

"Lift your head up, Attorney Roundtree," she said. "It's going to be all right."

By the time I reached the gate out front of 1808, she'd dispatched the young fellow in her shop with a red carnation. Without a word, he handed it to me and ran back to the floral shop. And I opened the outer door to the vestibule and walked into the waiting room.

The office was dark. As I stood in the doorway peering into the early morning greyness, I saw our secretary, Haywood Johnson, sitting absolutely still at his desk.

"Mr. Johnson," I said, "you are here in the dark."

"Yes, Attorney Roundtree. The lights are off, and so is the typewriter," he answered, bursting into tears. I walked over and put my arm around him, and he said to me, "I don't know what you're going to do, Mrs. Roundtree."

"I am going to get the lights turned on," I told him. "Is the telephone working?"

At that, he laughed, reached for the phone, and handed it to me. I dialed Gwen at her office at the Pentagon, explained to her that the electric bill must have come due after Julius was stricken, and that we were without power. It was the first time in the ten years of our practice I'd had to attend to the payment of any bill, since Julius handled that end of things, and until this moment I hadn't given the electricity a thought. Gwen left work immediately to give me a hand, and when she arrived, we walked to the Industrial Bank on the corner, where Julius had all our accounts, and paid the bill. The electricity came on at noon or thereabouts, by which time a whole lot of "God's light," as Grandma loved to call the sunshine, was streaming through the bay window that fronted on Eleventh Street. I stood up and headed for the staircase that led to Julius's second-floor office, to review his files.

Gently, Gwen dissuaded me from that plan. Perhaps I should see what I had on my own calendar first, she suggested, and determine which cases could be postponed, which could be settled, which required my urgent attention. This I did, sifting and sorting through my files all afternoon. Then I picked up the phone and, one by one, I placed calls to the people who cared about me, people I knew I could count on: Rev. Charles Green, Mr. and Mrs. Chisley, Professor George Hayes, Julius's real estate colleague Ernest Eiland, and two of our mainstays from the "old days" at Lindsay Cain's, Wilhelmina Rolark and Jesse Lewis. I invited them all to the office, and when they gathered round me in the waiting room, I asked Rev. Green to say a prayer. And then, lifted by his blessing, I set about the lonely task of building a law practice of my own.

Only the fact of my ministry sustained me through that bleak winter, pushing me in a forward direction when a part of me longed to stand still. Just three and a half weeks after Julius's death, on November 30, 1961, at the historic Campbell AME Church where Professor Nabrit had led the charge in the *Bolling* case, I was ordained an Itinerant Deacon in the AME Church, and launched on the two-year path toward full ministerial status that would culminate in 1963 with my becoming an Itinerant Elder. With the laying on of his hands, Bishop Frank Madison Reid, Jr., "set me apart," as the AME discipline says, to preach, to distribute communion, to baptize, to preside at weddings and funerals.

And there was ever so much more, I discovered, so much that was ineffable in the role into which I was thrust on the Sunday following my ordination. For all my preparation for the ministry, I had never imagined just how profoundly I would change, both within myself and in my relationship to the people of Allen Chapel, once I became "Reverend Roundtree." To teach Sunday school and even to preach an occasional sermon is one thing; to minister formally is quite another, and, once ordained and appointed to the staff at Allen, I felt with stunning force and from every direction the press of human need from a congregation now numbering in the hundreds. I was the only female on the ministerial staff, and I saw how deeply that touched the women in the pews. I loved that. I reached out to everyone, but I confess I took particular delight in the intensity with which older women, younger women, married and unmarried looked to me for counsel and advice, for guidance in things temporal as well as things spiritual, looked to me in a way that required me to summon myself and set aside my own grief, my own sense of aloneness, in order that I might minister to them.

On my block of Eleventh Street, too, all was noise and bustle and rebuilding—literally. With Julius's property at 1808 tied up in the processing of his estate, I put in a contract on a rowhouse a few doors down at 1828 Eleventh Street, which had housed, of all things, a mortuary. Even in my somber mood I couldn't resist joking about that maudlin coincidence to the architects and builders I hired to transform the Latinee Funeral Home into my law office. It was a conversion worthy of a christening, I told them upon completion of the remodeling that spring. For that grand occasion I summoned once again the circle of friends who'd gathered round me the day after Julius's funeral, along with attorneys George Knox and Bruce Harrison, who'd rented space from us at 1808 and were making the move down the street with me to the new quarters. Once again, Rev. Green did the honors with a magnificent prayer, and I proudly announced a new beginning.

I'd been reared to keep up a good front in public, to behave as though I was fearless even when I didn't feel that way, and I daresay not even those close to me saw how deeply I grieved. I missed Julius more than I'd thought possible, missed his brilliance and his common sense and his hardheadedness and his "what difference does it make if you're a woman" attitude. I also missed his protective presence, though I wouldn't have admitted that to a living soul. Julius himself would have vigorously denied that he'd acted as a shield for me, and in his lifetime, I would have been reluctant to acknowledge anything remotely resembling dependence. But the fact was that I *had* depended upon him, and it was also true that at a time when a female lawyer of any race was regarded skeptically, I'd derived a significant measure of credibility from my association with him. Now, I had to build that credibility alone, and there were times when I felt truly vulnerable.

The darkness inside me lasted a long, long time, and it had to do with more than Julius's death. His passing marked the beginning of a three-year season of loss for me, a time of anguish and of questioning. Like all of us who witnessed the brutality that unleashed itself across the Deep South beginning in the summer of 1963, I struggled to hold fast to my faith and my optimism. I believed to my depths in the power of what Dr. King called "soul force," in the transformative love he called "agape," in the redemptive power of "unearned suffering." But the kind of searing hatred that burst forth in Birmingham was of an order different from anything I'd seen in my years in the South. Medgar Evers's demand for simple justice resulted in his assassination; a year later, the three young men who'd come from the North to register black voters in Mississippi were brutally murdered. What I could not accommodate, anywhere in my mind, was violence done to children, and children were among the protesters who were blasted by Bull Connor's fire hoses and set upon by his police dogs; it was children who died in the bombing of the Sixteenth Street Baptist Church in Birmingham, just two weeks after Dr. King spoke to us about sitting down "at the table of brotherhood" at the March on Washington. "We must not lose faith in our white brothers," he told the mourners at the funeral for the four little girls killed at that church. He held out hope for the "high road of peace" he believed would come, eventually, from the deaths of those martyred children.

I wanted to believe that, and my religious faith demanded that I do so. But I struggled mightily to square my fundamental belief in human goodness with the brutality that came in waves, each more hideous than the last, as though the country was caught in some kind of monstrous and protracted birthing process that gave way at last to the signing of the Civil Rights Act of 1964. I felt every pang more acutely, I am certain, because in the midst of that overpowering national turmoil, I lost the greatest mentor of my life, Mae Neptune, and the soul to whom I was more deeply bound than anyone on earth, my grandmother. Mae Neptune embodied in her person the essence of Dr. King's vision; all my life she would represent for me concrete hope for the world of racial harmony he described. In the Christmas card I'd received from her the year she'd retired, she sent out an essay to all her former students laying out the ideal toward which she had worked all her life, the ideal toward which she wished us all to labor, a world where "every child would have the freedom to become his best self, be as happy as possible, and always have justice among his fellows." When on January 4, 1964, I learned of Miss Neptune's death in her childhood home, Barnesville, Ohio, I grieved at the passing of the person who had made the impossible possible for me, and left me a legacy of hope forever after.

For my grandmother's death there are no words, nothing that adequately describes the emptiness that overtook me when Mama called me before dawn on the first day of November in 1964 to tell me that Grandma was gone. Her death was not untimely; like Miss Neptune, she'd lived out ninety years and a few months more, and almost to the end, she was ever so much herself. Just a year earlier, she and I had been sitting on the porch together in Charlotte when word came over the radio of the assassination of our beloved President Kennedy, whom Grandma placed in almost the same category as President Lincoln. Together, we'd mourned the slain president, she and I, and Grandma had prayed with me for an end to the violence lashing across the land. In the months after that, her mind had begun to fail, and when I'd visited Charlotte a month or so before her death, I'd looked out the front window to find her wandering in the street. Horrified, I'd rushed to gather her up in my arms and lead her back into the house. The moment I heard she was gone from us, though, she became the fierce and beautiful young Grandma of my girlhood, the force of nature who'd shaken her fist at thunder and come at white hucksters with her broom and whipped me off the trolley rather than see me endure the insult of Jim Crow.

A hundred times in my adulthood I'd returned to the nest she'd made for us all. I'd returned to celebrate the awarding of my captain's bars, my law school graduation, my victory in the matter of Sarah Keys that was ever so much Grandma's victory, too. And I'd come home to find my way back out again after the war, and to grieve when my marriage ended. At the most important juncture of my life, when I'd first contemplated the ministry, she'd been far wiser than I and had sent me on my way with more understanding than I knew. I had, somehow, never truly believed the day would come when I would return home and my grandmother would not be standing at the gate, summoning me into the kitchen for a feast.

I was the minister in the family, Mama said, and so it fell to me to lead the procession from the home I'd bought Mama and Grandma through the streets to Ebenezer Baptist, the church they'd joined after Grandpa's death. There could be but one hymn for such an occasion, and as I began it I thought of the dozens upon dozens of processions she and Grandpa had led from the parsonage to his church, the whole neighborhood singing in unison.

Blessed Assurance, Jesus is mine.
O what a foretaste of glory divine.
This is my story, this is my song,
Praising my Savior, all the day long.

Alongside me marched Mama and Bea and Rachel and Eunice and their husbands, and our "little" brothers, Pete and Tom, our "forty 'leven" cousins, and behind them all the neighbors who'd looked to my grandmother, even when she was well into her eighties, for sustenance of every sort. The whole neighborhood echoed with the mighty sound of her home-going, and despite my sadness, my heart sang.

It was Mama, alone now in the house on East Hill Street, to whom my thoughts turned, even as I struggled with the emptiness I felt at Grandma's passing. With my sisters and me all gone from home, I dreaded to think of Mama by herself in Charlotte. For years I'd been pressing both her and Grandma to move to Washington and live with Gwen and Mrs. Winslow and me in our home. Now, with Grandma gone, I could think of nothing except that Mama should join us, become a part of the family we'd made, a family that just a few months earlier had expanded to include my young cousin Jerry Hunter, who'd enrolled that fall at Howard law at my urging and had set up his student quarters in my attic. Jerry was the grandson of my mama's beloved brother, Ally, and his wife, Cleadie, and Jerry's mother, Annie Belle, was one of one of Mama's favorite nieces. With Mama in the home, we'd have a regular Bryant reunion going. All of this I urged upon Mama, and Gwen and her mother joined in my campaign as well.

But Charlotte had been my mother's home for seventy years, and she was surrounded by friends, neighbors, and most of all, by her church family. In my careful selection of a property for Mama and Grandma within walking distance of Ebenezer Baptist, I'd put the two of them right "in the briar patch," as Grandma liked to say, and they'd bonded to the congregation there so thoroughly they'd made their home a sort of annex to the church. I knew exactly what it meant to be attached to a church family; I myself could not have contemplated parting from my Allen Chapel congregation. And so, when Mama insisted she'd best stay put, I understood.

Yet my home filled up, so quickly and unexpectedly I scarcely had time to plan, or even to think. The sudden arrival of a child of any age, in any home, at any time, turns things on end, and when the brilliant and sad and bewildered Peggy Pledger reentered my life at the end of 1964, at the age of seventeen, I was overcome. One moment, I was lost in grief for Grandma, the next moment I was turning myself inside out trying to understand the heart of a teenage girl so wounded by her father's death she barely spoke.

It was the court that brought Peggy to my doorstep, the court that turned to me with a request that I assume the role of legal guardian when the task of rearing and overseeing such a deeply troubled teenager proved too much for John Pledger's aging father and his brother. For me, there could be no other answer than an unequivocal "yes," though I knew even before Peggy stepped off the bus from North Carolina to spend her boarding-school break at my home that this was a child who would need far more than ordinary mothering.

She actually flinched when I reached out to hug her at the bus station, and I saw that in the three years since I'd seen Peggy, she'd turned in on herself in a way that made it almost impossible to connect with her. My every instinct was to take her up like a little child, but I knew that was the wrong thing to do.

I had no idea, however, about the right thing to do. She refused to ride to the office with me, insisting she wanted to spend her three weeks in Washington with Mrs. Cora Green, the elderly lady who'd been her childhood babysitter. When I offered her cab fare for the trip over to Mrs. Green's, she turned down the money, insisting on making the mile-long walk in the cold. She sat at the dinner table, sullen and withdrawn, and some evenings, she'd jump up abruptly and run to the den to watch television or down to the bedroom we'd outfitted for her in the basement.

She was so profoundly hurt, so damaged, that she put me in mind of the little wounded birds I was forever bringing home as a child. I'd put them in shoeboxes, with a little fine seed, and watch as they'd get to pecking at the seed. Then I'd chop up an earthworm, and give them some of the earthworm, tempting them with bigger and bigger chunks. I learned I couldn't heal those birds all in one lump. And so it was with Peggy. Patience had never been my long suit, but I had to cultivate it in dealing with that wounded child.

More than anything, it was her aloneness that touched me. I'd known that awful feeling of unbelonging many times over the course of my life, in the hours after my father died when my mother had seemed to disappear from our midst, at Spelman, as a poor working girl in a sea of wealthy classmates, as a black woman in a white man's army, as a female law student and then a lawyer in a male world that regarded me as an outsider. It was Miss Neptune who'd pulled me from my shell by appealing to my mind, and it was that same route that led me to a connection with Peggy.

She was, I noticed, drawn into one activity in the household in spite of herself, and that was the discussion of various points of law in which I engaged Jerry Hunter at the dining room table every evening. By the end of the first semester, when Peggy arrived for her holiday stay, Jerry and I had a tutorial regime in place. After supper we'd clear the table and "have at the law," as I liked to say, with Jerry summarizing cases from his torts and contracts classes and my quizzing him on the legal principles buried in them.

When Jerry and I started up in January at the outset of the new semester with our ritual of recitation and cross-examination, Peggy took to lingering nearby, instead of disappearing into the basement or heading upstairs to the den. And one night, as I awaited Jerry's response to a question I'd put to him on a case he'd just briefed for me, Peggy called out the answer from the living room, where she'd been sitting by the fire, reading—or pretending to.

Jerry and I looked up, astonished.

"How in the world did you figure that out?" Jerry asked her.

"Simple logic," Peggy said. And she walked across the hall into the dining room and stood at the end of the table and began explaining her answer to us. She'd been paying strict attention, I realized, not only to the case Jerry had just summarized, but to every other case we'd dealt with that week and, apparently, every word of analysis I'd spoken.

And so with that answer, and that moment, and the tiny smile of satisfaction I caught on Peggy's face as she saw how much she'd impressed

Jerry and me, she and I connected. In every other matter save the legal discussions, Peggy continued to wall herself in for the duration of her visit and for many visits afterwards. Yet we had made a tiny beginning. And over time, over spring breaks and winter breaks and the long summer vacations she spent with me through her college years, I would build a whole relationship with Peggy with my own peculiar style of mothering. I took pains to expose her to all things legal, assigning her what amounted to paralegal responsibilities in my office, bringing her with me to the law library and to court, where I'd have her take notes and review the cases with me afterwards. In every way I could think to do, I reached out to Peggy through her brilliant and inquisitive mind until finally I won her trust, and eventually her love.

We moved forward, kindred spirits that we became, to a relationship I would come to treasure as one of the greatest of my life, a relationship that would over the years alter me as deeply as the tragedy that had made it possible. In the season of loss that followed hard upon her father's death, Peggy, broken as she was, became the agent of my own healing.

She was not the only one. There had come into my life, just weeks before I brought Peggy into my home, another human being even more helpless than she, a little, little man so limited in his mental powers and so abject and pitiable in his circumstances that the United States government that had charged him with the murder of Washington socialite Mary Pinchot Meyer viewed him as entirely expendable.

His name was Raymond Crump, and he sought me out—or rather, his mother, Martha, did—on the eve of my grandmother's death, and his case, along with my mothering of Peggy, wound itself around my grief in a deep and powerful way, pulling me back into the fight for justice even as Peggy worked on my heart. The matter of *The United States v. Ray Crump* was to consume me for the better part of a year as I faced down the U.S. government and the Washington legal establishment in his behalf. His case, more than any other, was the one that defined my very essence as a lawyer, and that caused me, ultimately, to move beyond the law.

11. "Peer of the Most Powerful"

So far as I am concerned, there is in the complex and tangled web of certain truth and unconfirmed rumor, of inference and speculation and intrigue that surrounds the life and death of Mary Pinchot Meyer a single critical fact: Raymond Crump's innocence in her murder.

What actually occurred a few minutes past noon on October 12, 1964, when Mary Meyer was shot to death as she took her daily walk along the C & O Canal outside Georgetown, the identity and motivation of her true killer, the disposition of his weapon and the manner of his escape—these are questions to which I have no answers. Indeed, at the time of her murder I knew almost nothing about Mary Meyer herself, except what the newspaper accounts of her funeral at the Washington National Cathedral suggested about the world of power and privilege in which she moved. She was a niece of the famed conservationist and Pennsylvania governor Gifford Pinchot, and she was mourned, the press reported, by writer Arthur Schlesinger and Kennedy aide McGeorge Bundy, by *Washington Post* publisher Katharine Graham, by the wife of the French ambassador, and by her sister, Antoinette, who was married to *Newsweek*'s Washington bureau chief, Ben Bradlee.

That her ex-husband, Cord Meyer, Jr., was a top CIA official rather than the "author and lecturer" described in the press, that she had for two years been a lover and confidante of the late President Kennedy and had recorded their affair in a diary the CIA's counterintelligence chief was charged with destroying after her death were facts unknown to me at the time, and for more than a decade afterward. There were whispers of such things abroad earlier, vague suggestions about her White House access and her CIA connections, but the stuff of rumor couldn't be brought into a court of law. So I have told the reporters who sought me out in the years since her death, all of them searching for some piece of information, some insight or impression of mine that might, finally, illuminate the nature of her murder. If, as several researchers have suggested to me, Mary Meyer's access to the late president and her familiarity with certain facts surrounding his assassination made her a target of the CIA, I have no knowledge of such matters.

What I understood very clearly in 1964 was that this was a woman of great importance. At the age of forty-three, in the prime of her life, she'd been shot to death, execution-style, in a manner so ruthless it chilled the blood. Someone had to pay for a death like that. And I was absolutely determined that the child-man named Raymond Crump, Jr., not be that person. Or rather, to be absolutely precise about the matter, I *became* determined. In the beginning, I was dubious about his innocence, so persuasive were the facts the government had arrayed against him.

They had an eyewitness who couldn't have been more definite in his identification of Ray Crump nor in his account of what had happened. A mechanic, he'd been servicing a stalled car on the thoroughfare running along the C & O Canal when he heard screams, then two shots, and looked over the retaining wall to see a Negro male he said looked just like Crump standing over a body later identified as that of Mary Meyer. The man's clothing—golf hat, tan jacket, dark pants— was similar to what Crump had worn that day. The newspapers said that another witness, Lt. William Mitchell, reported having seen a black man, dressed in much the same fashion, following Mary Meyer as she walked along the towpath. It also appeared that Ray Crump had lied to the police when they'd arrested him near the scene, soaking wet and disheveled. He told them he'd been fishing on the rocks and had slid into the river while trying to retrieve his fallen pole, yet police had found nothing on the rocks but a half-empty liquor bottle, a bag of potato chips, and a pack of cigarettes. They'd found his fishing gear later that day, at his home.

Against all of this, I had, to begin with, only the word of Raymond Crump's mother. She'd come to me two weeks after the murder on the recommendation of her minister, pleading with me, as so many mothers had before in my practice, to help her child. To her, he was plainly a child, despite the fact that he was twenty-four years old, married, and a father of five children. "He's a good boy," she said of Raymond, the oldest of her three sons but the youngest in her eyes because he was so puny and so slow-witted. The other boys had picked on Raymond all through school, and then, a couple of years ago, after he was beaten by a gang of men trying to rob him, he'd begun having blackouts and terrible headaches. He'd been arrested once for petit larceny, and another time for urinating in public when he was drinking, but he worked, steady, on whatever construction jobs he could pick up day to day, provided for his family and pretty much stayed out of trouble. He drank too much for his own good, she said, but he'd never done anything serious, nothing like the awful thing he was accused of now.

Martha Crump spoke with such conviction and such purity that I compared her, consciously, to my grandmother, fighting ever so ferociously for Tom and Pete and all us "chillun" against onslaughts of every sort. I also knew that no mother's vision of her child is entirely accurate, sometimes not even remotely so. Perhaps Raymond Crump was truly a victim, as his mother believed; perhaps the beating she recounted at the hands of the gang of men really had been unprovoked. But by 1964 I'd seen too much of hideous, "unexplained" violence to fully credit any undocumented account of a person's conduct. No hardened criminal could have perpetrated more brutality than John Pledger, whom I knew to be a decent, responsible, and sensitive human being. I had John's profoundly wounded orphan-child Peggy in my life to remind me, as if I could forget, that good people are under certain circumstances capable of the most horrific deeds—deeds like the murder of Mary Meyer.

But when I met with Raymond Crump in the DC jail for the first time, the word that came to my mind was "incapable." He was, I remember thinking, incapable of clear communication, incapable of complex thought, incapable of grasping the full weight of his predicament, incapable, most of all, of a murder executed with the stealth and precision and forethought of Mary Meyer's. According to the coroner's report, she'd been shot in the head at point-blank range by someone who'd approached her from behind, overpowered her, shot her a second time in the shoulder blade, then either fled with the murder weapon or hidden it so well that police had been unable to find it. That the little slip of a man sitting before me in a state of such bewilderment could have planned, perpetrated, and hidden a crime of that magnitude struck me as preposterous. As I introduced myself to Raymond, spoke to him of his mother and how she had her church folks praying for him, how she'd asked me to take over his case from the young lawyer the court had appointed for him, he looked upon me with the air of a man who'd fallen asleep and awakened in a foreign country. I saw no indication that he was taking in anything I told him, except possibly the fact of his mother's prayers. His gaze wandered from me to the walls of the jail cell, and then back to me again, and when he finally spoke, my heart sank.

"Lawyer," he asked me, "what is it they say I done?"

This, I thought, was indeed the child his mother had described to me. I put down the pages of the indictment I'd been planning to read to him, reached across the table and put my two hands on both of his.

"They say you killed a lady, Mr. Crump."

Looking straight at Raymond, I began, slowly, to explain to him in the plainest language I could the single charge of first-degree murder the United States had brought against him. On the afternoon of October 12, 1964, I told him, the government said that he had shot a woman named Mary Pinchot Meyer as she was walking along the canal tow-path, that he had set out deliberately to kill her, and that she had died of the gunshot wounds she'd suffered. I laid out what little I'd been able to glean from the coroner's report about the case against him, and then I began asking him the questions to which I needed answers to build any kind of defense. He appeared so disoriented that I undertook to draw him into the circle of reality with a ridiculously simple question: had he been near the C & O Canal that day, in the area near Key Bridge in Georgetown? Yes, he told me, he had. Had he heard gunshots? Had he heard screams? Had he seen or heard any sound at all that told him something was wrong? He answered each of those questions in the negative, growing more frightened all the time.

"Are they gonna come after me again?" he wanted to know.

It was such an odd question that I had trouble responding. But this time, Ray explained himself, and as he did, he began to shake. The police officer who'd brought him in, he told me, had beaten him when he told him he hadn't done anything. The more he'd tried to explain to the officer that he knew nothing about the murder, the angrier the officer became, and the harder he beat him. I looked at Raymond, horrified. Such things had occurred in the DC jail when Julius and I had first begun practicing in the early fifties, but the courts had taken a hard enough line that I'd not heard stories of prisoner abuse of that type in a good while. Raymond, though, was truly frightened, and of something nearer to him, and more menacing, at least in his mind, than the prospect of a trial. I'd sensed immediately the disgust the white prison guards felt for Ray, and I'd been unsettled by it, knowing as I did that most people in Washington felt that Mary Meyer's murderer deserved the worst punishment the state could dole out.

"I'm here to look out for you, Raymond," I told him, promising him I'd pursue the matter of the policeman's behavior with the court as soon as I established who it was that had taken him into custody. "If anyone bothers you, I want to know about it right away. If you're frightened, and I'm not here, call out my name, as loud as you can, and tell 'em, 'My lawyer's on her way.'" I repeated my name for him, put my card in his hand, and then I looked straight across the table at him, straight into his eyes.

"Raymond," I said, "there are other people besides that policeman who believe you murdered that lady. What do you say about that?"

"I don't know nothin'," he told me. "I don't know why they got me."

"Are you telling me you're innocent?"

He seemed not to understand the word. I tried again.

"*Did you do it*? If you did, tell me now so I can try to help you. You need somebody to help you, man, because you're in a bad fix. It's going to take fighting, and prayers."

At that, he began crying.

"I didn't shoot nobody," he said.

"Then you'll be all right. You have a praying mother, and the grace of God. And you must pray, Raymond, even in this awful place. You must pray, hard. Because this is serious."

Indeed, the eyes of the whole city were trained upon the crime Raymond Crump was alleged to have committed, as law enforcement officials continued looking for the .38 caliber Smith and Wesson pistol that had killed Mary Meyer. Never in any murder case I'd tried had there been a weapon search on that scale. When police officers walking four and five abreast in the woods along the canal had failed to turn up a weapon in the forty-eight hours following the murder, the government brought in navy scuba divers to search the canal and the Potomac River, to no avail. Finally, the FBI had the canal drained, the mud at the bottom sieved, and the bed scanned with minesweepers.

I'd been following the reports of the officers' progress—or lack thereof—and as I dug more deeply into the basis for the case against Ray, I sensed that something was deeply wrong. Completely absent from the record was any evidence linking him to the victim. None of her blood had been found on his clothing, nor any gunpowder marks on his fingers. Ray Crump had never owned a gun. Solely on the basis of the car mechanic's identification, the police had arrested him. And that eyewitness had not even testified at the coroner's inquest held on October 19, one week after the murder, where Raymond had been represented by a young attorney assigned him by the Legal Aid office. Only the DC police detective in charge of the case had appeared for the government at the inquest, and he'd testified that the car mechanic had seen the man standing over the corpse at a distance of *three-quarters of a mile.* On the basis of that hearsay testimony, impossible on its face, the government had moved forward. Ray's Legal Aid attorney, a brilliant and eager young lawyer named George Peter Lamb, told me he'd been so outraged by the government's rush to judgment that he'd protested the legitimacy of the coroner's inquest by refusing to participate, and demanded a preliminary hearing so he'd have a chance to subpoena witnesses, cross-examine them, and learn the basis of the government's case. The court had granted his request for the hearing but denied his repeated motions to subpoena witnesses for it, then held that the indictment handed down by the grand jury on the same day as the coroner's inquest made the preliminary hearing unnecessary. By the time I entered my appearance in the case on October 28, it seemed Ray's fate was sealed. And the worst of it was, no one cared.

So swiftly that it took my breath away, the court brushed aside my contention that Ray had been beaten, as well as my petition for a writ of habeas corpus in which I held that without a preliminary hearing, my client's detention was illegal. The U.S. court of appeals ruling that a coroner's inquest was no substitute for a preliminary hearing, handed down just a few days earlier, was deemed irrelevant to Ray Crump's case. And while the court went through the motions of responding to my request for a mental evaluation of Raymond, the seven-line psychiatrist's report, delivered to me without attachment, made a mockery of the examination process. Raymond Crump, the doctor wrote, had been examined by "qualified psychiatrists" and been found "mentally competent for trial." Raymond's blackouts, his excruciating headaches, the effects of the beating he'd suffered in 1962, his probable addiction to alcohol—none of the issues I'd cited in my motion appeared to have been addressed, let alone weighed in any serious way. Ray's wife, too, washed her hands of him, leaving their five children with his mother and fleeing the area, and his two younger brothers wanted nothing to do with the case. In the midst of that wholesale desertion, the one person in the city of Washington in a position to actually help Raymond turned her back on him.

Her first name was Vivian, and she'd been with him on the day of the murder, he told me when I began pressing him about the crazy fishing story he'd told police. He'd been frightened of what his wife might do to him if she found out he'd been with another woman, and afraid, too, that the police might come after his girlfriend and hurt her. His very life, I explained to him, might depend upon her testimony, and I assured him I'd protect the woman.

He told me that she'd picked him up very early that morning, at the corner where he caught his ride to the day's construction job, and together they'd set out for the area of the canal where he sometimes fished, stopping on the way at a liquor store to buy a bottle of whiskey, some cigarettes, and some chips. They'd done a little drinking down in the woods together, "fooled around a little," he said, and then fallen asleep on the rocks at the water's edge. Or at least, Ray had—so soundly he'd slipped into the river, been jerked awake in the cold water, and climbed up the bank and into the woods to find Vivian gone. He'd looked all over for her, to no avail, and finally headed down the towpath in the direction he thought would lead him to a bus stop. There, walking toward him, was a policeman who began asking him what he was doing in the area. Afraid he was in trouble, he'd told the man he was fishing.

I pretty nearly turned the city of Washington inside out, looking for that woman—or rather, my assistant, Purcell Moore, did. Purcell had helped me on many a murder investigation since my earliest days with Julius, and although we had only a name to go on in this instance, I'd known him to locate witnesses based on descriptions alone. When he finally managed to track down the woman and I reached her by phone, I was certain that Ray's alibi was absolutely true, and equally certain that it would be absolutely useless in court.

Vivian corroborated his story, down to the details about the liquor and the potato chips and the sex on the rocks, but she had no intention whatever, she told me, of telling a judge what she knew. Her voice was full of fear, just as Raymond's was, but she had none of his gentleness. She was hard, and tough, and angry—angry that Ray had talked about her, angry that I'd called her at home, angry that I thought she might actually be stupid enough to come forward and get mixed up in a mess like Ray was in and risk being killed by her husband, if he found out what she'd been up to that day.

Only when I began speaking of the probability of a death sentence for Ray did she soften. She would sign a piece of paper, she told me, stating she'd been with him and telling what they'd done, and when, but that was all she would do. No matter how many times I explained that this would not suffice in a murder trial, that the court would admit her written statement only if she were personally present to testify under oath that it was true, she would not relent. When I hung up the phone that night, I knew I was as alone in this case as I'd ever been. The only two people who cared whether Raymond Crump lived or died were his mother and I.

And I cared. I cared so profoundly that Ray and every client in his position be given a chance at justice that once I committed to the case on October 28, nothing, not even my grandmother's death, coming as it had five days later, diminished my fervor. In fact, Grandma's death worked upon me in quite the opposite way, vaulting me back into the fight for Raymond with a force I would not have thought possible. On one hand, of course, I was numb with sadness when I returned to Washington after Grandma's funeral, and there was a part of me so mired in sorrow that I felt oblivious to the buzz and patter of ordinary things. Yet even in this was God ordinant, as He is in all things. Right in the midst of my grief and my desire to come to a standstill, He was pulling me back into the world with a matter so grave in its implications I had no choice but to embrace it.

Stripped by the court of just about everything except my right to appeal the habeas corpus ruling, which I did promptly, I turned my entire concentration to the one place I believed might yield up the answers: the mile-and-a-half stretch of the towpath that ran along the canal from Foundry Underpass to Fletcher's Boathouse. In every murder case I'd tried, the crime scene had proved critical. Only at the actual spot, I believed, was it possible to breathe in that which remained hidden in cold witness statements and police records and minutes of grand jury proceedings. And so, in the chilly days of late November and early December, I headed with George Knox, whom I'd made my new partner, and with Jerry Hunter to the place where the police reports pinpointed the murder. There, in the woods, on the river, along the canal, on the towpath, at the stone retaining wall where the mechanic had stood and observed the man he said was Ray Crump, I looked for the truth I was certain lay just beneath the surface.

It had not occurred to me that there were people who did not want me to find it. I cannot pinpoint the date on which I received the first phone call in the middle of the night that shattered the peace of my household and left me with the sense that my investigations along the canal had not gone unnoticed. But I remember the queasy feeling with great clarity, for I knew then, and felt more and more definitely as the weeks passed and the calls continued, that my movements were being tracked by someone with a keen interest in the outcome of the trial. Sometime after midnight the phone would ring. The caller never spoke, yet he or she stayed on the line, breathing into the phone until I hung up. Days would pass, and then once again would come the dreaded ring. As Christmastime came and Peggy Pledger arrived for her first visit with us, I worried that her already fragile state of mind might be affected by such disturbing goings-on. Peggy was well aware of the Crump case, and was fascinated by it, and while I discussed certain aspects of the facts that were known to everyone, I was intent on shielding her from danger.

The calls, it became clear, were tied to my visits to the crime scene. I often had the sense, there, that I was being watched. The sun shone, the park and towpath echoed with the shouts and laughter of runners and picnickers and fishermen on the autumn afternoons when we visited, but I could not shake off the sense of something sinister. The more we visited the crime scene, the more persistent the calls became, but I kept returning to the towpath area with George and Jerry because I was so absolutely convinced that only by memorizing the area, every tree and blade of grass, would I be fully prepared for anything the prosecution might bring up at trial.

Again and again, the three of us reenacted the scene as we understood it: the woman, walking westward from Key Bridge toward Fletcher's Boathouse; the man, hands in pockets, trailing her; the jogger, Lt. William Mitchell, three feet from the man he passed on the path. And then the gunshots and the screams, heard by the car mechanic and his assistant up on Canal Road. This, too, we reenacted, smashing paper bags to mimic the sound of gunshots and taking turns at the spot at the low stone wall where the witness Henry Wiggins claimed to have seen the man standing over the body, placing something in his pocket, walking down the embankment into the woods.

What had ensued immediately thereafter couldn't be reenacted, because no one had any idea what transpired. When Wiggins took off for the Esso station at Key Bridge to phone police, he'd left his assistant, William Branch, at the wall to monitor the area. But Branch had been frightened, he told the police later that day, and he'd gotten back into the stalled car and stayed there. So no one saw the movements of the man who'd turned away from the corpse and walked into the woods, its trees heavy with leaves in mid-October. Those woods stretched for miles along the canal, and ran parallel to the Potomac River.

"A person could do anything here," Jerry said, "and get away without anyone ever knowing what happened."

Often, I thought of what Julius used to say when he and I would map out a case: "It's got to make sense, D. J.," he'd tell me. "If it doesn't make sense to us, it sure isn't going to make sense to a jury." And this case made no sense. Everywhere I looked, there were missing pieces. The absence of a murder weapon and of any trace of the victim's blood on Raymond and his clothing troubled me, of course, as did the lack of information about the stalled car on Canal Road. Who owned the car, and why had the police not tracked him down? I had tried to do so, to no avail, going personally to the Key Bridge Esso to speak with the manager and ask for his records, and then, when he put me off, sending Purcell Moore to the station. They couldn't produce a work ticket or any other record of a car stalled at that location on that date, and they had no information about the owner.

More than anything else, I needed to fill out the minutes before the murder, to have an idea of who'd been moving about in the woods and along the towpath or the river's edge. The afternoon of October 12 was cool, but bright and sunny, the kind of day that drew visitors, even on a weekday. If only I could find someone else who'd been in the area besides the jogger from the Pentagon, I thought, perhaps I might learn something.

I knew, and had known from the beginning, that I couldn't look to Raymond for any help in that regard. He'd been preoccupied with the woman; he'd been drinking; he'd fallen asleep. But even if he'd been wide awake at 12:25 PM, when Henry Wiggins said he heard the shots, I doubted Raymond could have given me a description of any other person he might have seen in the park. He'd been confused from the beginning, and once he returned from his psychiatric evaluation at St. Elizabeths, he deteriorated daily.

I hadn't thought a person could become more anxious or overwhelmed than Ray was at the outset, but his mental state worsened so drastically in the jailhouse that I became truly alarmed. I'd seen men far tougher and smarter than he was broken by prison, but unless they'd suffered some trauma, either through rape or beatings, it generally happened over a period of years. As the weeks passed, and then the months, and the trial date was pushed into the summer, Ray's disorientation gave way to abject fear—fear of the guards he said browbeat him constantly to confess, fear of beatings, fear of anything and everything within the walls of the prison, including the food, which he believed was poisoned. I counseled him to run his hands through it to check for foreign objects, and to tell me immediately if anything was amiss. If ever a prisoner needed psychological help, Raymond did, but given the way in which the psychiatrist had washed his hands of him, I knew I couldn't expect any assistance in that regard.

And so I became to Raymond Crump not simply a lawyer, but a protector. Ray was more inaccessible to me even than Peggy Pledger, in all her woundedness. Peggy, at least, I could reach through her intellect. I had no avenue into Ray Crump's inner self. I tried, by making myself a continuing presence for him, even as his own mother did, to prevent him from sinking any further into desperation, and over time Ray came to trust me and to count on my visits. His was a horrible situation. Apart from the obvious fact of his legal predicament and the possibility of the death penalty if he were convicted, he confronted a prison existence in the DC jail that was worse than usual, if that comparison has any meaning in such a context. The guards' hatred for him was so palpable that I began making daily appearances at the jail, something I had never done for any other client. Between his mother's visits and mine, I hoped we stood a chance of establishing a watchful presence that might give ill-doers pause.

"Do you pray, Raymond?" I asked him once, as he sat before me crying and shivering. He gathered himself together, and looked across the table at me.

"Yes, ma'am," he said. "I prays."

Prayer was pretty much all we had as we moved toward trial. I'd thoroughly exhausted the crime scene, and despite all my motions and petitions, I had nothing more from the government by February than their list of witnesses and exhibits. I was reduced to building the case on what I could piece together from the signed statements given to police by

Wiggins and Branch and the jogger Mitchell, and the police records themselves.

The file was thick with form after numbered form, recording as it did every action taken by the police from the moment Wiggins had phoned them. I'd reviewed the file many times since I'd taken the case, and found nothing remarkable about it. I have no doubt that I'd seen the document numbered PD-251, a standard form that records the information police put out on their radio lookout for a suspect. But I hadn't paid it much attention. Perhaps I'd been distracted with my worries about Ray's deteriorating mental state and my losing battle for access to the government's witnesses, or unduly persuaded that the crime scene itself would yield up some critical fact none of the investigators had seen. In any event, I'd never taken a good, hard look at the description Wiggins had given the police to aid them in their search.

I saw that, contrary to the testimony of the DC police detective at the coroner's inquest, who'd stated that Wiggins had seen the suspect at a distance of three-quarters of a mile, Wiggins placed himself at a distance of about 120 feet. The suspect, he told police for the purposes of the lookout, was a Negro male wearing a dark hat with a peak, dark slacks, and a light jacket. Beneath that was printed his estimate of the size of the person he'd seen. The man had been five feet eight inches tall, weight estimated at 185 pounds. I read the statistics a second time: *five feet eight, 185 pounds.* When I checked the height information on the lookout against the description William Mitchell had given police of the black man he'd passed walking behind Mary Meyer, I saw that it matched, to the inch. The man Wiggins and Mitchell had seen was almost certainly the same person. But that person was not Ray Crump. He was too small. Raymond, when he raised himself up straight, stood eye to eye with me at five feet three. Even accounting for the two-inch heels on the shoes he'd had worn that day, he fell short of the height given by Wiggins and Mitchell by at least three inches. Even more significant was the weight difference, I thought. A man who weighed 185 pounds was stocky, burly, on the heavy side in fact, if he stood five eight. At 130 pounds, Raymond was as slight as a slender woman.

It was a discrepancy, I told my partners, that without question cast doubt upon the prosecution's case. Whether that doubt would rise, in the minds of a jury, to the level of "reasonable doubt" required for acquittal in a court of law, I did not know. Nothing, in my mind, argued more persuasively for Raymond's innocence than his mental limitation, but unless I put Ray on the stand, I had no way of demonstrating that to a jury. And I had the gravest reservations about subjecting him to cross-examination by U.S. attorney Alfred Hantman, who had a reputation as a relentless and aggressive trial lawyer. Under a barrage by Mr. Hantman, I feared Raymond would collapse, probably into tears. Without testimony from Vivian to corroborate his alibi, he'd be alone on the stand to explain what he'd actually been doing out on the river when he told police he'd been fishing. The prospect of exposing him to Mr. Hantman's ridicule made me shudder.

As we moved toward our July trial date, I fought with all I had, without gaining any ground. I argued my habeas corpus appeal in March, contending that the court had, in denying Ray a preliminary hearing, compromised his right to due process. But the U.S. court of appeals ruled against me in June, and although I derived a measure of moral satisfaction from the blistering dissent of Judge George Thomas Washington to the majority ruling, that didn't help my case for Raymond, nor my sense that what we were up against was a web of circumstantial evidence too formidable for anyone to puncture, given the heinousness of the crime. A young woman of forty-three, a mother of two sons, a much-beloved citizen of Washington had been gunned down in cold blood. Juries were reluctant to let deeds of that magnitude go unpunished. And juries didn't like liars. What person, listening to the silly little fishing story Ray had given police and hearing he had no fishing gear with him that day, would fail to think he'd lied to save himself? And what, now, could I do about that? I studied the police documents. I met with Raymond daily, soothing him and praying with him, and I met with his mother at least that often, trying to calm her wild fear that her son was going to die. I went to Ray's neighborhood to round up character witnesses to speak in his behalf—his neighbors, the minister of his mother's church, the head of the Sunday school. And they came forward, anxious to tell the court, every one of them, that they'd known him for many years as a person of peace and good order. And that was it. That was all I had. Upon their word, and my own certainty about Ray's innocence, and the little matter of inches and pounds, I would build my case.

No time would have been propitious for trying a case like Ray Crump's, but the summer of 1965 was surely one of the worst. Washington was not Selma or Montgomery, but black folk everywhere were raw with shock at the brutality that had exploded on March 7 at the Edmund Pettus Bridge outside Selma, where six hundred protesters marching for passage of the Voting Rights Act clashed with police, who let loose with tear gas, whips, and clubs, beating men, women, and children back into the churchyard from which they'd come. "Bloody Sunday," they called that day. Those of us who thought we'd seen southern hatred and violence peak with the Freedom Riders in the summer of 1961, and then again in the summer of 1963 during Dr. King's Birmingham Campaign, wondered in the spring of 1965 where it would all end, what price would finally have to be paid before the demon spent itself and we could claim what was rightfully ours, in peace. Such times breed a particular kind of distrust and suspicion even among well-meaning people. In midsummer, as the Voting Rights Act came before Congress, the racial tension floated all around us in the nation's capital, in the streets and the buses and the stores and the public places. And it settled so heavily in the courtroom on the morning of Tuesday, July 20, the opening day of Raymond Crump's trial, that I felt the actual weight of it in my shoulders.

My very presence, I knew, irritated and threatened many of the white judges and lawyers in the courthouse, male and female alike. There'd been bitter protests just a year or so earlier when my name had been proposed for membership in the all-white DC Women's Bar Association by the brave and bold attorney Joyce Hens Green. There were board members who'd resigned over the matter, and it had required all of Joyce Green's influence to force the issue to a vote of the entire membership, something that had never been done before. I sat in the U.S. district court on the first morning of the Crump trial keenly aware that there were many who wanted me to fail.

I also felt, even more acutely than I had during all those months in the jailhouse, the smallness of Raymond. He sat between George Knox and me at the defense table in the new blue suit his mother had bought him, shaking and reaching out to touch my hand every few minutes, sensing, as I did, the press of the enormous crowd behind us. I'd never seen the courtroom as packed as it was that day. Martha Crump had brought along at least a dozen of her church friends from Second Baptist, and they jammed into the seats along with the newspaper and television reporters and what looked to me like a veritable sea of men in grey suits, along with two or three fashionably dressed white women, friends, I assumed, of Mrs. Meyer's. Across from us at the prosecution table sat assistant U.S. attorney Alfred Hantman, flanked by his legal team. The case he'd mounted against Ray was formidable: twenty-seven witnesses and more than fifty exhibits, including the blood-stained tree trunk to which he said Mary Meyer had clung as she struggled with her murderer, and a fifty-five-foot-wide topographical map of the area surrounding the murder scene. He intended to spread it out, he'd announced to the judge the preceding day, across one entire wall of the courtroom.

Truth be told, I was angry that it had come to this, angry that a man who'd never even had a preliminary hearing now sat at the defense table on trial for murder, that the system that purported to protect the rights of the accused had shunted him aside, that he'd been disposed of by a psychiatrist in the space of a few lines and allowed to languish without help in the jailhouse, where he'd crumbled, mentally, to the point that I feared he might already be lost.

Yet I could still save his life, I believed, if I fought hard enough. And so even before the jury was brought into the courtroom, I was at the bench, arguing each of my pretrial motions, by which I hoped, among other things, to lay the foundation for an appeal, if Raymond were convicted. His clothing had been taken from him without a warrant, and his hair cut from his head for laboratory testing outside my presence, and with such force that he'd been injured and had required medical treatment. I moved to suppress both the clothing and the hair as evidence. I then took up the matter of the government's denial of a preliminary hearing, so prejudicial, I said, as to "taint all the proceedings." I requested that Raymond Crump be granted a preliminary hearing, or in the alternative, that the indictment be dismissed. I also moved to have witnesses removed from the court once they'd testified if they were going to be recalled, lest they be unduly influenced by other witnesses' statements. The judge denied every motion except the last, and held off ruling on the admissibility of Raymond's hair. George Knox fought at the bench, too, about the huge map Mr. Hantman proposed to paste to the courtroom wall. Hantman argued it was necessary; we argued that it was prejudicial, sensational, inflammatory.

I was walking a fine line, and I knew it, in pressing so hard and so aggressively before a judge whose predilections—what Julius used to call "the judicial lean"—were unknown to me. Judge Howard Corcoran, a brother of the legendary Washington lobbyist Tommy "the Cork" Corcoran, was brand new to the federal bench, and he had the air of a man who was not going to tolerate one bit of foolishness in his courtroom, from counsel or anyone else. He'd barred me from making any mention of Mary Meyer's life, habits, friends, and possible enemies during the trial as well as from referring to the fact that Ray had five children. There'd be no undue sympathy or prejudice, he made it clear, for either side.

This was a man I could not afford to alienate. And so I asked his indulgence.

"We are advocates and we hope the court will feel no hesitancy in admonishing us or letting us know if we become too overanxious," I told him, "because I am anxious about this case. It is an important case."

"It is an important case," Judge Corcoran agreed. "We all realize that."

There was no question that the jury understood the gravity of the matter. Each and every one of them wore an expression of the most intense concentration from the moment they took their seats. I watched them closely, those seven women and five men the prosecutor and I had selected with such care. They were hardworking, decent, ordinary people, black and white in equal numbers, to the best of my recollection, housewives, government clerks, a taxi driver, a social worker, a nurse, a counselor. Upon them hung Raymond's fate, and I tracked their reactions to Mr. Hantman's minute-by-minute account of the murder of Mary Pinchot Meyer as he laid it out before them in his opening argument, his voice growing louder and louder with each horrifying detail. I hadn't known until this moment exactly how the prosecution had reconstructed the events of October 12, nor how they'd fit Raymond Crump into that reconstruction. No one had witnessed the murder itself, but only its aftermath, and thus the government's theory of the killing remained just that, a theory.

This was, according to prosecutor Hantman, murder for the sake of murder—lacking in motive, meticulous in execution. Mary Meyer had been carrying no wallet or purse, wearing no jewelry, nothing, he said, that would have attracted the attention of a thief. The man who'd gunned her down at 12:23 or 12:24 PM on the afternoon of October 12, 1964—a time he pinpointed based upon the statement of the car mechanic who'd heard the screams and shots—had set out deliberately to kill her, then followed her as she took her customary walk along the towpath in the direction of Fletcher's Boathouse, surprising her from behind, placing his .38 caliber revolver to her head just behind her left ear, and firing. She'd screamed, they'd struggled, hard, judging by the twenty-foot drag marks police had found leading to a blood-stained tree, to which she'd apparently clung as she fought for her life. Then the killer had shot her a second time, also at point-blank range, in the shoulder blade.

The jury looked horrified, and with good reason, so graphic was Mr. Hantman's evocation of the bloody crime. Equally dramatic was the picture he painted of a desperate Raymond Crump, racing westward from the murder scene, flinging into the Potomac River first his cap and then his tan jacket—the same cap and jacket, Hantman maintained, that the eyewitness Henry Wiggins had seen on the man standing over the corpse—then zigzagging eastward through the woods past the place where the body lay. When he'd spotted police on the towpath, Mr. Hantman said, he'd jumped into the river until he figured the coast was clear, whereupon he climbed up the bank and onto the trolley tracks, and encountered a police officer.

I could not recall ever having seen a prosecutor so certain that each piece of evidence pointed to the defendant, so confident of the impenetrability of the police dragnet. Within four minutes of the murder, every exit from the area had been closed, he said. Raymond Crump had to have been the murderer, because he was the only one there.

"After listening to this testimony, ladies and gentlemen, carefully and impartially," he concluded, "the just, the honest, the fair verdict would be . . . a verdict of guilty as indicted."

The courtroom was quiet, expectant, as I rose for what the prosecution assumed would be my opening statement. But there are times, in trial, when it is best to hold one's peace. I judged this to be one of them, and I therefore announced to the court that I'd be reserving my statement for the defendant until later in the proceedings. To reveal anything about the basis of my case to the prosecution placed me at great risk. I thought it best to tread lightly, and watch, and make my move when I saw an opening.

If I'd known then what I know now about Mary Meyer's diary and the apparent importance placed upon it by the CIA, I'd have found my opening during the testimony of the prosecution's first witness, Mrs. Meyer's brother-in-law, Ben Bradlee. He'd taken the stand simply to testify to his identification of her body at the morgue, and neither Mr. Hantman nor I saw fit to put to him anything but the most superficial questions. How differently my line of cross-examination would have run had I been aware, on July 20, 1965, of the story Mr. Bradlee told thirty years later in his autobiography, about the occurrences at his sister-in-law's Georgetown home and art studio immediately following her death. On the night of her murder, he wrote, he and his wife had received a phone call from a friend of Mrs. Meyer's in Japan, alerting them to the existence of her diary and her wish that it be destroyed in the event of her death. The diary, as it turned out, corroborated what had been rumored for years: that Mary Meyer had been a lover of President Kennedy.

More shocking to me than that revelation was Mr. Bradlee's description of his encounter with CIA counterintelligence chief James Angleton at the door of the residence and studio. The CIA official's presence had startled him and his wife, Mr. Bradlee said, and they were utterly astounded to find him attempting to pick the lock at both places in an effort to gain access to the premises for the purposes of locating her diary, which he, too, knew about, somehow. Because he was a personal friend of theirs and an associate of Mary Meyer's ex-husband, they permitted him access and then, discovering the diary, prevailed upon him to destroy it. James Angleton's awareness of the diary's existence and his interest in finding it, reading it, and destroying it—all of that unsettled me deeply when I read Mr. Bradlee's 1995 account, as did his insistence that the diary was a private document. "The fact that the CIA's most controversial counterintelligence specialist had been caught in the act of breaking and entering, and looking for her diary" was, he said, not something he thought appropriate for public discussion or press coverage. He and his wife had given it to James Angleton to be destroyed, but after reading it, Angleton had returned it to them for destruction. Its ultimate fate and the extent of the CIA chief's surveillance of Mary Meyer prior to her murder are, I understand, matters that remain under investigation.

The mere existence of the diary was, of course, so suggestive of keen governmental interest in Mary Meyer's activities that had I been aware of it, I would have felt compelled to pursue it. But Mr. Bradlee's answers on the stand indicated nothing out of the ordinary. All he'd found in Mrs. Meyer's home and studio, he told prosecutor Hantman, was her purse, which contained her wallet, some cosmetics, some pencils, and her car keys.

In retrospect I see myself in that moment like a player at blind man's bluff, groping for a truth that hovered just beyond reach of my fingertips. Unaware of a critical piece of Mary Meyer's existence, I moved on to what lay right before my eyes in the courtroom—the enormous topographical map of the area between Key Bridge and Fletcher's Boathouse, which Mr. Hantman had placed upon the wall in preparation for the testimony of the Department of the Interior employee whose office had provided it, Mr. Joseph Ronsisvalle.

Four black stars on the wall map and on the smaller copies the jury and I held in our hands designated four spots by which a person might exit the area of the C & O Canal where Mary Meyer had been murdered. I'd walked each of those exits dozens of times, with George and Jerry: the steps leading up to Water Street at Key Bridge, the steps at Chain Bridge, an underpass at Foundry Branch, another underpass at Fletcher's Boathouse.

I listened to the mapmaker's answers, his careful measurements of the exact distances from one exit to the other, his delineation of each of the four points of egress with a pointer. There were four, and only four of them, he said with absolute certainty. And I knew, then, that every single visit I'd made to the murder scene, every mile I'd covered in the mud and the ice in the months since the murder, had been worth it. The map, as Mr. Ronsisvalle described it, portrayed a wide-open range of dense woods as though it were a room with four doors, each one equipped with lock and key.

I rose and walked to the witness stand.

"Now, Mr. Witness," I said, "all along in the area of this diagram is a heavily wooded area. Is that true, or do you know?"

Yes, he answered. The area was wooded.

"It is heavily wooded?"

"Yes."

"And it would be possible, would it not, for a person to take a path which you have not indicated and which counsel, through his questions, has not asked about which you do not know. Is that true?"

Mr. Hantman objected, and was overruled.

"Now, have you—I noticed you looked at counsel—have you, yourself, walked in this area?"

"No."

One by one, I named the exits, asking the mapmaker each time whether he'd ever walked them. Each time, he answered in the negative. He had never, in fact, been in the area at all.

Again Mr. Hantman objected. "If Your Honor please, I submit that we are now far outside the scope of the direct examination."

Judge Corcoran disagreed, and instructed me to proceed.

Again, I asked Mr. Ronsisvalle whether he'd ever walked or explored any of the areas indicated. Again, his answer was no.

"Then, can you positively say there is no way out from this area other than that which you have enumerated?"

"I can only indicate from the records in my office that the records indicate that these are the exits of the towpath between Chain Bridge and Key Bridge."

"But you do not know, and this map does not show, does it, the fact that this is a wooded area?"

"This particular map does not show, no, it does not."

"The fact that it is possible to roam far in the area, it doesn't show that either, does it?"

"No."

"That is all," I said.

The court recessed, and I glanced over at Mr. Hantman, sitting with his team at the prosecutor's table. He looked tense, I thought. But the truth was I hadn't done much, really, except to show how wide open the police dragnet had been. The jury had yet to see Mrs. Meyer's blood-stained clothing and the bloodied tree trunk she'd allegedly clung to in her struggle. I'd raised the strongest objections at the bench to having those items brought into court, but which way Judge Corcoran would rule, I did not know. There were more than twenty witnesses yet to come to the stand, including every one of the policemen at the scene, a slew of crime experts, the jogger from the Pentagon, and, of course, the car mechanic, Henry Wiggins, who swore Ray Crump was the man he'd seen standing over the victim. Of everything that sways a jury—inflammatory evidence, impressive experts, a sympathetic victim, a flimsy alibi—a credible eyewitness is far and away the most persuasive.

Henry Wiggins looked younger in person than he had in his newspaper photograph, I remember thinking, as he entered the courtroom on the second day of trial to tell the jury what he'd seen from his place at the stone wall. He was twenty years old, a nice-looking young black man who exuded confidence from the moment he took the stand. He described how he and his assistant, William Branch, had come to fix the stalled car in the 4300 block of Canal Road at about 12:25 PM on October 12, how they'd heard a scream, then a shot. Wiggins had crossed the road to the stone wall, at which point he'd heard a second shot. He'd looked over the wall to see a black man standing over the body of a woman. He'd been standing about 120 feet from the man, and he'd gotten a "glance" at the man before ducking behind the wall. Then he'd come up for another half minute to get a second look before the man put a dark object into the pocket of his jacket, turned, and walked away, into the woods behind him. The man had a medium build, he said. He hadn't been able to estimate his height, but he guessed the man weighed about 185 pounds.

When Mr. Hantman showed Wiggins the shoes, jacket, and hat Ray Crump had been wearing that day, he testified that they were the exact clothes he had seen on the man standing over Mary Meyer. Then he pointed to Ray, sitting beside me at the defense table, and identified him as the man he'd seen that day.

"From where you looked over the stone wall, sir, can you tell us whether or not you had a clear, unobstructed view of what appeared on the other side of the canal?" Mr. Hantman asked him.

"There was nothing in the way of my vision," the witness answered.

I rose from my place at the defense table, walked toward the witness stand, and looked at Henry Wiggins.

"This morning," I asked him, "do you remember that you said the defendant weighed 185 pounds?"

"Oh, yes, ma'am, I did."

"Do you remember, Mr. Witness, that you also said you had only a glimpse of the person you saw on the scene?"

"I remember that."

"This morning, nevertheless, Mr. Witness, you are prepared to tell this court and this jury that these are the pants?" I asked, indicating Ray's dark corduroy slacks on the evidence table.

"That's right."

"Positively?"

"Positive."

"You are prepared to say that this is the cap?"

"That is the cap."

"And that these are the black shoes?"

"That is right."

"And that this is the jacket?"

"That is right."

I looked over at the black wingtips Ray had been wearing that day, entered into evidence.

"Do you find any difference in black shoes?" I asked Mr. Wiggins. "If you see from a distance that a man has on black shoes, could you find any difference in those shoes than in other black shoes?"

"There isn't too much difference," he said. "The design on the shoes at a distance you cannot tell."

"You can't tell the design?"

"I can tell whether the shoes are dark, whether the shoes are light or brown or black," he said.

"But you can't tell if one pair is a particular pair of black shoes, or a particular pair of brown shoes if you see them two blocks away, can you?"

Mr. Wiggins shifted uneasily in the witness box. "I wouldn't say that," he answered.

"Could you describe the shoes?" I asked. "Did you know exactly how the shoes looked, which you say you saw this day?"

"Well, I can say that these shoes appear to be sort of a dress shoe. They were dark."

I waited, then, feeling the jury waiting right along with me.

"Do you recall telling anyone that this defendant, the person that you saw, was five feet and eight inches tall?"

"Well," he answered, "I believe I told one of the policemen which came down in the cruiser with me."

"Would that, then, be an accurate estimate of what you saw, the man you saw weighed 185 and was five feet eight?"

Wiggins looked over at Ray.

"That wouldn't be an accurate estimate, no, ma'am."

I turned to face the jury.

"Well, now, are you telling us now you gave them information which was not accurate?"

Wiggins hesitated. "I give it to them as close as I could remember," he said.

"And you gave them, though, what you thought you saw from across the canal?"

"I tried to do my best."

"All right. One hundred eighty-five pounds; five foot eight."

"That's right."

Mr. Hantman came forward to question his witness again. He asked him if he'd had a clear view of the murder scene, whether anything had obstructed his vision.

"No," Wiggins answered.

I rose again. I asked Wiggins how Raymond Crump was dressed that day, when he'd seen him on the towpath with the two police officers and said, "That's the man."

"I didn't look at him that hard," he answered me.

The courtroom went absolutely still. I looked again at the jury, at each of their shocked faces, and back at Wiggins.

"Did you ever, Mr. Witness, look at this man hard?"

Wiggins did not reply.

But every man and woman on the jury was looking at Raymond Crump—hard—and repeatedly as the trial moved into its third day, on Thursday of that week, and then resumed the following Monday with testimony from the seven policemen on the scene. One by one, they recounted the height description incorporated into the lookout based on the information Wiggins had provided. And as each one took the stand, the jury studied Ray, until at last the government called a witness who erased any remaining question about the height of the suspect. Former army lieutenant William L. Mitchell took the stand and described the black man he'd passed as he jogged past Mary Meyer. He had looked at the man from a distance of two or three feet, he said, and he'd measured him eyeball to eyeball by his own height of five feet eight inches. He would not be able to identify the man if he saw him again, he testified, not as Ray Crump or anybody else.

All of this I pondered as I retreated each evening to the quiet and solitude of my back screen porch, a place enshrouded in trees and set away from the traffic that moved up and down Sixteenth Street just a block and a half away. Every case I'd ever tried, I'd mapped out on this porch, where complex matters invariably reduced themselves to simplicity. The nights in that last week of July were hot, humid, heavy, even under the trees, but my back porch was my sanctuary, my thinking place, as screen porches had been for me all my life, and there, with a glass of lemonade and a legal pad in my lap, I read my notes and I assessed where I stood as we moved forward into the sixth and then the seventh day of trial, when at last the prosecution rested. I was disturbed by the way the chief detective on the case had equivocated about his verification of the spot at the retaining wall where Wiggins claimed he'd stood. He hadn't returned to the spot with Wiggins on the day of the murder, he said, and he couldn't recall when he did return. Neither he nor the other police officer involved had taken notes of the visits they claimed to have made with Wiggins to the site of the stalled car on Canal Road, though both insisted they'd been there, sometime.

There was nothing equivocal about the results of the government's effort to tie Ray Crump to the victim. They had nothing. When all was said and done, there was not one shred of credible evidence in that regard, for all the elaborate testimony Mr. Hantman had introduced in an effort to prove otherwise. The firearms expert who'd testified that Raymond's hands had borne no trace of powder burns only because such burns wash away in water admitted under cross-examination that a suspect's hands were often washed after the first evaluation, and the test repeated on the washed hands. So too with the so-called hair and fiber expert Mr. Hantman brought into court to try to demonstrate that the hairs that had been forcibly cut from Raymond's head—admitted over my objection into evidence—matched those found inside the little golf hat police had fished from the Potomac. I'd come to the courtroom on that particular day armed with a stack of textbooks on the subject, none of which the witness had read. And he'd acknowledged that there was a "great controversy raging" over the reliability of hair-matching techniques. No one really knew, he admitted, whether positive identification of hair was possible.

I considered, too, the contradictory statements of the witness William Branch, who'd been with car mechanic Henry Wiggins in the service truck on Canal Road. He'd told police in the written statement he signed on the day of the murder that he'd been too frightened to remain at the retaining wall and that he'd returned to the truck when Wiggins left. On the stand, though, he said otherwise, insisting under cross-examination that he'd stayed at the wall throughout Wiggins's absence, monitoring the scene. Even when I read his October 12 statement back to him, and pressed him about his changed version of the facts, he stuck to his new story. What the jury might make of that, I didn't know. I was certain, however, that I'd managed to call into serious question the tightness of the police dragnet over a park that every person in Washington—indeed every person who'd ever walked through a woods, anywhere—knew to be filled with multiple escape routes.

When all was said and done, Ray Crump had been brought to the bar of justice on the word of a single witness who now admitted that he'd caught only a "glimpse" of the individual standing over Mary Meyer, and that his identification of Raymond as that individual had been made with something less than a glance. "I didn't look at him that hard," he'd said under cross-examination. The fact of the matter was that Wiggins had based his description of the suspect on a fleeting impression of clothing that might have been worn by dozens of men on a fall day, rather than on his face. And when he saw Ray with the policeman down on the towpath and shouted out, "That's the man," Ray had been wearing just his slacks and a white T-shirt. The only person who had actually gotten a close look at the suspect's face was the jogger who'd passed him on the towpath, and he had not been able to identify Ray Crump as that man. He had, however, solidified in the minds of the jury the all-important height estimate of five feet eight inches.

And so I ended where I'd begun, with a little case for a little man. I thought much of Raymond each evening as I rocked on my porch swing and scribbled on my legal pad, of the human being I'd struggled to protect from the destructive forces of prison, the human being in whose innocence I believed, and whose life I was striving to save. Raymond Crump was not a great man, to be sure. He had none of the qualities of mind that the world prizes. He was limited in his mental powers. He drank too much. He'd been unfaithful to his wife. He was the sort of person society considered so expendable that if he were subtracted from the human population, no one would miss him except his mother. But he was a human being, and he counted in the eye of the Lord, and in the eye of the law as well, which regards men as God does, all equal one to another. That was the ideal I had embraced in my first weeks at Howard law school when Professor Nabrit had held up to us the dissent of Justice John Marshall Harlan in *Plessy,* lest we despair in our fight for justice: "There is no caste here. Our Constitution is color-blind, and neither knows nor tolerates classes among its citizens. In respect of civil rights, all citizens are equal before the law. The humblest is the peer of the most powerful. The law regards man as man, and takes no account of his surroundings or of his color when his civil rights as guaranteed by the supreme law of the land are involved."

My case was twenty minutes long. It consisted of three character witnesses from Raymond's neighborhood and one exhibit. The exhibit was Raymond himself. At five feet three inches tall and 130 pounds, I told the jury in my opening statement, he was my Exhibit A.

One by one, the church folk took the stand, his mother's minister, the Reverend Jesse Brown, then the superintendant of the Second Baptist Sunday School, Louise Wester, and finally another man from the church,

Roach Young. They'd all known Raymond for many years, they told the jury. They knew him to be peaceful and orderly, and so did everyone they'd talked to about him in the community. Their testimony lasted perhaps twenty minutes. When it was over, I rested my case.

There wasn't a sound in the courtroom, except Mr. Hantman's chair scraping as he stood up and looked at me, and then at Judge Corcoran, in pure astonishment.

"If Your Honor please, I am caught completely flat-footed at this moment," Mr. Hantman said. "I never in my wildest dreams anticipated that counsel would rest her case."

But I had done all I needed to do. The prosecution had given me my case, and I'd tried it.

I rose and walked to the jury box to deliver the closing argument I had been preparing for days, or perhaps, as I think of it now, for my whole life. Every principle for which my grandmother and Miss Neptune and Dr. Bethune and Dr. Nabrit had taught me to fight was on trial in this case, and as I walked toward the jury and began speaking, I felt as though everything I'd ever done had been moving me toward this moment.

"This, as the court told you at the outset, is a serious case," I began. "You hold in your hands the life of a man—a little man, if you please."

His fate depended now, I told them, on whether they believed that the man seen by the government eyewitnesses was the man seated at the defense table.

"I told you in my opening that one exhibit you had before you for eight days. You had it from the moment you took this case—Raymond Crump, Jr. When you go into the jury room, you will take with you his image, and you must answer, I submit, the question: does he weigh 185 pounds? That was the lookout given to the world at large, that there was a man five feet eight on the towpath that did indeed murder this poor lady. This is not Raymond Crump, Jr."

This case that had seemed so very complicated was really very simple, I told the jurors.

"You can remember everything, these mountains of evidence presented by Mr. Alfred Hantman, remember all of that, if you please—place the jacket on him, give him a light-colored jacket, give him a cap, if you please. Well, then you must make him grow, and you must fill him out in dimensions which simply do not exist."

That alone, I said, should be enough to create reasonable doubt in anyone's mind. But there was more. The government had not produced the single piece of evidence central to any murder case: a weapon. And why not? Because it was never there to be found. "The man who committed this dastardly murder left," I said, "and he took with him this gun.

"All through this case counsel has attempted to explain things away. He attempted to say to you that gunpowder which would be on the hands of a person in firing that gun, that all of this is washed away. It had to be.

"He attempted to say that all the blood was washed away. He has to say that, ladies and gentlemen of the jury, to try and fit Raymond Crump, Jr., into this package, into this dramatic presentation he is making, weaving together facts here, half facts there, and saying to you that you have no choice. There is only one person, and only one person could have done it, and that person is Raymond Crump, Jr.

"I say to you, you must have reasonable doubt from all of the evidence that has been adduced before you. You must have reasonable doubt, if for no other reason than that the dimensions of the person out on the towpath, the dimensions of the person seen by two persons, exact in every particular, simply do not fit Raymond Crump, Jr."

I looked into the faces of the jury—the twelve people who'd listened so closely to every word of the trial. They had the power to take Ray's life away from him. But they also had the power to set him free. This was what I'd fought for.

"We have brought you character witnesses who testified before you this morning. Perhaps when I called them, you said: well, she is not giving much evidence. I gave you the most important evidence anyone can present for another person. 'He who steals from me my purse steals trash, but take away from me my'—what?—'my good name' and you have taken all that I have."

I turned and looked over at Ray, and then I turned back to the jury.

"I leave this little man in your hands."

The courtroom was silent when the jurors filed back in and took their seats.

"Mr. Foreman," the clerk asked, "has the jury agreed upon its verdict?"

"It has."

The clerk handed the slip of paper to Judge Corcoran and asked the jury to rise.

"Members of the jury," the judge said, "we have your verdict, which states that you find the defendant, Ray Crump, Jr., not guilty. And this is your verdict, so say you each and all?"

The jurors nodded.

"Raymond Crump," Judge Corcoran said, "you are a free man."

Mrs. Crump cried out, and so did her minister and her friends from church.

I hugged Ray and he hugged me back. I took him by the arm and led him through the press of people out onto Constitution Avenue.

"Is there anywhere you want to go, Ray?" I asked him.

He looked at me and answered, "I wants to go home."

12. Healing the Brokenness

In the eight months during which I had Raymond Crump in my keeping, and the eight days of the trial when I acted as his advocate at the bar of justice, I reached into every part of my mind, drew upon nearly every area of my legal training, tapped every recess of my heart, and looked into my soul for the understanding that neither the law nor my intellect could provide. No case, before or since, consumed me in quite the same way. And no case left me so changed.

It brought me, to begin with, the kind of success of which many lawyers dream. If success is defined as volume of cases, notoriety in the press, and respect in the legal community, then it can fairly be said that in the wake of the Crump case, I achieved it. Judges appointed me to some of the toughest murder cases to come before the court in the District of Columbia, and I was honored and proud to serve at their behest, proud to win acquittal for other men who, like Ray, had no chance at all. I believe, too, that the wall of prejudice that had kept me and my black colleagues at the margins of the system truly began to crumble in the months following the Crump acquittal. I'd gone into the trial with the sense that I was being tested and watched by many who resented my presence in such a high profile case, but I felt, afterwards, that at last I'd won acceptance, and in so doing, helped to make a way for young attorneys of every color. I took a great many of them to my bosom, opened my office for seminars, coached and trained and mentored them, even as I'd been mentored by Professor Nabrit and Professor Hayes. Magnificent young Howard law students like Norma Holloway Johnson, who rose to become chief judge of the U.S. District Court for the District of Columbia, the same federal court where I tried the Crump case, were, they told me, inspired by what they witnessed in that fourth-floor courtroom in the last two weeks of July in 1965. These things are precious to me, more than I can say.

I believe, too, that in winning acquittal for Ray Crump, I made it impossible for the matter of Mary Pinchot Meyer's murder to be sealed off and forgotten, as the government so clearly wanted to do. There is much about the crime that bears the most serious and sustained investigation, and to the extent that my efforts in defending Raymond opened the path for researchers seeking to know more about the troubling circumstances surrounding her death, I am gratified.

But if the way was made for further probing into Mary Meyer's murder, and if the District of Columbia became a place of fair play for black lawyers through my efforts, and if women attorneys have an easier path in part because of my battle in the summer of 1965, it is also true that there was a great and heartbreaking loss in the matter of *United States v. Ray Crump*. That loss was Raymond himself.

He did not lose his life. I saw to that. But he lost himself. That which I had feared, and over time felt as a near certainty, came to pass. The little man who disintegrated before my eyes in the eight months of his imprisonment was in fact truly shattered. I had seen it before, with men whose minds were broken by what happened to them in jail, and I would see it again, but I never grew quite so heartsick as when I learned, piece by piece, of the deadly and destructive effect prison had wrought upon Raymond Crump. He was not a remotely violent man when he was jailed for Mary Meyer's murder in 1964, but he became one afterward, both in the District of Columbia and later in North Carolina, where he eventually moved with his second wife. Never did he commit murder, but he lashed out in any number of ways at people he believed had wronged him, setting fires, torching the car of a mechanic he'd fought with, threatening two of his girlfriends with violence, and moving constantly in and out of prison. Could he have been helped, if at some point he had sought me out? The answer, I believe, must be no, because I am now prepared to say that it was too late for Raymond on the day of his acquittal of the Meyer murder, when he'd stood on Constitution Avenue and told me, "I wants to go home."

I grieve for Raymond, and the disintegration of his life, and my grief is for more than just the loss of one individual person. For the truth is that what happened to Raymond Crump in the years following his acquittal on July 30, 1965, was but a mirror, an emblem, of the chaos and the violence and the self-destruction I saw taking hold of my own beloved community of Anacostia. *The beloved community*: how many times I embraced that magnificent phrase, spoken by Dr. King in speech after speech from his earliest days in Montgomery. It captured for me the Charlotte of my childhood, expanded wide to include people of all races, after the vision of Miss Neptune and Dr. Bethune, and it seemed to me no idle, foolish dream but something that with enough tough-mindedness we might actually achieve. The beloved community, King told us, was the redemption and reconciliation that would follow upon nonviolence, the love that would "bring about miracles in the hearts of men." Yet it eluded us, moving forever and forever as we moved, vanishing in the wake of each victory. Somehow, it seemed all of a piece, the forward motion and the backward. The summer of the Crump case became for America the summer of the passage of the Voting Rights Act, but also of the Watts riots. I watched the civil rights movement splinter and become riven with voices of hatred and separatism. And then, on that terrible afternoon of April 4, 1968, when Dr. King was gunned down in Memphis, the dream of brotherhood and peace he had evoked seemed to vanish all together.

My city, the city I loved despite its hurts, the place where I had made my home and fallen in love with the law and pressed the cause of justice, exploded into flames. In one great paroxysm of rage and pain, Washington turned in on itself and tore its insides out. To those who may find that characterization hyperbolic, let me say that it expresses more accurately than the facts of the newspaper accounts what happened inside me after the assassination of Dr. King. History records that the burning and looting and rioting that took place in Washington, DC, concentrated itself around Fourteenth and U streets, but as I walked to my office on Eleventh Street from the courthouse on the first day of the madness, as I saw the smoke billowing and heard sirens wailing and passed people running, I felt as though the whole world had come to an end.

A single catastrophic event can never truly be said to alter the universe, of course. But I see the death of Martin Luther King, Jr., as the marker of a deep and rapid descent into chaos. My own Anacostia, already torn by the first infestation of drugs, spiraled downward, and it became an emblem for cities and communities all over America, where once peaceful streets began to turn to killing fields. All of society seemed to become infected. I wondered whether any place was immune from the brutality of the times. And I thought of my girlhood, and the place in Charlotte we called Blue Heaven.

When the summer breezes blew our way, we could smell the open stills of Blue Heaven's bootleggers from our porch. We could hear its sensuous, swaying music, the raucous laughter of the women of the night, and the frightening sound of gunfire exploding from time to time, mostly in the hours between Saturday evening and Sunday morning, when desperation and drunkenness mixed with each other and became murderous. But we were children of the day, my sisters and my little brothers and I, and Blue Heaven did not touch us. Our backyard fence and a narrow creek separated us from that world of damnation, and if a storm had ever demolished those barriers, we had Grandma and Mama and Grandpa to draw the line up tight, to wall us in, and keep Blue Heaven out.

In the years after Dr. King's death, I began to see Blue Heaven everywhere about me. Where was the line, so very clear in my childhood, between the good and the bad, the wholesome and the vulgar, the nourishing and the destructive? I looked for it, and I saw it vanishing before my eyes, and with it, our children, those who if their hearts were whole and their minds untainted, might be the builders of the beloved community. More and more, as I labored at the bar and in the pulpit and in the privacy of the counseling room, I confronted shattered children, children caught between warring parents, children who'd borne witness to the most horrific crimes, children neglected and shunted aside, children preyed upon by those entrusted with their care. Seeing this, I began to shift the direction of my law practice in the seventies and eighties, even as I had chosen a different path in the fifties, in the wake of the Sarah Keys case. It was the pain of ordinary men and women who had no voice, no money, and no chance that had moved me then. But that pain began to pale beside the wreckage I saw among children. And so I threw myself into yet another war, a war for the children. My legal practice and my ministry at Allen Chapel, tightly bound from the beginning, became almost indistinguishable, one from another.

What I sought couldn't be found at the defense table, nor was it primarily a legal endeavor. More often than not I found myself doing battle outside the courtroom, moving from one side of the courthouse hallway to the other, brokering agreements between spouses over the matter of child custody, sowing peace as best I could between people whose hatred was often palpable. I represented one side or the other, as I had to do, but the party for whom I fought was the child. I'd work on the mothers and fathers the way I'd worked on my juries in criminal cases, and when I went before the judges in the family court I pled not for simple justice, but for what I called "a little healing." Some of the wisest judges I have ever known presided over my domestic and juvenile cases, but I began to understand that no amount of judicial wisdom or lawyerly eloquence could fix what was broken.

I had known for many, many years, of course, the devastating effects of trauma upon children. I'd understood that from the day I reached out to hug Peggy Pledger when she arrived at the bus station for her first visit at Christmastime, 1964, and she'd put her hands up and pulled away from me. Over the years, I managed to break through that wall, but I never doubted that there was at the core something I couldn't touch, a void so great no outpouring of love could fill it. How I begged Peggy, when she graduated from high school in 1967, to come to college in Washington, under my protective wing. Her answer hurt to hear, it was so filled with bitterness and confusion. She told me that people "knew about her" in Washington, knew what her father had done, and they would hold it against her.

I listened, stunned, understanding that this was a child so wounded, so crippled by her pain that she saw the whole world as her enemy, saw contempt where there was none, imagined rejection in the minds of total strangers. No matter how I argued and cajoled and reasoned with her about the irrelevancy of her family's history, she would not bend. And so with great misgivings, I watched her set out for St. Augustine's College in Florida in the fall of 1967, knowing she'd excel academically and that she would, in all probability, flounder in every other way. I was right on both counts. Peggy's logical mind stood her in good stead as a mathematics major, but for all her stellar accomplishments in that realm, she wrestled with depression and anger and just plain hurt. She phoned me constantly, and I was glad for the calls, believing that so long as she continued to reach out to me, I could help, somehow. I'm not sure, in retrospect, what I did, except love her.

Each time she appeared at my doorstep, as she did every other weekend when she graduated from college and began teaching, I welcomed her, and sat her down and talked and talked. I often spoke to Peggy about her father, about how much I'd thought of him, how trapped he'd been, how much he'd loved her and her little brother, Vincent. I'm not sure she believed me. She'd been betrayed, as she saw it, by the person dearest to her, and she saw betrayal everywhere—in every boyfriend, every professor, every classmate, and as I tried to counsel her,

I felt something akin to the powerlessness I'd experienced in dealing with her father. Knowing Peggy's pain so intimately, I came to see every wounded child who crossed my path in the most intense and urgent way. And as I grew up with Peggy, and grew older, I witnessed yet another shift in the world at large, a change that pushed me to the brink of despair—the realization that with stunning frequency, children were not merely victims of violence, they were perpetrators.

There can be no greater horror, I think, than this. I saw the evidence of this disease of our time not only in newspaper statistics and the reports of the many task forces on which I served, but right in front of me, in my neighborhood, in the streets of Anacostia where I'd found such peace during my law school years, which now rang with gunfire and the screech of sirens. And the children who came into court, charged with murder and gang violence, were young, and young, and younger. To officiate at the funeral of a little boy gunned down by other boys, as I did in 1996, to visit boys imprisoned for murder and assault and know that theirs would likely be the fate of Raymond Crump, to see the demon of violence infecting even our young girls—these were the markers of a time I had never imagined, even in nightmare.

None of us dares stand idle or silent in the face of this plague. Age has taken my strength, and it has robbed me of my eyesight, but I have yet a voice, and I raise it this day, at this hour, for our little children, that we may do right by them, that we who are their parents and their grandparents, their teachers and their pastors may nurture them and hold them to our bosoms, that we may baste them in love, that we may weave about them the cocoon of family, and that we may do this from the moment they are born. To do less than this is to leave them vulnerable to the corruption of our times, to the seductive power of the world outside the home. In every pulpit to which I have access at this stage of my life—legal conventions, bar association meetings, women's gatherings and symposia all over the country—I plead this cause, the cause of our little children. I have battled in my time for so many kinds of justice, fought for integration in the army, pressed for racial fairness before the ICC, argued for the rights of hundreds upon hundreds of men and women in courts of law, but no battle of my half century at the bar has been so urgent as the one for the next generation. If every matter before every court in America were foreclosed this moment as a litigable issue, there would yet remain the cause of our little children. They are the case at bar. Theirs is the case I plead now.

The kind of justice I seek today is older by far than the law, and it resides in people's hearts. It is nursed into being not primarily in the pulpit or the classroom or the courtroom, but in the home, at the fireside and the dining room table, in the thousands of intimate moments when mother and father and children weave their bond. It is in this sanctuary that the passing on takes place, that the "miracle in the hearts of men" of which Dr. King spoke unfolds itself. I know this to be true. I know it in my mind, and also in my heart, and I know it in the most intensely personal way, because I was granted, in my last years, the miracle of motherhood and grandmotherhood, and with that, a way of understanding the world that had eluded me even in the deepest moments of my ministry. In the magnificent young woman named Charlene Pritchett, who came into my life on a Sunday morning in 1992 when she gave me a ride home from services at Allen Chapel, I found not only a companion and helpmate in my increasing infirmity, but a true and faithful and much beloved daughter. And in her son, James Andrew, I was given a grandson, and a whole world.

That such a fate should have been visited upon me in my ninth decade defies all logic and certainly the laws of chance. Yet that is the way of every great miracle of my ninety-four years—the improbable intersection of Mary McLeod Bethune's life with that of my grandmother; Miss Neptune's orchestration of the loan that enabled me to finish Spelman College; the presence, at critical points in my development, of mentors like Dr. Nabrit and colleagues like Julius; the wisdom of judges who helped me to save children when the odds of time and place argued that redemption was impossible. These are blessings so rooted in the Divine that we exhaust ourselves in trying to account for them in earthly terms.

In that first ride home from services at Allen Chapel in 1992, Charlene and I forged a bond unlike any other I had known—she a health education graduate with her mind set on a master's degree in health services, I a woman in physical decline but bent nevertheless on practicing law and remaining in the pulpit. She had lost her own mother at the age of twenty-one, and in my debilitation and my aloneness in my empty house after the death of my friend Gwen in 1985, Charlene became my salvation. It was she who, along with my incomparable helpmate, driver, and personal assistant, Carroll Johnson, enabled me to continue to practice law and preach on Sundays even as my diabetes overtook me. When there came into Charlene's life the crisis of an unplanned pregnancy and she faced the prospect of single parenthood, we took it on together, she and I. And so it was that on the fifteenth of May in 1995, as I stood beside Charlene in the delivery room for the birth of James Andrew Pritchett, I became a grandmother.

I had thought, when Peggy Pledger came into my home in 1964 as a girl of seventeen, that I had known domestic upheaval. And I'd seen, in small doses, what joyful havoc little children can wreak when Peggy began visiting me with her son, Jonavin, and later, her little girl, Paloma. But James Andrew Pritchett was in my home to stay, and from the moment his tiny fist grasped my forefinger and held on tight, he had ahold of my heart.

At last I understood the overpowering devotion Julius had for his four children and the intensity with which he regarded the Supreme Court's decision in *Brown v. Board of Education*. To me, *Brown* was a monumental blow for justice; to Julius, it was a personal promise for his children. So it is with all parents and grandparents. James Andrew became for me not only my much-treasured and, I freely admit, much-indulged little boy. He became for me the whole future. The stakes, already high, became for me higher still. I preached after his birth with a new understanding, and more often than not, when James grew old enough to stand, I had him right by my side.

But it was not at the lectern or in the pulpit, and certainly not in the courtroom that I fought my final battle for justice. I fought it with James in the wide open spaces and peaceful fields of the Virginia countryside, where I moved with him and his mother to a life of retirement. There, in Spotsylvania, Virginia, at the edge of the site of the Battle of Chancellorsville, James and I would take long walks, and have great and winding talks and much sharing of wisdom, back and forth, and endless telling of stories, his about his adventures in kindergarten and day camp, mine about Grandma Rachel. Little boys do not, I discovered, sit still for any length of time, so I told my "Grandma stories," as James called them, on the run. In the center of Charlene's backyard we placed one of my most prized possessions, the enormous cast-iron cauldron in which Grandma made her lye soap, and that cauldron, converted into a giant flower pot, became the starting point for many a story. We'd begin there, James and I, of a morning, and I'd tell him of the bubbling and foaming that took place as my grandmother poured in her fat drippings and her Red Devil lye powder, and how she'd whack me with her wooden spoon to keep me away from the flames. I told of how she'd stand out on the porch and shake her fist at the lightning, how on summer mornings when the rest of Charlotte was asleep, she'd take me into the forest with her just before sunrise to pick blackberries, read the darkness, call to the birds. I do a pretty fair imitation of any number of bird calls, and James does a pretty fair imitation of everything, and between the two of us, calling and crowing to each other around the edges of the cornfield that was once a battlefield, the two of us really got some storytelling going.

One story cannot change the world, I know. But one child can. In every child like my James Andrew, there is infinite potential, untarnished and whole, and it is in ministering to our children that we stand to alter the future. It took James to teach me the final lesson about King's "beloved community," and to make me believe, really *believe*, that it could be achieved. It took James, too, to bring me to a full understanding of the miracle making of my grandmother, of what she accomplished in the humblest ministrations of daily life. With all the ugliness outside us in Charlotte, it was good around our table. It was good when Mama sang, and Grandma hummed. It was good when Grandpa brought home a watermelon, or a cantaloupe, or a bushel of ripe tomatoes for Grandma to can, or a sack of peaches we'd peel for pies, and, every once in a while, steal a slice on the sly. That was good. That was *good* good. All of that hurt, out there and over there, somehow could not and did not disturb that sense of precious fellowship that Grandma created with corn pudding, or rice pudding, or bread pudding with raisins all plumped up. She is the reason I am able to look at the darkness and confusion of our times, and know that if we minister to our children as she ministered to me, redemption is truly possible. It is, indeed, inevitable.

No world could have been darker than mine on the night my father died. Our home was filled with whispering, weeping adults who moved about, consulting with Grandma about whatever it is that people find to consult about in death, and doing their best to comfort my mother, but failing entirely, so far as I could tell. The entire house seemed to my four-year-old's ears to be filled with the sound of her weeping, and I could not bear the sound. I wandered about, and watched the visitors, and at last I crawled under the kitchen table. The oilcloth cover reached almost to the floor, and made a kind of fort for me. I unlaced my shoes, and curled up and held my ears against the sound of the crying.

I didn't know I'd fallen asleep until I heard my sister Bea's voice, calling for me. She must have seen my feet, for she whooshed down upon me and took me in her arms, and led me out into the kitchen. The company was gone, and my grandmother was moving about, heating water on the stove and pouring it into the great metal tub in which we children took our baths.

The autumn air was chilly but next to the stove it was warm.

"It's bedtime, Dovey Mae," Grandma said to me, unbuttoning my jumper and lifting it over my head. She hugged me to her, and then she hoisted me into the tub. The water was warm, and I sank into it and breathed in the smell of Grandma, so near, and of the lye soap she was swooshing across my back. She was humming, as she loved to do whenever she worked, and every once in a while, she'd start singing the words of whatever hymn had filled her mind that evening. It may have been a hymn of mourning—it must have been—but to me it sounded like angels' singing, because it drowned out the sound of my mother's crying, coming from the bedroom. Grandma left nothing to chance where cleanliness was concerned. She had a system for everything, including the bathing of little children. Methodically, she cleaned my back, my arms, my underarms, behind my ears, my neck, my scalp. When she was satisfied that she and her lye soap had done everything they possibly could, she had me stand. She lifted me out, reached for the towel she had warming next to the stove, wrapped me in it, and rubbed me dry, head to toe.

And then she gave me a great, great hug.

"*Now*, Dovey Mae, you're ready for bed," she said.

With that there came a peace over me. Young as I was, I understood that there was a time, and a place, and a way of doing a task that must be followed, a system that she would adhere to no matter what, and that I was a part of that orderly stream of things. And I knew that she loved me. That bath, that night, was my real beginning. The undisturbable thing, so fragile and yet so strong that it abides with me yet, began with a bath and the humming of hymns.

It was the beginning of true goodness, of the time I remember so clearly and with such joy, the times of singing and lye-soap making and canning and cooking and bread making and berry picking, those most magical of forays into the woods that I, and only I among all my sisters, would take with Grandma.

So it is for every child. In these small things, in the moment to moment, in the thousand acts of loving, the future is built, society molded. As I look back upon the great mentors who have shaped me, Edythe

Wimbish and Miss Neptune, Dr. Bethune and Professor Nabrit, I am awed, and profoundly grateful for their brilliance, their erudition, their wisdom. But we live in times that require a particular kind of healing, and urgently so. And in my quest for the answers to the crisis of our children, it is my grandmother I turn to, more than any other person, for it is she who led me out of the darkness, who put the world right, who made for me the way out of no way.

BENEDICTION

[T]here will arise the sun of justice with its healing rays.

MALACHI 3:20

In my memory, it is midsummer, in the hour before dawn, dark and cool and shadowy. It is a time so etched in my heart that, a thousand mornings later, I can call it up fresh and whole, smell the damp earth, feel the dew-laden air on the back of my neck, hear the swish, swish of my grandmother's skirts as we move through the darkness toward the woods where blackberries grow.

Silently, we pad along, my grandma Rachel and I, the only two people awake in the still-sleeping world, her long skirts brushing the dirt path, the tin berry pail that is almost as big as I am banging against my knees as I trot behind her. How quiet the world is, as though holding its breath for one last, long moment before darkness gives way to daybreak. I hold my breath, too, trying my best to be as noiseless as Grandma as we pause at street corners and wait for the other berry pickers to join us.

One by one, as if by some secret signal, they appear in doorways and fall into line behind us. By daylight, these are the grown-up ladies who come to quilt with Grandma, pass food over the fence, gather in our backyard for soap making. But now they are just shadowy figures in our grand, silent procession, our secret mission, our berry picking.

It grows cooler as we enter the forest, and darker. There was a time, when I was four or five, when the darkness frightened me. But now I'm six and I know, because Grandma has taught me, that darkness isn't something to be afraid of. If you wait just a little, she says, your eyes will learn to see, and you can find your way. So I stand blinking, knowing that in a minute or two, things will begin to come clear. In the meantime, Grandma's voice cuts through the shadows, pulling me to her.

"Dovey Mae?" she calls out. "Where is you?"

"I'm right here," I answer. "Right over here."

"Well, you hold on to my apron, child. Might be some snakes in these woods."

I reach out, take a fistful of starched apron in my hand, and we begin to walk. Grandma's steps are swift and sure, and I move as she does, stopping when she stops to poke the underbrush with her snake-whacking stick. In the leaves ahead of me, I can just make out the flash of her high-top shoes. I fix my eyes on the shiny heels. And I listen.

The darkness holds a thousand sounds. Softly, somewhere very near, a family of birds, disturbed by our passage, flutters in the bushes, while from off in the distance comes the shrill, hollow caw of a crow, and farther away another, answering. As we push deeper and deeper into the woods, the blackness turns to gray, and sleepy birds begin calling to each other, setting the treetops echoing.

Grandma says the birds'll lead you to the best berries, every time. Sure enough, as we follow the sound of beating wings just ahead, we come into a clearing ringed with berry-studded bushes. The ladies swoop down, pails clanging, but I move closer to Grandma, following the sweep of her hand as it grazes a bush and comes back with the first berry of the day, frosted with dew. I open my mouth, she drops in the berry, and I bite down hard, and suck the juice, and know that there is no blackberry anywhere like this one, so fat it squirts seedy blue juice down my overalls and so sweet I keep licking my lips to get the taste. Grandma looks down at me and laughs. Then she turns to the bushes and commences to hum, the way she does when it's time to get to work.

The clearing fills with the sound of berries hitting tin pails, and jealous birds squawking, and flies buzzing, and laughter, and Grandma's humming, and the grown-up-lady talk I love better than anything. From my spot in the bushes I pick berries as fast as I can and listen to the whispers of the goings-on at church, of who's courting and who's marrying, who's just had a baby and who might have a baby next, of when the circus is coming to town, and what'll happen when it does.

Already, heat is rising from the forest floor, making me think of the feast that is coming in just a little while, of how I'll eat berries from the minute I get home to the minute I go to bed. Soon, there'll be blackberries from one end of our screen porch to the other—berries soaking in big tubs of cool water, berries, sugar-sprinkled, spread out across newspapers to dry. And all around the edges, on every spare inch of wooden ledge, will be the greens and roots and wild onions and seed pods Grandma is gathering now.

I watch her bend down, poking away in the underbrush, and I wonder how in the world she knows, in all that leafy mess, what to bother with. Some of the things in the forest are hurtful, she says, and some are healing—but how to tell one from another? Sometimes I think that my grandmother must have just about everything in the world buried down in that head of hers, things about what to pick and what to leave behind, about which leaf will stop a cough, or suck the pain from a cut, or clear your lungs. Again and again, as we move along the creek bank, she reaches low or stands a-tiptoe to pluck a green fruit from up high, berry picking all the while.

And then, suddenly, in the middle of her rush, she stops.

"Look, Dovey Mae," she whispers. "Over yonder."

I follow the line of her pointing finger to a spot off in the distance, outside the forest, where sky meets earth. All is gray there, but I am sure even before Grandma announces it that this is the place where the dawn will break, because I know that in the midst of watching me and watching the birds and snake whacking and berry picking and filling her bag with medicine makings, my grandmother waits for the sun. She waits, and she watches, and when she spots it, she sets down her pail and puts out the word, calling the sun, the way she does just about everything else she loves, by name.

"She's comin'!" she whispers. "Comin' up right over there!"

Slowly, slowly, the horizon pinkens.

"Here she comes! Here she comes!" Grandma whispers. She draws me to her, and together, we watch the pink turn to red, the red to gold. Then, all at once, as if at my grandmother's command, the orange ball that is the sun shows its face.

It rises up over the edge of the world, and as it does, Grandma rises, too, and stands, just looking. She is so still, so quiet, her face shining in the light, that I wonder whether she is even breathing.

I don't know how long we stay there watching the colors shift, but when Grandma claps her hand on my shoulder and shakes out her skirts, dawn is day.

The sun lights up the clearing, shining on the berry bushes, dancing on the creek, coloring pink and gold everything we've collected in the darkness. The heat and the light and the rising birdsong overhead all push us along, toward berry rinsing and berry sugaring and berry eating for some time to come. My grandmother turns and heads down the path, as quick and hurried now, leading me homeward, as she was motionless at the moment of daybreak. In that whisper of time between the work of the night and the work of the day, how still she stood, celebrating.

Always, in memory, I see her there, standing in the clearing, pail and sack at her feet, face upturned to meet the dawn.

Always, I see her waiting for the sun.

NOTES

Dovey Roundtree and I set out in *Justice Older than the Law* to render the story of her life in as personal and intimate a manner as possible. Yet her life is also history with important implications for scholars seeking a deeper understanding of the black experience in the World War II military, of the events and influences that led to the *Brown v. Board of Education* decision and the dismantling of Jim Crow in public transportation, and of the renowned figures who influenced Dovey's formation as a lawyer and civil rights activist. I have therefore provided citations and, in the case of her military history, notes on additional sources for readers who may wish to further investigate the events chronicled in this book.

The World War II period presents particular difficulties for those seeking a comprehensive and balanced view of the African American experience in the military. Those readers interested in further context for the account presented in this book are referred to Martha S. Putney's *When the Nation Was in Need: Blacks in the Women's Army Corps During World War II* (Metuchen, NJ, and London: Scarecrow Press, 1992). Basing her account on correspondence and contemporary press accounts and on interviews with pioneers in the WAAC/WAC (including extensive interviews with Dovey Johnson Roundtree), Putney provides the most extensive analysis available of the U.S. military's approach to race and segregation as it affected black servicewomen during the war, as well as a detailed history of black recruiting from 1942 to 1945.

The experience of black military personnel during this period is also dealt with in two publications of the Office of the Chief of Military History, Department of the Army, Washington, DC: Mattie E. Treadwell's *The United States Army in World War II: Special Studies: The Women's Army Corps*, 1954, and Ulysses Lee's *The Employment of Negro Troops*, 1966. As noted below, the account of WAAC segregation in Treadwell differs in important particulars from the account presented herein as well as from the account in Putney's *When the Nation Was in Need*.

The Mary McLeod Bethune Papers (Bethune Museum and Archives, Washington, DC) contain extensive correspondence files pertaining to Dr. Bethune's role in overseeing black women's participation in the military during World War II. The papers of Dovey Johnson Roundtree, which include her military records and contemporary press accounts of her recruiting activities for the WAAC/WAC, are housed in the Bethune Museum and Archives.

Chapter 2. Making Somethin' of Yourself

p. 12 *Dr. Bethune presided over the education of college students*: In 1924, Mary McLeod Bethune merged the girls' school she had founded in Daytona Beach, Florida, in 1904 (the

Daytona Educational and Industrial Institute, later the Daytona Normal and Industrial Institute) with the coeducational Cookman Institute in Jacksonville to form a junior college. The institution changed its name to Bethune-Cookman College in 1929. In 1943 its standing was upgraded to a senior college, and it awarded its first bachelor of arts degrees.

Chapter 3. "Pass It On": Spelman and the Legacy of Mae Neptune

p. 29 *or return to a Fatherland now entirely controlled by the Nazis*: "Plebiscite in Saar Has Wide Bearing: Vote on National Destiny Next January May Determine Fate of Europe," Dorothy Thompson, *New York Times*, September 9, 1934, p. E2.

p. 30 *would prove just how widely his doctrine was accepted*: "Dorothy Thompson Home from Berlin: Writer Expelled from Germany Lays Financial Plight to Hitler's Extravagance," *New York Times*, September 15, 1934, p. 15; "Hitler Main Factor in Saar Plebiscite; Without Him There Would Be No Problem to Solve in Worried Territory," Dorothy Thompson, *New York Times*, September 16, 1934, p. E2; "Saar Foes Charge New Nazi Killings; Newspaper Declares 100 Have Been Slain and 1,000 Seized in Hitler Clean-Up," Associated Press, *New York Times*, December 28, 1934, p. 1; "Saar Goes German by 90%; League Deliberates Today; Anti-Nazis Already Fleeing," Associated Press, *New York Times*, January 15, 1935, p. 1; "Saar Nazis Hail Victory As Foes Go Into Hiding; League Decision Today: Joyous Hitlerites March; Unfurl Swastika Flags and Bury 'Old Man Status Quo,'" *New York Times*, January 16, 1935, p. 1.

Chapter 4. My America

p. 42 *rushing toward us*: "President Solemn; Congress Gives Ovation as He Requests Arms to Smash Invader," *New York Times*, May 17, 1940, p. 1; "Auto Plants Ready to Pour out Arms; Industry Already Prepared to Make Tanks, Guns, Plane Motors, Boats, Ammunition," *New York Times*, May 18, 1940, p. 8.

p. 43 *likened it to the Emancipation Proclamation*: "F.D.R.'s Executive Order," *New York Amsterdam Star-News*, July 5, 1941, p. 14. The article says EO 8802 is "epochal to say the least. It marks the first time an American President has issued an executive order affecting the status of the Negro since Abraham Lincoln signed the Emancipation Proclamation . . . the recent order of President Roosevelt is designed to end, or at least curb, economic slavery."

p. 43 *"without discrimination because of race, creed, color or national origin"*: "President Orders an Even Break For Minorities in Defense Jobs: He Issues An Order That Defense Contract Holders Not Allow Discrimination Against Negroes or Any Worker," *New York Times*, June 26, 1941, p. 12.

p. 46 *a stateswoman in Washington*: Gunner Myrdahl, *An American Dilemma: The Negro Problem and Modern Democracy* (New York,: Harper and Row, 1944), p. 987; and Elaine M. Smith, note 2 (p. 206) to "Politics and Public Issues," in *Mary McLeod Bethune: Building a Better World, Essays and Selected Documents* (Bloomington, Indiana: Indiana University Press, 2001), citing columnist Edward Lawson (1937) and philosopher Alain Locke (1939).

p. 49 *the way of things in the military for black folk*: *Pittsburgh Courier*, January 31, 1942; "Remember Pearl Harbor . . . and Sikeston Too!," "Remember Pearl Harbor! Remember Sikeston! Japan and Sikeston, Both Must Fall!," "Japan Lynched Pearl Harbor; Sikeston Lynched Democracy!," *Chicago Defender*, March 14, 1942.

p. 49 *reports of southern "peace officers" . . . at army bases in the South*: *Atlanta Daily World*, May 7, 1942; "Even Axis Cannot Make Dixie Give Up Its Hate" and "Free Us Now, Not After the War," Baltimore *Afro-American*, June 27, 1942; "Soldiers Throughout the World," *Atlanta Daily World*, June 22, 1942.

p. 49 *the idea of women in the military*: *The Congressional Record*, 77th Congress, 1st Session, March 7, 1941, pp. 2014–18, documents the contempt with which congressmen Everett Dirksen and Frank Keefe viewed Eleanor Roosevelt's private White House meeting of February 1942 on the subject of mobilizing American women for the war effort. They condemned the First Lady's plan as a threat to democracy, terming it a conspiracy among women to regiment themselves in the mold of German women.

p. 50 *Marshall himself entered an appearance*: Letter to Hon. Andrew J. May, Chairman of Military Affairs, House of Representatives, December 24, 1941, cited in Report No. 1320 from Hon. Warren R. Austin to accompany H.R. 6293, Report No. 1320 of Committee on Military Affairs, US Senate, 77th Congress, 2nd Session, May 11, 1942.

p. 50 *a new bill authorizing an auxiliary corps had reached the floor of Congress*: Hearings before the Committee on Military Affairs House of Representatives, 77th Congress, 2nd Session on H.R. 6293, A Bill to establish a Women's Army Auxiliary Corps for Service with Army of the United States, January 20 and 21, 1942; hearing before the Committee on Military Affairs United States Senate, 77th Congress, 2nd Session on S. 2240, A Bill to establish a Women's Army Auxiliary Corps for Service with Army of the United States, February 6, 1942.

p. 51 *launched against "Hitler abroad and Hitlerism at home"*: *Pittsburgh Courier*, April 11, 1942, full-page display ad with the headline " 'Double V' Incentive for Unity Among the Races." (The "Double V Campaign" had its genesis in the letter of James G. Thompson, a cafeteria worker at Cessna Aircraft, to the *Pittsburgh Courier*, January 31, 1942, that read in part: "The V for Victory sign is being displayed prominently in all so-called democratic countries . . . then let we colored Americans adopt the double VV for double victory. The first V for victory over our enemies from without, the second V for victory over our enemies from within. For surely those who perpetuate these ugly prejudices here are seeking to destroy our democratic form of government just as surely as the Axis forces.") An account of Mary McLeod Bethune's advocacy of the "Double V Campaign" appeared in the *New York Times*, November 14, 1941, "U.S. Negroes Held Foes of Fascism; Head of National Council of Negro Women Stresses Loyalty of Her Race," p. 20.

p. 52 *right after Pearl Harbor*: "We, Too Are Americans," Mary McLeod Bethune, *Pittsburgh Courier*, January 17, 1942, p. 8.

p. 53 *the arguments of a single woman*: Hearings before the Committee on Military Affairs, US Senate, 77th Congress, 2nd Session, on H.R. 6293, May 1 and May 4, 1942, pp. 44–45 (testimony of Helen Douglas Mankin); "WAAC to Follow Jim Crow Policy: Plan to Train 40 Women as Officers; Organization to Adopt Army Pattern; Texan Named Director," *Chicago Defender*, May 23, 1942, pp. 1, 2.

p. 53 *the bill that passed and was signed into law*: Report No. 1320 (to accompany H.R. 6293) of Committee on Military Affairs, US Senate, 77th Congress, 2nd Session, May 11, 1942; "WAAC to Follow Jim Crow Policy: Plan to Train 40 Women as Officers; Organization to Adopt Army Pattern; Texan Named Director," *Chicago Defender*, May 23, 1942, pp. 1, 2.

p. 53 *on War Department letterhead*: Memorandum, May 1942, War Department, Women's Army Auxiliary Corps, Office of the Director, Washington, Mary McLeod Bethune Papers, Part II (Correspondence File).

Chapter 5. "Everybody's War"

p. 57 *"We are not going to be agitators."*: *Birmingham World*, July 24, 1942, pp. 1, 7.

p. 61 *lawyer and newspaperman Charles Howard*: Letter and report from Charles Howard to Mary McLeod Bethune citing multiple examples of unnecessary discrimination beyond the level of housing Negro candidates in separate barracks, August 26, 1942, Bethune Papers, Part II (Correspondence File). The account of the Office of Military History, which states that "Reports from the first Negro trainees indicated that these prohibitions against discrimination were being upheld to the satisfaction of national Negro organizations" (Treadwell, *Women's Army Corps*, p. 590), differs substantially from Dovey Roundtree's experience as well as from the account in Putney's *When the Nation Was in Need*, pp. 48–70.

p. 61 *had publicly endorsed segregation in the WAAC*: Letter from NAACP executive secretary Walter White to Mary McLeod Bethune, October 28, 1942 (enclosing his letter of same date to Secretary of War Stimson and WAAC director Oveta Culp Hobby), stating that post commandant Col. Morgan had told officers Dovey Johnson and Irma Cayton that they were "agitators," that Bethune had approved segregation, and that they could resign if they could not accept this condition.

p. 62 *from the time the WAAC bill reached Congress*: Undated report of the National Council of Negro Women to the War Department, stating that the council was "working towards the goal of full integration" in the WAAC, demanding that black officers be trained for all specialized assignments for which white officers were trained, and that black enlisted women be assigned to the adjutant general's office, to the Pentagon, and as counselors at Fort Des Moines (War Department WAAC 291.2, Report of the National Council of Negro Women, decimal file Record Group 165).

p. 62 *to bring Mrs. Roosevelt into the fray*: Letter and report from Charles Howard to Mary McLeod Bethune citing multiple examples of unnecessary discrimination beyond the level of housing Negro candidates in separate barracks, August 26, 1942; personal memo from Eleanor Roosevelt to Mary McLeod Bethune discussing September 17 meeting, August 26, 1942; letter from Mary McLeod Bethune to Eleanor Roosevelt's secretary, Malvina Thompson, confirming meeting for September 17 and enclosing Charles Howard's report on discrimination at Fort Des Moines, August 29, 1942 (Mary McLeod Bethune Papers, Part II ([Correspondence File]).

p. 62 *since my commissioning were lily white:* Putney, *When the Nation Was in Need*, appendix 2, Number and Percentage of Blacks in the WAAC/WAC, 1942–1946, p. 155, and appendix 3, Number of Blacks and Their Officer Candidate School Class, p. 156.

p. 63 *they talked privately of resigning:* According to figures provided by Putney, the attrition rate for black servicewomen in World War II exceeded 35 percent (Putney, *When the Nation Was in Need*, p. 46).

p. 64 *sufficient to form an all-black platoon:* This strategy is discussed at length by Putney, *When the Nation Was in Need*, pp. 54–56. Her account and the personal experience of Dovey Roundtree differ from that in the official account of the Office of Military History, which states that "In November of 1942, officers' housing and messing at Fort Des Moines were merged, and also service club facilities, and officer candidate companies became nonsegregated, there being precedent for these steps at some men's schools" (Treadwell, *Women's Army Corps*, p. 591). Correspondence between NAACP executive secretary Walter White and the War Department documents that White and William Hastie, civilian aide to the Secretary of War, were told in November 1942 that "the segregation of colored WAAC officers had been abolished" (letter from Walter White to Natalie Donaldson, November 25, 1942, NAACP Papers, Manuscript Division, Library of Congress). However, when White requested assurance that the OCS would not be resegregated in the event that there were "sufficient number of [black] officers candidates to form a company," the War Department refused to give such assurance. At the time that White and Hastie were told that segregation had been "abolished," the blacks in the OCS class were in fact "organized as a separate squad and quartered in a separate squad room." The twelfth class, which began on November 30, 1943, and had fewer black students than the eleventh, was the first class to be desegregated (Putney, *When the Nation Was in Need*, p. 54).

p. 64 *a press release she issued that fall:* Baltimore *Afro-American*, November 21, 1942.

p. 65 *at posts all over the country, unwanted and unassigned:* Putney, *When the Nation Was in Need*, p. 120.

p. 66 *placed me in the gravest danger:* In November 1943, Congress rejected a bill that would have granted protection to Negro military personnel traveling in Jim Crow states. In July 1945, three uniformed black WACs were brutally beaten by local policemen and incarcerated when they refused to vacate a bench in the white section of the waiting room in a Kentucky bus station. All three were court-martialed, though the court returned a verdict of not guilty. When black leaders pressed for the prosecution of the two policemen, the War Department disclaimed jurisdiction in the case (Putney, *When the Nation Was in Need*, pp. 65–69).

p. 67 *black recruits failed . . . the army's Mental Alertness Test*: Treadwell, *Women's Army Corps*, p. 593.

p. 67 *that white women with the same test scores were commissioned as officers*: Putney, *When the Nation Was in Need*, pp. 120–121, citing Treadwell, *Women's Army Corps*, p. 59.

p. 68 *to eradicate the integrated training regiment*: This memorandum is reprinted in Putney, *When the Nation Was in Need*, appendix 7, p. 174.

p. 70 *I hadn't needed to*: According to records of the Detroit office of the NAACP, two captains and five first lieutenants offered their resignations rather than accept the Jim Crow regiment (291.2, Detroit Office of the NAACP to Mr. Leslie Perry, director of the Washington, DC, office, September 29, 1943, decimel file National Archives Record Group 165).

p. 71 *if not a personal visit*: Undated letter from Mary McLeod Bethune to WAAC director Oveta Culp Hobby, 291.2, historical file National Archives Record Group 165.

p. 71 *issued a memorandum . . . revoking the plan in its entirety*: This memorandum is reprinted in Putney, *When the Nation Was in Need*, p. 17.

p. 71 *urging my return to the field*: Letter from L. Virgil Williams, executive secretary of the Dallas Negro Chamber of Commerce, to WAC director Oveta Culp Hobby, July 2, 1943, WAAC/WAC decimel file National Archives Record Group 165.

p. 72 *who served in the WAC during World War II*: Putney, *When the Nation Was in Need*, p. 126, citing "Strength of the Army" reports for July 1, 1945.

p. 72 *6,500 were black*: Putney, *When the Nation Was in Need*, p. 40, citing unpublished study prepared by the Division of Doctrine and Literature, United States Women's Army Corps School, Fort McClellan, Alabama, 1963.

Chapter 6. Uneasy Peace

p. 74 *"this is what American democracy means to me"*: Mary McLeod Bethune, NBC radio address, "What Does American Democracy Mean to Me?," America's Town Meeting of the Air, New York City, November 23, 1939.

p. 85 *"the essence of the American tradition"*: Pauli Murray, "The Right to Equal Opportunity in Employment," *California Law Review*, vol. 33, no. 3 (September 1945), pp. 388–433.

p. 85 *in behalf of a young law school applicant named Lloyd Gaines*: Missouri ex. rel. Gaines v. Canada 305 US 337 (1938).

Chapter 7. Making War on a Lie: The Assault on *Plessy v. Ferguson*

p. 96 *the assault that would climax in* Brown v. Board of Education: *Brown v. Board of Education of Topeka* 349 US 294 (1954).

p. 96 *the notorious case of* Plessy v. Ferguson: *Plessy v. Ferguson* 163 US 537 (1896).

p. 98 *whose Texas law firm had led the charge for black voting rights in the years before the war*: Nixon v. Herndon 273 US 536 (1927) and Nixon v. Condon 286 US 73 (1932).

p. 101 *with a Boston school segregation case from the days of slavery*: Roberts v. City of Boston 5 Cushing's Reports 198 (1849).

p. 101 *and one which flatly contradicted its own reasoning in* Plessy: *Yick Wo v. Hopkins* 118 US 356 (1886).

p. 102 *"cannot put them upon the same plane"*: Plessy, supra.

p. 103 *in behalf of the Baltimore woman named Irene Morgan*: Morgan v. Virginia 328 US 373 (1946).

p. 103 *outside the reach of the government*: Chiles v. Chesapeake & Ohio Railway Co. 218 US 71 (1910).

p. 104 *against the University of Missouri*: Missouri ex. rel. Gaines v. Canada 305 US 337 (1938).

p. 104 *her name was Ada Lois Sipuel*: Sipuel v. Oklahoma State Board of Regents 322 US 631 (1948).

p. 106 *the Court sided with the school board*: Carr v. Corning 182 F. 2d 14 (1950).

p. 107 *in an Austin office building*: Sweatt v. Painter 339 US 629 (1950).

p. 107 *the University of Oklahoma granted admission*: McLaurin v. Oklahoma State Regents for Higher Education 339 US 637 (1950).

p. 108 *five cases that would make history under the caption "Brown v. Board" was born*: Bolling v. Sharpe 347 US 497 (1954).

p. 110 *using every weapon available to a lawyer at that time* (p. 110) to *separateness was inherently unequal* (p. 111): Brief for Elmer Henderson, September 8, 1949, U.S. Supreme Court, October term, 1949, docket no. 25.

p. 111 "... *which segregation manifests and fosters"*: Brief for the United States, October 5, 1949, U.S. Supreme Court, October term, 1949, docket no. 25.

p. 114 *and emphasized "the artificiality of a difference in treatment"*: Henderson v. U.S. 399 US 816 (1950).

p. 114 *handed down its ruling in* Henderson v. United States: *Henderson*, supra.

p. 117 *"supreme law of the land are involved"*: Plessy, supra.

Chapter 8. Taking on "The Supreme Court of the Confederacy": The Case of Sarah Louise Keys

p. 118 *for* Plessy v. Ferguson *was about to come under full-scale attack*: Plessy, supra.

p. 119 *In his own school case,* Bolling v. Sharpe: *Bolling*, supra.

p. 119 *" 'All men are equal, but white men are more equal than others' "*: From transcript of James M. Nabrit's speech, "An Appraisal of Court Action as a Means of Achieving Racial Segregation in Education," reprinted in *The Journal of Negro Education*, vol. 21, no. 3 (Summer 1952), pp. 421–430.

p. 128 *a 1941 railway segregation case known as* Mitchell v. United States: *Mitchell v. United States* 313 US 80 (1941).

p. 129 *with the Interstate Commerce Commission as well:* Mitchell v. Chicago, Rock Island & Pacific Railway Co., 229 ICC 703 (1938).

p. 131 *as a result of her exposure to "ridicule, contempt . . . and grievous indignities"*: Complaint for False Arrest, Refusal to Honor Contract of Interstate Passage, Violation of Civil Rights, and Unlawful Discrimination Under the Interstate Commerce Act and for Other Causes, *Sarah Keys v. Safeway Trails, Inc. and Carolina Trailways, Inc.,* US District Court for the District of Columbia, Nov. 19, 1952, Civil Action No. 5234–52.

p. 132 *read the headline of the* Courier *article*: Pittsburgh Courier, November 20, 1952.

p. 132 Brown v. Board of Education, *the case from Topeka, Kansas: Brown*, supra.

p. 132 Briggs v. Elliott, *the case from Clarendon County, South Carolina: Briggs v. Elliott* (1951) 347 US 497 (1954).

p. 132 Davis v. County School Board of Prince Edward County, *the case from Virginia: Davis v. County School Board of Prince Edward County* 347 US 483 (1954).

p. 132 *the District of Columbia case Professor Nabrit had taken from Charles Houston upon Houston's death in 1950:* Carr v. Corning 182 F. 2d 14 (1950).

p. 132 *shepherded to its final incarnation as* Bolling v. Sharpe, with a new group of plaintiffs: *Bolling v. Sharpe*, supra.

p. 132 *the case from Delaware,* Belton v. Gebhart: *Belton v. Gebhart* (and *Bulah v. Gebhart*) 347 US 483 (1954).

p. 135 *the full caption of the South Carolina case: Harry Briggs, Jr., et al., Appellants, v. R. W. Elliott, Chairman, J. D. Carson, et al., Members of Board of Trustees of School District No. 22, Clarendon County, S.C. et al., Appellees,* Case No. 101, Tuesday, December 9, 1952.

pp. 135–36 from *Marshall, too, moved and gestured* (p. 135) to: *had to be faced* (p. 136): Text of Oral Argument, Case No. 101, Tuesday, December 9, 1952.

p. 136 *to hear Marshall deliver the rebuttal*: Text of Oral Argument, Case No. 101, Wednesday, December 10, 1952.

p. 137 *they were a Virginia corporation, their affidavit stated*: Order to Quash Return of Service of Summons, and attached affidavit, *Sarah Keys v. Motion of Carolina Coach Company*, US District Court for the District of Columbia, Civil Action No. 5234–52.

p. 138 *on February 23, 1953, they dismissed the case*: Order Dismissing Complaint as to Defendant Safeway Trails, Inc., *Sarah Keys v. Safeway Trails, Inc. and Carolina Trailways, Inc.*, US District Court for the District of Columbia, Civil Action No. 5234–52 (February 23, 1953).

p. 141 *to see a photographer from the Washington bureau of the* Afro-American *show up*: Photograph in the *Washington Afro-American*, August 15, 1953.

p. 141 *Congressman Arthur Mitchell, with his 1937 complaint against Jim Crow seating for first-class Pullman passengers, Mitchell v. Chicago, Rock Island & Pacific Railway Co.,* 299 ICC 703 (1938).

p. 141 *or FEPC representative Elmer Henderson, when he'd protested the Southern Railroad's dining car segregation policy five years later—Henderson v. Southern Railway Co.,* 258 ICC 413 (1944).

p. 142 *when the commission evaluated Arthur Mitchell's complaint*: *Mitchell v. Chicago, Rock Island & Pacific Railway Co.,* supra.

p. 142 *when Elmer Henderson came before the commissioners for the second time in 1946*: *Henderson v. Southern Railway Co.,* 269 ICC 73 (1947).

p. 142 *from September 1, 1953, when Sarah Keys became the first black petitioner*: Complaint for Unlawful Discrimination, Undue Preference, and other Violations of the Interstate Commerce Act and for Damages, *Sarah Keys v. Carolina Trailways, Inc.,* ICC Docket No. MC-C-1564. (The *Keys* case file, along with all other ICC Motor Carrier files, was destroyed by the National Archives and Records Administration. A copy of the case file is available in the files of the Department of Justice Anti-Trust Division, DOJ Case Number 144-54-56.)

pp. 144–45 from *Warren's methodical march through the history of the Fourteenth Amendment* (p. 144) to *"deprived of the equal potection of the laws guaranteed by the Fourteenth Amendment"* (p. 145): *Brown*, supra.

p. 145 *Professor Nabrit's District of Columbia case*, Bolling v. Sharpe: *Bolling*, supra.

p. 146 *to golf courses, public housing, and amusement parks*—Holcombe v. Beal 347 US 974 (1954); *Housing Authority of San Francisco v. Banks* 347 US 974 (1954); *Muir v. Louisville Park Theatrical Association* 347 US 971 (1954).

p. 147 *so Julius and I argued in the brief we filed with the ICC on June 17*: Brief for Complainant, ICC Docket No. MC-C-1564, supra.

pp. 147–48 from *"The Examiner Finds that Carolina Coach Company"* (p. 147) to *invoking them as if they were Holy Writ* (p. 148): Report and Order Recommended by Isadore Freidson, Examiner, September 30, 1954, *Sarah Keys v. Carolina Coach Company*, ICC Docket No. MC-C-1564 (DOJ 144-54-56)

pp. 150–52 from *We began at the beginning* (p. 150) to *and so now must the ICC* (p. 152): Exceptions to Proposed Report and Order, October 19, 1954, *Sarah Keys v. Carolina Coach Company*, ICC Docket No. MC-C-1564 (DOJ 144-54-56).

p. 150 *Whiteside v. Southern Bus Lines, it was called*: *Whiteside v. Southern Bus Lines*, 177 F.2d 949 (6th Circuit 1949).

p. 151 *quoting the words of the justices in* Hirabayashi v. United States: *Hirabayashi v. United States*, 320 US 100 (1943).

p. 152 *against segregation on railroads and in terminal waiting rooms*: NAACP v. St. Louis–San Francisco Railway Company, 297 ICC 335 (1955).

pp. 152–53 from *"We conclude that the assignment of seats in interstate buses"* (p. 152) to *all signs separating waiting rooms into "Colored" and "White" sections in the terminals serving those buses and trains must be removed* (p. 153): Report of the Commission, *Sarah Keys v. Carolina Coach Company*, 64 MCC 769 (1955).

p. 153 *"as soon as practicable"*: Brown v. Board of Education 349 US 294 (1955).

p. 153 *as a legal breakthrough*: "Segregation's End On Buses, Trains Ordered by I.C.C.," *New York Herald Tribune*, November 25, 1955; "Whistling in the Dark," Baltimore *Afro-American*, December 10, 1955; "ICC Outlaws Travel Bias," *Pittsburgh Courier*, December 3, 1955; "ICC Ruling: End of an Era," *Pittsburgh Courier*, December 10, 1955.

p. 153 *the New York Times announced*: *New York Times*, November 25, 1955.

pp. 153–54 *Newsweek called the Keys case "a history-making ruling"*: "Segregation: Anybody's Seats," *Newsweek*, December 5, 1955, p. 23.

p. 154 *on Thanksgiving weekend*: "Balky Dixie Keeps Jim Crow in States," *New York Post*, Sunday, November 27, 1955.

p. 154 *touched me most deeply*: "We Ride Together," Max Lerner, *New York Post*, Monday, November 28, 1955.

p. 155 *two more rulings by the Supreme Court in the field of bus travel*: Gayle v. Browder 352 US 903 (1956) and Boynton v. Virginia 364 US 454 (1960).

Chapter 9. At the Threshold of Justice

p. 156 *and pressed them to deliver on it*: Before the Interstate Commerce Commission, Petition for Rule Making Filed by Attorney General on Behalf of the United States, ICC Docket No. MC-C-3358, May 29, 1961.

p. 156 *and began enforcing them*: Discrimination in Operation of Interstate Motor Carriers of Passengers, 86 MCC 743 (1961).

p. 174 *who cared for his daughter, Peggy*: "GSA Guard Slays Wife, Doctor, Self: Shoots 2 Others at Navy Tempo in Jealous Rage," *Washington Post*, January 12, 1961, pp. A-1, A-27.

p. 176 *in the most recent travel desegregation case*, Boynton v. Virginia: *Boynton*, supra.

p. 177 *an international embarrassment*: Letter from Secretary of State Dean Rusk to the Honorable Robert F. Kennedy, Attorney General, May 29, 1961, attachment to Petition for Rule Making, supra; see also "Bus Segregation Assailed by Rusk: He Backs Robert Kennedy in Bid for I.C.C. Action," *New York Times*, June 2, 1961.

p. 177 *in the pages of New York Times*: "Excerpts From Bus Petition to I.C.C.," *New York Times*, May 29, 1961.

p. 178 *and in the terminals that serviced them*: Discrimination in Operation of Interstate Motor Carriers of Passengers, supra.

Chapter 11. "Peer of the Most Powerful"

p. 189 *who was married to* Newsweek's *Washington bureau chief, Ben Bradlee*: "Grand Jury to Hear Evidence Today in Mary P. Meyer Death," *Washington Post*, October 15, 1964, p. C18.

p. 189 *for more than a decade afterward*: Reports of an affair between Mary Pinchot Meyer and the late President Kennedy first appeared in the tabloid press in 1976, along with the suggestion of CIA involvement in her murder. Later that year, the story was covered by reporters Philip Nobile and Ron Rosenbaum in the *New Times* ("The Mysterious Murder of JFK's Mistress," Philip Nobile and Ron Rosenbaum, *New Times*, October 1976, p. 25). Meyer's romantic relationship with the president and the role of CIA counterintelligence chief James Angleton in the destruction of her diary was eventually corroborated by her brother-in-law, Ben Bradlee, in his 1995 autobiography, *A Good Life: Newspapering and Other Adventures* (New York: Simon & Schuster, 1995), pp. 267–268.

p. 194 *at a distance of three-quarters of a mile*: *Crump v. Anderson*, 352 F.2d 649, June 15, 1965, footnote 10.

p. 194 *handed down just a few days earlier*: *Blue v. U.S.*, 342 F2d 894.

p. 194 *and been found "mentally competent for trial"*: Letter from Dale C. Cameron, M.D., Superintendant, St. Elizabeths Hospital, Washington, DC, to Clerk of the Criminal Division of US District Court for the District of Columbia, January 13, 1965, *U.S. v. Ray Crump, Jr.*, Criminal No. 930-964.

p. 201 *blistering dissent of Judge George Thomas Washington to the majority ruling*: *Crump v. Anderson*, supra.

p. 203 *prejudicial, sensational, inflammatory*: *U.S. v. Ray Crump, Jr.*, Criminal No. 930-64, US District Court for the District of Columbia, Trial Transcript, p. 25.

p. 204 *"We all realize that."*: Trial transcript, p. 30.

p. 205 *"a verdict of guilty as indicted"*: Trial transcript, p. 17.

p. 205 *identification of her body at the morgue*: Trial transcript, p. 43.

p. 206 *that Mary Meyer had been a lover of President Kennedy*: Bradlee, *A Good Life*, p. 268.

p. 206 *Angleton had returned it to them for destruction*: Bradlee, *A Good Life*, p. 271.

p. 207 *and only four of them, he said with absolute certainty*: Trial transcript, p. 111.

pp. 207–8 from *I rose and walked to the witness stand* (p. 207) to *"That is all," I said* (p. 208): Trial transcript, pp. 121–126.

pp. 208–9 from *He described how he and his assistant* (p. 208) to *"There was nothing in the way of my vision," the witness answered* (p. 209): Trial transcript, pp. 128–234.

pp. 209–11 from *I rose from my place at the defense table* (p.209) to *Wiggins did not reply* (p. 211): Trial transcript, pp. 235–272.

p. 211 *couldn't recall when he did return*: Trial transcript, p. 631.

p. 212 *repeated on the washed hands*: Trial transcript, pp. 767–768.

p. 212 *none of which the witness had read*: Trial transcript, pp. 801–802.

p. 212 *whether positive identification of hair was possible*: Trial transcript, p. 803.

p. 212 *he stuck to his new story*: Trial transcript, pp. 298–299, 306–307.

p. 213 *"supreme law of the land are involved"*: Plessy, supra.

p. 213 *he was my Exhibit A*: Trial transcript, p. 882.

p. 214 *talked to about him in the community*: Trial transcript, pp. 883–892.

p. 214 *"that counsel would rest her case"*: Trial transcript, p. 893.

pp. 214–15 from *"a little man, if you please"* (p. 214) to *"in your hands"* (p. 215): Trial transcript, pp. 927–944.

pp. 215–16 from *"has the jury agreed upon its verdict?"* (p. 215) to *"you are a free man"* (p. 216): Trial transcript, p. 995.

INDEX